Ethics, Economy and Social

This book is a collection of critical engagements with Andrew Sayer, one of the foremost postdisciplinary thinkers of our times, with responses from Sayer himself.

Sayer's ground-breaking contributions to the fields of geography, political economy and social theory have reshaped the terms of engagement with issues and debates running from the methodology of social science through to the environment, and industrial development to the ethical dimensions of everyday life. Transatlantic scholars across a wide range of fields explore his work across four main areas: critical realism; moral economy; political economy; and relations between social theory, normativity and class.

This is the first full-length critical assessment of Sayer's work. It will be of interest to readers in sociology, economics, political economy, social and political philosophy, ethics, social policy, geography and urban studies, from upper-undergraduate levels upwards.

Balihar Sanghera is Senior Lecturer in Sociology at the University of Kent. His research has focused on neoliberal reforms in post-Soviet Central Asia and charitable giving and philanthropy in the UK. In both areas, he uses moral economy to emphasise the ethical dimensions of economic and social life. His book *Rentier Capitalism and Its Discontents; Power, Morality and Resistance in Central Asia* (Palgrave Macmillan, 2021) is co-authored with Elmira Satybaldieva.

Gideon Calder is Associate Professor of Social Philosophy and Policy at Swansea University. His ten books include, most recently, *How Inequality Runs in Families: Unfair Advantage and the Limits of Social Mobility* (2016) and the co-edited *Routledge Handbook of the Philosophy of Childhood and Children* (2018). He has written extensively on issues in social, political and ethical theory and their application to various issues of policy and practice, and is co-editor of the journal *Ethics and Social Welfare*.

Routledge Advances in Sociology

For more information about this series, please visit: www.routledge.com/
Routledge-Advances-in-Sociology/book-series/SE0511

Ethics, Economy and Social Science

Dialogues with Andrew Sayer

Edited by Balihar Sanghera
and Gideon Calder

Routledge
Taylor & Francis Group

LONDON AND NEW YORK

First published 2022
by Routledge
4 Park Square, Milton Park, Abingdon, Oxon OX14 4RN

and by Routledge
605 Third Avenue, New York, NY 10158

Routledge is an imprint of the Taylor & Francis Group, an informa business

British Library Cataloguing-in-Publication Data
A catalogue record for this book is available from the British Library

Library of Congress Cataloging-in-Publication Data
Names: Sanghera, Balihar, editor. | Calder, Gideon, 1971– editor. |
Sayer, R. Andrew, honoree.
Title: Ethics, economy and social science : dialogues with Andrew Sayer /
edited by Balihar Sanghera and Gideon Calder.
Description: Abingdon, Oxon ; New York, NY : Routledge, 2022. |
Series: Routledge advances in sociology |
Includes bibliographical references and index.
Identifiers: LCCN 2021061731 (print) | LCCN 2021061732 (ebook) |
ISBN 9781032161617 (hardback) | ISBN 9781032161631 (paperback) |
ISBN 9781003247326 (ebook)
Subjects: LCSH: Sayer, R. Andrew. | Social sciences. | Sociology.
Classification: LCC H59.S336 E84 2022 (print) |
LCC H59.S336 (ebook) | DDC 300.1–dc23/eng/20220401
LC record available at https://lccn.loc.gov/2021061731
LC ebook record available at https://lccn.loc.gov/2021061732

ISBN: 978-1-032-16161-7 (hbk)
ISBN: 978-1-032-16163-1 (pbk)
ISBN: 978-1-003-24732-6 (ebk)

DOI: 10.4324/9781003247326

Typeset in Times New Roman
by Newgen Publishing UK

Contents

Contributors

Ted Benton is Professor Emeritus at the University of Essex. He has worked on critical realist philosophy and ecological sociology and has contributed to the formation of ecological historical materialism and eco-socialism. He was a founder member of the Red-Green Study Group and is involved in local environmental activism. He is also the author of numerous books on natural history.

Gideon Calder is Associate Professor of Social Philosophy and Policy at Swansea University. His ten books include, most recently, *How Inequality Runs in Families: Unfair Advantage and the Limits of Social Mobility* (2016) and the co-edited *Routledge Handbook of the Philosophy of Childhood and Children* (2018). He has written extensively on issues in social, political and ethical theory and their application to various issues of policy and practice, and is co-editor of the journal *Ethics and Social Welfare*.

Nick Crossley is Professor of Sociology at the University of Manchester and Co-Founder/Co-Director of the Mitchell Centre for Social Network Analysis. His work covers a range of sociological themes, including theory, embodiment, social networks and music. His most recent book is *Connecting Sounds: The Social Life of Music* (Manchester University Press, 2020).

Justin Cruickshank's research concerns ontology and the politics of knowledge. He has written on critical realism and the justification of categories and the problems facing the enhancement of a post-Habermasian dialogic approach to democratic politics. As regards the latter, he has used Rowan Williams' critique of the 'functionalist' (instrumentally rational) public sphere and Gadamer's work on hermeneutics, to criticise Habermas' approach to religion in the public sphere, contributed to the growing field of critical university studies from a hermeneutics-informed perspective, and criticised the Government's 'Prevent Strategy' using the work of James Scott and the decolonial critic S. Sayyid.

Dave Elder-Vass is Honorary Fellow in Sociology at Loughborough University. His latest book *Profit and Gift in the Digital Economy* (Cambridge University Press, 2016) theorises appropriative practices, economic diversity and their implications for social theory and politics. He has also published extensively on social ontology and social theory from a critical realist perspective, including *The Causal Power of Social Structures* (Cambridge University Press, 2010) and *The Reality of Social Construction* (Cambridge University Press, 2012).

Steve Fleetwood is Professor of Human Resource Management and Employment Relations at the University of the West of England. He specialises in the application of philosophy and methodology of social science, especially critical realism, to disciplines like labour economics, organisation studies and human resource management.

Bob Jessop is Emeritus Professor in Sociology at Lancaster University. He is best known for his contributions to state theory, critical governance studies, critical political economy, cultural political economy and the philosophy of social science. His most recent sole-authored book is *Putting Civil Society in its Place* (2020) and two recent co-edited editions are *Transnational Capital and Class Fractions* (co-edited with Henk Overbeek, 2018) and *The Pedagogy of Economic, Political and Social Crises* (co-edited with Karim Knio, 2019). His work is available through ResearchGate.net and Academia.edu.

Jamie Morgan is Professor of Economic Sociology, Leeds Beckett University. He co-edits *Real-World Economics Review* with Edward Fullbrook. He has published widely in the fields of economics, political economy, philosophy, sociology and international politics. His recent books include: *The Inequality Crisis* (2020); *Modern Monetary Theory and its Critics* (2020); *Economics and the ecosystem* (2019); *Trumponomics: Causes and consequences* (2017); *Piketty's capital in the twenty-first century* (2014), all edited with Edward Fullbook; and *Realist responses to post-human society* (Ed. with I. Al-Amoudi 2018); *Brexit and the political economy of fragmentation* (Ed. with H. Patomäki, 2018); *What is neoclassical economics?* (Ed. 2015).

Kevin Morgan is Professor of Governance and Development in the School of Geography and Planning at Cardiff University, where he is also the Dean of Engagement. Andrew Sayer was one of his PhD supervisors at Sussex University and together they co-authored *Microcircuits of Capital: Sunrise Industry and Uneven Development* (Polity Press), one of the first radical accounts of the spatial structure and strategies of the emergent 'high-tech' sector in and beyond the UK. Despite co-authoring a book, they have remained close friends ever since.

John O'Neill holds the Hallsworth Chair in Political Economy at the University of Manchester and is director of the Political Economy Institute. He is on the editorial boards of a number of journals, including *New Political Economy*, *the Journal of Applied Philosophy* and *Historical Materialism* and has written extensively in areas including political ecology, ethics and the environment, the market, deliberative democracy, socialism and meta-ethics.

Jamie Peck is Canada Research Chair in Urban and Regional Political Economy and Professor of Geography at the University of British Columbia, Canada, and Global Professorial Fellow at the Institute for Culture and Society at Western Sydney University. With long-term research interests in geographical political economy, labour studies and critical studies of statecraft, Peck's current research is focused on the political economy of capitalist transformations and 'marketcraft' in Hong Kong and South China. He has been listed since 2015 by Clarivate/Web of Science as one of the world's most highly cited social scientists.

Douglas V. Porpora is Professor of Sociology in the Department of Communication at Drexel University, and the current president of the International Association of Critical Realism. His work alternates between the political and philosophical. His most recent book is *Reconstructing Sociology: The Critical Realist Approach* (Cambridge, 2015), and he is working now on the concept of structural racism. He is co-editor of the *Journal for the Theory of Social Behaviour*.

Diane Reay grew up in a working class, coal mining community before becoming an inner city, primary school teacher for 20 years. She is now a visiting professor at the LSE and Emeritus Professor of Sociology of Education at the University of Cambridge. She has researched extensively in the areas of social class, gender and ethnicity across primary, secondary and post-compulsory stages of education. Her latest book is *Miseducation: Inequality, Education and the Working Classes* published by Policy Press in 2017.

Balihar Sanghera is Senior Lecturer in Sociology at the University of Kent. His research has focused on neoliberal reforms in post-Soviet Central Asia, and charitable giving and philanthropy in the UK. In both areas, he uses moral economy to emphasise the ethical dimensions of economic and social life. His book *Rentier Capitalism and Its Discontents; Power, Morality and Resistance in Central Asia* (Palgrave Macmillan, 2021) is co-authored with Elmira Satybaldieva.

Elmira Satybaldieva is Senior Research Fellow at the University of Kent. Her main area of research interest is politics in the post-Soviet space, with a particular focus on grassroots activism and international development in Central Asia. She is currently researching Chinese, Russian and western investment strategies in Central Asia and their varied implications for the region. Her book (co-authored with Balihar Sanghera) is *Rentier Capitalism and Its Discontents; Power, Morality and Resistance in Central Asia* (Palgrave Macmillan, 2021).

Andrew Sayer is Emeritus Professor of Social Theory and Political Economy at Lancaster University, UK. His work in these areas has been mainly concerned with uneven spatial development, divisions of labour, culture and economy, the production, effects and experience of inequalities, moral economy and ethics in everyday life, and values in social science. While many of his publications on these topics develop a dialog between social science and philosophy, he has also written specifically on critical realist philosophy of social science. His two most recent books are *Why Things Matter to People: Values, Ethical Life and Social Science* (Cambridge University Press, 2011) and *Why We Can't Afford the Rich* (Policy Press, 2015).

Graham Scambler is Emeritus Professor of Sociology at UCL and a visiting professor of Sociology at Surrey University. His main interests include social theory, health, health inequalities and relations of stigma. Recent books include: *Sociology, Health and the Fractured Society: A Critical Realist Account* (Routledge, 2018), which won the Cheryl Frank Memorial Prize; *A Sociology of Shame and Blame: Insiders Versus Outsiders* (Palgrave, 2020); and, with Aksel Tjora, *Communal Forms: A Sociological Exploration of the Concept of Community* (Routledge, 2020). He was a founding editor of the international journal *Social Theory and Health* and is a fellow of the Academy of Social Sciences, UK.

Richard Walker is Professor Emeritus of Geography at UC Berkeley, where he taught from 1975 to 2012 and served as Chair for five years. His books include two co-authored classics in economic geography: *The Capitalist Imperative* (1989) and *The New Social Economy* (1992), and four books on California: *The Conquest of Bread* (2004), *The Country in the City* (2007), *The Atlas of California* (2013) and *Pictures of a Gone City* (2018). Walker has received awards from the Fulbright program, Guggenheim Foundation, Association of American Geographers, California Studies Association and Western History Association. He is currently director of the Living New Deal, a project to document and map all New Deal public works.

Introduction

Balihar Sanghera and Gideon Calder

Since the early 1980s, Andrew Sayer has made a series of incisive, influential and ground-breaking contributions to the fields of geography, political economy, social theory and the study of issues arising from industrial development to class, political-economic change to the environment and the ethical dimensions of everyday life to the methodology of social science. In the process, he has both beaten a path for postdisciplinary thinking and become one of its pre-eminent exponents. A series of acclaimed and award-winning books – from *Radical Political Economy: A Critique* (1995) and *The Moral Significance of Class* (2005) through to *Why Things Matter to People* (2011) and *Why We Can't Afford the Rich* (2015) – have reshaped the way crosscutting issues are understood and explained, while bringing together distinct theoretical traditions in original and fertile ways. His two works on the place of realism in social sciences – *Method in Social Science: A Realist Approach* (1984, 1992) and *Realism and Social Science* (2000) – are exemplars of how to advance distinctive and fresh takes on the nature of the subject while providing accessible routes into difficult areas for those unacquainted with the terrain. His work since 2000 has developed a distinctive position on the importance of normativity in social relations, critical of both modernist and postmodernist orthodoxies. His writing has drawn fruitfully on diverse theoretical resources – among them Marxism, Adam Smith, Pierre Bourdieu, the 'capabilities' approach and fellow exponents of critical realism – while staking out fresh conceptual ground of its own. Achieving cross-disciplinarity to a rare degree, he has reached an extraordinarily wide range of academic audiences and has shaped debates along lines extending far beyond his starting points in economic geography.

This book offers a critical assessment of his work, with contributions from critics, collaborators and interlocutors from across the intersecting fields on which it has touched. Its four parts, outlined below, address his work under the headings of realism, moral economy, political economy and social theory and class. The book closes with Sayer's own response to those contributions.

DOI: 10.4324/9781003247326-1

Part I: The Nature and Scope of Realism

Douglas Porpora's account of why Andrew Sayer matters centres first on his role in the development of critical realism (CR) and its critique of positivism in the social sciences. For Porpora, the core of CR lies in a basic orientation towards political economy – as an articulation of the philosophical underpinnings of Marx's historical materialism. What Sayer's work does is make explicit what many proponents of materialism have denied: the 'humanistic concerns', or moral dimension necessarily present in any such mode of enquiry. In the process, it has also fleshed out the implications of critical realist thinking for ethics, and vice versa.

Porpora then offers a sympathetic critique of positions adopted by Sayer in *Why Things Matter to People*, specifically regarding the rationality of emotions. Where he diverges is on Sayer's rooting of morality in human sociality, and his 'embodied, naturalistic, sociological account of our ethical nature'. It is the naturalistic element by which Porpora is left unconvinced. For Sayer, human rights might be founded in needs – in 'basic capacities for flourishing and suffering', or in other words, well-being (Sayer 2011: 230). Porpora argues that rights should be grounded in aspects more exclusively human than those. He also departs from Sayer's definition of truth in terms of practical adequacy, which is in favour of a correspondence theory of truth.

Ted Benton similarly signals agreement with the bulk of Sayer's positions on the relationship between social science, social criticism and the possibility of human flourishing, and also focuses on the positions put forward in *Why Things Matter to People*. His own point of divergence is located in the status of 'nature'. Benton focuses specifically on Sayer's distinction between 'biological' and 'cultural' nature, and he argues that it hinges on a reductionist understanding of the biological – reflecting a tendency in Sayer's work to 'hold "biological nature" at arm's length, while at the same time not wanting to ignore it'.

Benton proposes an alternative philosophical anthropology 'more strongly rooted in (a critical appreciation of) what the life-sciences have to offer'. Departing sharply from Porpora's position in the preceding chapter, Benton argues for the relevance of a strain of naturalistic thinking that runs through the works of Darwin and Marx and Engels, in which humans are 'beings whose socially combined populations coexist with, depend upon and share kinship with all other forms of life'. This is, in significant respects, a situation shared in common with other animals, and in tune with our best accounts of evolutionary history and adaptation. While it differs from Sayer's philosophical anthropology, this conception is in tune with its key focal points – for example, caring, dependency, solidarity and cultural variability.

Justin Cruickshank also addresses Sayer's account of the foundations of critical social science, and specifically his appeal to an objective conception of human well-being. For Sayer, much of what has passed for critical social science has slipped into versions of the scholastic fallacy, wherein agency is defined in (modernist) terms of socially detached contemplation, rather than as something exercised in the thick of embodied social practice. Sayer's alternative position is based on Aristotelian appeals to flourishing and practical knowledge – but is also one in which a certain kind of epistemic authority resides with the social scientist, rather than the lay agent.

Cruickshank seeks to explore what he calls the 'dialog' arising from this relationship and the ways in which the conduct of the 'expert' may result in certain kinds of harm to the 'lay'. He finds in Gadamer's hermeneutics an account in which academic expertise is itself characterised by *phronesis*, or practical embodied knowledge. For Cruickshank, this provides the basis for an alternative conception of expert-lay dialog set on more co-productive terms, but retaining room for the kind of appeal to objective harm that Sayer sees as a necessary part of understanding the relationship between human well-being and the tasks of critical social science.

Steve Fleetwood's point of departure is an early article of Sayer's published in *Radical Philosophy* in 1981, offering a realist interpretation of 'abstraction' – an under-analysed concept, partly because it was assumed to be obviously necessary and self-evident. Fleetwood's chapter offers a kind of follow-up on that account, providing the missing groundwork to clarify just what is at stake in contrast between the 'abstract' and the 'concrete'. He proceeds by outlining four senses in which 'entities' might be 'real': material, conceptual, social and artefactual. He then moves on to an extended investigation of the term 'abstract', and then 'conception', and how practices of abstraction produce what he calls abstracted conceptions. The term 'concrete', as Fleetwood notes, is similarly taken for granted, albeit making regular appearances in social science discourse. He moves from it to three distinctions attaching to the term abstraction: abstraction as *extraction* versus abstraction as *exclusion*; abstraction as *process* versus abstraction as *product*; and finally *internal* and *external* abstraction. It is an extended and meticulous coda to the line of analysis broached in Sayer's original article.

Part II: Dimensions of Moral Economy

Bob Jessop examines the relationship between CR and moral economy. He discusses how Sayer contributes both to CR in general and critical realism in particular. Sayer's two most-cited books (*Method in Social Science* and *Realism and Social Science*) distinguish critical realism in general from opposing positions in the social sciences. Sayer offers a position of weak social constructionism and moderate essentialism that recognises reasons can be causes and identifies both necessity and possibility in the world.

Jessop argues that Sayer's analyses of critical cultural political economy and moral economy are particular applications of critical realism, moving from abstract, philosophical and meta-theoretical reflections on critical realism to specific, practical and theoretically grounded research programmes. Sayer integrates practical reason and lay normativity into his work, and is concerned with tendencies, counter-tendencies, capacities, liabilities and vulnerabilities that shape human flourishing and social suffering in specific conditions. His later books particularly explore the harmful effects of unequal power relations and class interests on people's evaluations, well-being and the environment.

Kevin Morgan notes that Sayer's embrace of the concept of moral economy was a way to rejuvenate radical political economy as a critical social science and reclaim an ethical stance that had been wrongly abandoned by radical scholars. The moral economy perspective addressed the tendency of radical political economy to displace ethical issues in favour of economic imperatives by reinserting human flourishing, lay morality and evaluations into economic analysis.

But Morgan claims that moral economy as ethical critique cannot by itself help to fashion alternative worlds that are necessary to create the conditions for human flourishing. Instead, the foundational economy as a political strategy is embraced to achieve concrete policies and practices that are necessary for the provisioning of 'mundane' goods and services to promote social justice and ecological integrity. The foundational economy perspective focuses on the 'mundane' sectors to secure the social and material infrastructure to meet household daily essentials, such as utilities, food, health, social care and housing.

Dave Elder-Vass explains that Sayer employs the moral economy concept in three ways. First, it embodies an important theoretical claim that all economies, including capitalist versions, are moral economies. Second, it is an approach to studying, describing and explaining moral economies. Moral sentiments and lay normativity receive particular attention. Third, it takes an evaluative stance. As economic arrangements affect human flourishing, social scientists cannot avoid the normative implications and assessments of economic institutions and practices.

But Elder-Vass maintains that moral economy does not in itself provide explanations or justifications. While the perspective recognises a general class of causal mechanisms, it does not define specific mechanisms and structures. Rather it is a framework that needs to be developed with specifics, taking account of various mechanisms at work and how best to capture them. Nor does moral economy provide a firm meta-ethical justification for human flourishing or solve practical ethical questions when people have different needs and beliefs about well-being. Instead, it functions as a manifesto that needs to be filled out with more specific claims about what contributes to flourishing.

Balihar Sanghera and Elmira Satybaldieva examine how resistance to unjust economic arrangements is less foundational in Sayer's moral economy perspective than in the classic texts of E.P. Thompson, James Scott and Karl

Polanyi. Although social suffering can be a source of resistance, Sayer believes complicity, resignation and accommodation are more likely. In situations of limited resources and alternatives, subordinate groups often accept and naturalise economic domination, rather than resist it.

But Sanghera and Satybaldieva suggest that Sayer's account of lay morality and economic responsibilities offers more space for resistance in his moral economy perspective than he usually allows. As evaluative beings, individuals can and do engage in active participation in civil society to pursue concerns related to social justice and change. Given economic responsibilities are unavoidable, people can respond to others' unmet needs, social suffering and injustice by making normative demands of institutions for greater responsibility. In their empirical study on rentierism in Central Asia, Sanghera and Satybaldieva identified how grassroots movements emerged to counter the harmful effects of the neoliberal commodification of land, money and labour.

Part III: Applications in Political Economy

Jamie Morgan explores some key themes in Sayer's book, *Why We Can't Afford the Rich*. Modern capitalism is a growth system that targets continual increases in national income. The very rich are incompatible with a sustainable future. First, they capture a significant proportion of economic share, leaving less for the majority. Second, they are incompatible with a steady-state situation, so threatening the Earth's bio-physical limits. Third, their consumption has a high ecological footprint. Fourth, unable to consume their income, they feed a financialised system that exacerbates extreme inequality and ecological harms.

Morgan argues that for climate and ecological purposes, 'the rich' constitutes a far broader base of people than it does in the case of other issues. It includes those in newly industrialised countries. Of course, the issue is not just 'who are the rich', but the unintended consequences of the system that leads to ecocide. The core question is, what is to be done? Sayer argues not merely for the decarbonisation of the economy, but for equality, democratisation and degrowth.

Jamie Peck recounts how Sayer's critical realist critique of human and economic geography provoked defensive responses from authority figures and gatekeepers in the 1980s and 1990s. He took issue with David Harvey's *Limits to Capital* for reading off specific and singular spatial outcomes from the abstract logic of capital, given the open and politically mediated nature of social systems. The spatial is largely a domain of contingent relations and cannot serve as the locus for grand proclamations. But this does not mean that space is unimportant.

Peck appraises the substantive research programme that Sayer pursued during the 1980s that became known as the restructuring approach. This explored how the concrete expressions of restructuring were not reducible to a single theoretical claim but were diverse in ways underestimated both in conventional and orthodox Marxist analyses. It was committed to qualitative research methods, coupled with a theoretically informed search for causal mechanisms and structures. Sayer insisted on the rigours of concrete research in open and messy systems. Sayer and Kevin Morgan's research project on the restructuring of the electronic industry culminated in their monograph, *Microcircuits of Capital*. The book was faithful to Sayer's position of the 'difference that space makes', and his commitment to explanatory specificity over bold claims, though its uncompromising narrative style alienated some in the discipline.

John O'Neill's chapter on the nature of unfree labour in modern capitalist societies owes much to his conversations with Sayer. Unfreedom in labour can occur at three sites. First, entry into the labouring process can be forced or involuntary; for example, debt-bondage. Second, the labouring process itself can be unfree, as a result of workplace violence, lack of control over the working day, personal dependence and domination. Third, unfreedom can arise at the point of exit.

O'Neill addresses a specific tension at the point of entry between the treatment of unfree workers as vulnerable victims and as agents who make choices about their own lives. He notes that humans are constituted by both passive and active powers. The exercise of choice and agency is only possible against the background of constraints and dependencies. Assessing the involuntariness of unfree labour requires a careful understanding of how individuals are compelled by necessity and (gendered) obligations, such as care for dependents.

Richard Walker reflects on Sayer's persistent radicalism from his much-anticipated book with Kevin Morgan, *Microcircuits of Capital*, to the critically acclaimed *Why We Can't Afford the Rich*. Their book together, *The New Social Economy*, urged scholars to examine more seriously the division of labour and criticised the bogus economic category of 'services'. Sayer took philosophical and methodological debates to another level with his path-breaking books, *Method in Social Science* and *Realism and Social Science*. Walker remarks that Sayer's *Radical Political Economy* was a masterpiece of clarity and rigour that fairly adjudicated the strengths and shortcomings of conventional and radical economic theories. In the 2000s, Sayer veered towards class relations and moral economy, as in *The Moral Significance of Class*, and then towards hermeneutics of social thought and embeddedness of social scientists, as in *Why Things Matter to People*.

For Walker, *Why We Can't Afford the Rich* serves to synthesise the qualities that distinguish Sayer from his peers. Hard and careful work went into the book. A key characteristic of the book is the rigorous logic involved, in particular the way Sayer dismantles bogus arguments in favour of enrichment. The book reveals the moral axis of his life and work – his moral stance against the rich and class society and his writings on moral economy. His commitment to political economy also comes through, especially reviving classical political-economic terms like value and rent. The book's most telling theme is his radicalism, arising from his commitment to truth seeking.

Part IV: Social Theory, Normativity and Class

Diane Reay's chapter develops two case studies: practices of wealth extraction from the UK welfare state undertaken by members of the post-2019 conservative government and what she calls the 'emotional violence' of class inequalities in English education. The first is a story of greed, corruption and elitism cloaked in rhetoric around the valorisation of the 'creation of wealth'. Reay shows how Sayer's analysis of the over-consumption of the rich and their abuses of power helps diagnose the patterns of how the current UK government has, even while invoking a spurious ambition to 'level up', done the opposite of 'challenging privilege, wealth and power in society'. It amounts to what Sayer describes in *Why We Can't Afford the Rich* as 'the infiltration and capture of the state by the rich' (Sayer 2015: 239).

Meanwhile, educational inequalities tell of 'shame, humiliation, despair and powerlessness', of contempt for the working classes, and how injustices of recognition are materialised in the distribution of resources. Reay relates Sayer's attention to the role of emotions in the experience of domination in *The Moral Significance of Class* to her own extensive analysis of how the English education system shames those placed in bottom sets at school, perceived as places of failure inhabited by the 'written off'. Even among children, the markers of class inflect their views of those in other sets and indeed reinforce a sense of their otherness.

Graham Scambler singles out those same two books, in addressing class relations in contemporary Britain. Sayer resists the conflation of *objective* class relations – which have exerted more causal power since the 1970s, indicated for example by the increasing capacity for those with wealth to buy those with power – with *subjective* class relations, the experience of which may be said to have become less salient in that same period. Meanwhile, health inequalities have substantially increased in ways highlighted and widened by the Covid-19 pandemic. Scambler presents this process in terms of asset flows (biological, psychological, social, cultural, spatial, symbolic and 'above all, material') – the virus having had the direst consequences for those, such as BAME communities, for whom those asset flows are weakest.

Scambler sets out a series of further theses, regarding the role of the postmodernisation of culture in reinforcing the power of the plutocracy, and the non-reducible but intrinsic relation of gender and racial relations to those of class. The effects of these tendencies are felt in the fracturing of society characterised by environmental threats, precarity and cultural disorientation among other current symptoms. In light of these, Scambler suggests four alternative possible eventualities, of which one – 'statist authoritarianism' – can be regarded as already being under way.

Nick Crossley's chapter considers the complex relationship between Sayer's work and that of Pierre Bourdieu, culminating in *The Moral Significance of Class* and related elaborations on the normative dimensions of social divisions. For Crossley, Sayer's account of the role of dispositions and sentiments is overly individualistic, in an important sense which reflects similar tendencies in the Bourdieusian notion of habitus, on which it draws. Specifically, it reduces phenomena that exist *between* actors to properties of the individual. Drawing on Mead and Habermas' accounts of intersubjectivity, Crossley argues that an appreciation of how and why we are moral requires instead due attention to the role of interaction and relationality in the formation of the moral self – and that this recuperates what for him, though not for Sayer, remains a crucial Kantian distinction between the right (that which is required as a matter of moral duty) and the good (that which contributes to flourishing). Indeed Sayer himself relies on the tenability of such a distinction, in some of what he says. In these respects, for Crossley, Sayer has not distanced himself far enough from the individualistic biases of Bourdieu's account of habitus to articulate a fully convincing sociological account of moral life.

Gideon Calder looks across from Sayer's work on inequality to recent debates in political theory. Calder presents the terrain of those debates in terms of three divides in late twentieth-century theorising: between liberals and communitarians, modernists and postmodernists, and different styles and vocabularies of egalitarian thinking. In each of these areas, he argues, Sayer's work has a good deal to offer, as a means of working across the divides and mobilising insights from either side. This makes it unfortunate that his work is not drawn upon more widely by political theorists, particularly as it has so much to say about why inequality is *wrong*, both at the macro level and in terms of everyday lived experience. (In both of these senses, as Calder suggests, it has become marked by a deep and pernicious kind of 'ordinariness'.) What Sayer's work helps with is the critical understanding of the social, political and economic settings of our lives, in ways that provide rich insights for any egalitarian seeking to articulate why inequality demands a response. It remains to be connected up with the kind of fleshed-out engagement with the political that those insights invite.

Andrew Sayer, in the closing chapter, responds to those discussions of his work, focusing on points of disagreement along the lines of six themes: space, theory and economic development; critical realism; ethical life, habitus and naturalism; moral economy; inequality and the rich; and environment. He also says something about his own debts and intellectual trajectory towards a postdisciplinary approach to social science.

Sayer's distinctive version of approach has borne many fruits, achieving in the process a rare degree (as Scambler puts it near the start of his chapter) of depth, delicacy and potency – and in ways sparking insights across a remarkable array of academic arenas. We hope that this book does some justice to this achievement. Our contributors mark their respect and gratitude in their own ways. As editors, we would like to add our own deep thanks to Andrew for his generosity, both intellectual and personal, and to say what a pleasure it has been to put this book together.

Part I

The Nature and Scope of Realism

Chapter 1

Why Andrew Sayer Matters

Douglas V. Porpora

I am very honoured to be included in this volume celebrating Andrew Sayer, whose work has mattered so much to the development of Critical Realism (CR). Sayer is one of the most prominent social scientists calling themselves critical realists, and as a social scientist myself, I look to him as a leader.

It has been commonplace to associate CR with Roy Bhaskar. Bhaskar's *A Realist Theory of Science* (2013) and *The Possibility of Naturalism* (2014) are indeed both important and emblematic of CR as a brand. The truth, however, as I have argued elsewhere (e.g. Porpora 2015), is that CR was born of an entire community of progressive scholars that included at the time Bhaskar's mentor in philosophy, Rom Harré, whose *Causal Powers* (Harré & Madden 1975) was equally formative. The formative CR community also included other philosophers like Andrew Collier and Peter Manicas. But the community was also interdisciplinary so as to include economists like Tony Lawson and Steve Fleetwood and, besides Sayer, sociologists like Margaret Archer, Ted Benton, William Outhwaite and Charlie Smith.

Although Manicas and Smith were Americans, they had strong British connections, and the community that gave rise to CR was mostly British. Thus, although I go back a long way in CR, actually through Manicas and Smith, as an American, I came to CR a bit later. When I did, for a long time, I would describe myself as 20 per cent of the critical realists in America, which was a bit of an understatement even then. Now, however, I am happy to report that I am likely less than one per cent of America's critical realists.

In contrast with me but like Margaret Archer, Tony Lawson and others, Sayer was there from the beginning – even before, that is, CR was CR. Along with other similarly minded scholars like John Urry and Bob Jessop, Sayer was already at the University of Lancaster, where there was held the first of what would become the annual meetings of the *International Association of Critical Realism* (IACR). Even before that first meeting, Sayer had already published his *Method in Social Science* (1992), which would do so much, even now, to move people away from a positivist understanding of social research.

DOI: 10.4324/9781003247326-3

Before that first IACR meeting, in addition to *Method,* Sayer had already published several books from a political-economic perspective, for me, most notably, *Radical Political Economy: A Critique and Reformulation* (1995). I say most notable for me because I would likewise describe myself as coming from the tradition of radical political economy. In fact, in my first address as president of IACR (Porpora 2019), I suggested that a non-reductive political-economic approach is the basic theoretical orientation of CR, one that takes full account of Archer's (2013) Structure, Agency and Culture (SAC). With the so-called cultural turn and practice turn and kindred other turns, most social science today effaces structure, especially what I would call material structure, and conflates agency with culture. It is with material structure, however, that on my understanding, the political economy begins.

In labelling political economy the basic orientation of CR, I likely overstate the case. Today, CR is a broad tent that includes many whose research has little to do with economy or politics – however applicable they should still find the SAC formula. When, however, I made my debut with CR at the second annual meeting of IACR, among CR's major constituents were self-identified Marxists or fellow travellers like Collier, Fleetwood, Mervyn Hartwig, Rachel Sharp, Sean Vertigan and Colin Wight.

I still tend to think, along the lines of Benton's (2014) *Three Sociologies,* that CR articulates the philosophical underpinnings of Marx's historical materialism. Although I do not have the space to make the case here, Marx's adoption of causal mechanisms and narrative history contrasts with the statistical, nomothetic approach of Durkheimian positivism while Marx's attention to material structural relations contrasts with Weberian individualism.

In any case, it has been important to me – especially now that I likely do represent near one per cent of the self-identified Marxists remaining in American academy – that Andrew Sayer stands as an important exponent of the political-economic approach. His more recent book, *Why We Can't Afford the Rich* (2015), continues in this tradition.

As a materialist orientation, non-reductive or not, the political-economic approach tends to be regarded as tough-minded, not usually associated with such humanistic matters as morality or ethics.[1] Yet the political-economic approach is in fact motivated by deep ethical concerns. It has been a significant contribution therefore for Sayer to make those concerns explicit, first in his *The Moral Significance of Class* (2005) and then more broadly in his *Why Things Matter to People: Social Science, Values and Ethical Life* (2011). The latter in particular has launched a salutary new attention to ethics, both in CR and beyond. It is truly seminal in this respect.

I perhaps should say upfront that I agree with and appreciate what Sayer says on most matters relating to CR. I judge, however, my saying so of less general interest than points of difference. Thus, I will also broach some points where I have a different point of view.

Why Things Matter to People

This heading is, of course, also the title of one of Sayer's most significant books, a title I think is beautiful. As Sayer notes, despite its fundamental importance, the question it raises has gone largely unaddressed by social science. The question is of fundamental importance because it addresses the very meaning of importance.

As doctoral students facing their defences know, the most daunting question they can face is: *So what?* However methodologically perfect and theoretically grounded their research, the question asks why anything they say is of any interest or importance. The question is daunting both because doctoral candidates often have difficulty articulating a satisfactory answer and because should there be none, the implication is that their research is not worth discussing or having been done in the first place.

To say that something is of interest or important means that it matters to us in some way, and that the more it matters, the more interesting and important it is. To say in turn that something matters to us means that it affects us somehow.

From the critical realist perspective, something can matter to us even without our knowledge or awareness, that is, in a way that is purely objective ontologically. That is because our well-being is not purely a subjective matter, a matter of what we think or feel. Even if we are unaware of it, for example, or, as in America, refuse to acknowledge it, climate change or the pandemic can nevertheless undermine our quality of life. Both already have.

As agents, however, we react to what matters to us objectively only if it comes to matter for us subjectively, that is, we come to see or appreciate its mattering. It is this subjective mattering that Sayer explores. Following Archer's (2000) usage, Sayer thinks of subjective mattering as a concern. I would agree but also think that concern is equivalent to care (Porpora 2001). I don't know that Sayer would disagree.

If I understand him correctly, Sayer unpacks care or concern in terms of emotions. Again, I would agree. Although Sayer again follows Archer (2000) in conceptualising emotions as commentaries on our concerns, I have alternately conceptualised emotions as more constitutive of care, as actually orientations of care or varieties of caring (Porpora 2001). It may come to the same thing, but I think of emotions as felt stances or relations of our entire selves to the objects of our emotions. To say that I had been outraged by the Trump administration is to say how I stood in relation to it and that I cared about it in this way as opposed to being merely annoyed by or frustrated with it.

If subjective mattering has to do with care or concern and if care and concern have to do with the emotions, then it matters or becomes important how and why we have the emotions we do. Thus, along with others of us who have argued similarly (Archer 2000; Porpora 2001), the next move Sayer makes is of great importance. It is to rebut the dominant view in social science, popularised in the United States by Arle Hochschild's (2012) otherwise admirable *The Managed Heart*, that emotions are to be equated with feelings.

Our emotions certainly are often accompanied by feelings, but our emotions are not distinguished by them. Outrage, annoyance and frustration may all evoke feeling, but we do not distinguish among them by what we feel but rather by the nuanced relation each identifies between us and the object of the emotion. Frustration can span a wide spectrum of contexts and need not connote any moral blame as when we are frustrated with uncooperative weather. Annoyance may convey some moral blame but the blame it signifies is mild. We become annoyed by breaches of etiquette or perhaps when someone is behaving with less rationality than we expect of a human being. Although outrage simpliciter can convey just very strong anger, it more distinctly identifies aptly strong anger directed at a much more serious moral transgression.

In a sense, because, as above, emotions represent how actors stand in relation to the objects of their emotions, emotions are, as Sayer says, cognitive appraisals or evaluations. It follows, as Sayer goes on to say, that we can argue about the aptness of our emotions. I may be annoyed that you have arrived at my office late for an appointment, and if you are late, some degree of annoyance might be justified, might be rational. If, however, you point out correctly that my clock is running fifteen minutes fast, only then would my continued annoyance become unjustified and hence irrational. Emotions, in short, like beliefs, may be either rational or irrational and are certainly not, contrary to conventional prejudice, the correlative contrast to rationality.

The rationality of emotions is important to Sayer's argument because he goes on to turn to moral emotions, that is, emotions about moral matters. As I have suggested above, outrage is one such.

Among the moral matters that emotionally engage us are our values, in which we are emotionally invested. Along with critical realists generally, what Sayer wants to say against positivism is that values and other moral appraisals are not utterly subjective but reflective of the ontologically objective, empirical world. So, although this may not be quite Sayer's line of argument, it follows that if emotions generally are rational as reflective evaluations of ontologically objective features of the world, so are moral emotions in particular.

Many of our descriptive terms are hybrids, that is, thick descriptors or moral facts. Although it remains an empirical matter whether or not such descriptors apply to a particular case, they have values ineluctably built into them. Consider murder, rape or genocide. Whether any particular case instantiates any of these categories is subject to argument over empirical evidence. Still, there is no getting around that all carry a moral valence. Thus, if a rape or murder occurred in a particular case, it is a fact, but it is a moral fact. Given their empirical nature and given that, as Sayer shows, moral facts are among the facts that matter most to us, moral considerations should not be excluded from sociological study. The fact/value distinction, therefore, does not hold and hence neither does the positivist stance of value neutrality.

In all the preceding, I am at one with Sayer. There are, however, ways in which I part company. These departures are not necessarily disagreements. Some are pursuits of different problems, which nevertheless rest on the same foundation Sayer lays. Principally, whereas Sayer concerns himself largely with what matters to people, my own work on morality (Porpora 1992, 2001, 2013) has largely tried to understand how certain important moral issues come not to matter. Put otherwise, my focus has been the social construction of macro-moral indifference to such matters as genocide and war. Of course, talk of moral indifference presupposes the opposite possibility, which is why I say this focus presupposes what we have seen Sayer say so far.

In other ways, I differ from Sayer more substantively. Even these differences, however, are not all so much disagreements as different ways of seeing things. I principally see things differently about the grounding of ethics. By the grounding of ethics, I mean their basis or warrant. The issue arises because ethics have a special status. One does not need to justify one's tastes. One cannot, for example, be asked reasonably to defend a preference for vanilla over chocolate ice cream. Part of the reason surely, along lines Sayer (2005: 44–46) suggests in *Moral Significance*, is that tastes generally are less serious or consequential than moral choices. Nothing much rides on my own preference for vanilla over chocolate.

It is not just, however, that tastes are generally inconsequential. They also are in some sense the opposite of commitments. I very much like Sayer's (2005: 40) understanding of commitments as *emotional, reasoned attachments*. In contrast with my commitment to, say, justice, I have no commitment whatsoever to vanilla. My preference for vanilla is not just inconsequential but also unreasoned. And I have no emotional attachment to it. Were some neuro-scientist to change my brain so that I would henceforth prefer chocolate, I would not much care. That would not be the case for justice, to which I feel myself emotionally called. I would not similarly describe myself as called to vanilla.

But the above considerations are still not the crux of the status difference between tastes and moral judgements. The crux of the difference is that tastes play no role at all in argument, whereas moral judgements are dispositive. Moral judgements are trumps. They generally override matters of prudence like self-interest, which may include taste but also concerns much more serious. Where moral duty calls, we may even put our very lives on the line. As Sayer (2005: 48–50) likewise acknowledges, moral judgements likewise trump or override social conventions (see Sayer 2011: 155–156), which can be called morally into question.

Morality in short is our highest criterion of judgement. That exalted status, I think, requires justification or at least explanation. Why, even over convention, does morality hold such status? Historically, morality has been rooted in religious ontologies, in terms of which, moral *oughts* are derived from what *is*. Most famously, the American *Declaration of Independence* roots human rights in the sanctity of human personhood. Hinduism similarly derives the sanctity of all life from an ontology in which we are all of one divine essence. Being admittedly of a religious sensibility myself, I am comfortable with what I observe to be a convergence of all the major religions on ideals of benevo-lence, leading me to infer something transcendental about love and kindness. As Bishop A.T. Robinson (2002) once commented in relation to Feuerbach, even if there is no divine person, there still may be personal qualities that are divine.

Not having similar religious sensibility, Sayer in *Moral Significance* roots morality ultimately in human sociality and in what he says is a human ten-dency to universalise the most general moral sentiments like empathy that are constitutive of it. It is 'the reciprocal character of relations with others' Sayer (2005: 48) says that 'produces not only a generalising tendency but a concern with consistency and fairness'. In *Why Things Matter*, Sayer (2011: 148–188) expands on this account. He again speaks of moral sentiments and social relations but also of how we are also socialised into them via, among other things, stories and moral exemplars.

In total, Sayer offers an embodied, naturalistic and sociological account of our ethical nature. It is an account certainly consistent with the perspec-tive of radical political economy or, what to me is the same thing, historical materialism. Here, however, I suppose I depart not just from Sayer but also from historical materialism. A completely naturalised, sociological account of ethical force – that is, of its emotional pull on us – does not convince me.

I accept, as does Sayer, that an ought can be derived from an is, but, I think, it cannot be just any is. The mere fact that as a result of evolution we humans possess certain sentiments does not explain to me the justification for ele-vating some but not all of them to governing ideals. Other sentiments we possess, like tribalism, I think we actually should endeavour to resist. I par-ticularly differ from what Sayer says about human rights.

> Although human rights are social constructions that are intended to be beyond question, they cry out for justification, and here we can only appeal to basic capacities for flourishing and suffering that seem to be common for all human beings. Among these, the right to be treated as an end in itself is preeminent.
>
> (Sayer 2011: 230)

I definitely agree with Sayer that human rights cry out for justification. I just don't think that Sayer's suggested justification suffices. Like Brian Turner (2006), Sayer suggests that human rights are to be founded in human need. In a footnote, Sayer reinforces the point, denying, in his opinion, that rights derive at all in Kantian fashion from the moral status of human persons, possessive of reason and free will, but solely from what is required for their well-being.

My own instincts are directly opposite. In the first place, the criterion of well-being does not distinguish human beings from any other animal. To be sure, like Peter Singer (1980), though not on utilitarian grounds, I do believe we have a moral obligation to avoid the suffering of any creature and therefore feel the call, to which I fall short, of vegetarianism. I further think that even if we eat animals or otherwise employ them, they deserve our respect along the lines that Andrew Collier (1999) outlines in *Being and Worth*. At the moment, however, I would not go so far as to say that even the higher animals possess rights, that my cats, for example, should be allowed to haul me into court for feeding them the same boring food over and over (which, actually, they seem to prefer).

Even when it comes to humans, I do not think that it is need per se that undergirds rights but that they are needs specifically of persons, which, I would follow Kant in assessing as in some sense sacred and therefore as obliging the deference we variously cash out in rights. So I suppose, again speaking from a religiously inclined perspective, I would say that if we are going to derive a moral ought from an is, it helps for the is to have high moral worth.

There is one other place where I differ with Sayer and that concerns truth. I bring it up here because with the rise of post-truth populism across many of our countries, particularly my own, I have come to think more about the ethics of belief (Porpora 2019; Porpora & Sekalala 2019). We think of ethics as pertaining to our actions, but we also bear responsibility for our beliefs. In particular, especially where our beliefs are socially consequential, we have an obligation to believe not just what is pleasing or in our interests but what actually is true (Clifford 1877).

But what is truth and how do we determine it? We critical realists all believe in truth and its determination but with differences. I agree with Bhaskar (2009) that we speak of truth in multiple senses but also agree with Groff (2000) that at its core, truth means the correspondence of what we say or believe with ontologically objective reality. Sayer (1999) demurs here in favour of what he calls *practical adequacy*. I certainly think that what is true will generally prove to be adequate practically, but I do not think that practical adequacy is either the meaning of truth or an adequate replacement for it, especially in moral matters. When we call on oppressors or exploiters to desist from their behaviour, the moral force of that call inheres not in the practicality of so designating them but in the ontologically objective deviation from virtue that the designations signify. It is another case where an is implies an ought. The determination of truth, I agree, is a fallible, rhetorical matter that may include, among other things, appeal to practical adequacy (Porpora 2015), but I think it also important to affirm, particularly in moral matters, the correspondence of our claims with the reality that we call truth and on some occasions speaking truth to power.

In closing, let me say that for the sake of interest, I tried to unearth some places where I differ from Sayer. I want to reaffirm therefore that I remain very closely aligned with most of what Sayer says and think what he says matters very much, not only to me but to CR and beyond.

Note

1 I agree with Sayer that any difference between ethics and morality is debatable, and I use them more or less interchangeably.

References

Archer, M. (2013). Social Morphogenesis and the Prospects of Morphogenetic Society. In M. Archer (ed.), pp. 1–24, *Social Morphogenesis*. Dordrecht: Springer.

Archer, M. S., & Archer, M. S. (2000). *Being Human: The Problem of Agency*. Cambridge: Cambridge University Press.

Benton, T. (2014). *Philosophical Foundations of the Three Sociologies* (RLE Social Theory). New York: Routledge.

Bhaskar, R. (2009). *Plato Etc: Problems of Philosophy and Their Resolution*. New York: Routledge.

Bhaskar, R. (2013). *A Realist Theory of Science*. New York: Routledge.

Bhaskar, R. (2014). *The Possibility of Naturalism: A Philosophical Critique of the Contemporary Human Sciences*. New York: Routledge.

Clifford, W. K. (1877). The Ethics of Belief. At: www.homeworkgain.com/wp-content/uploads/edd/2019/08/20190407071250clifford_ethics_of_belief__1_.pdf

Collier, A. (1999). *Being and Worth*. New York: Routledge.

Groff, R. (2000). The Truth of the Matter: Roy Bhaskar's Critical Realism and the Concept of Alethic truth. *Philosophy of the Social Sciences* 30(3): 407–435.

Hare, R., & Madden, E. (1975). *Causal Powers*. Totowa: New Jersey.

Hochschild, A. R. (2012). *The Managed Heart: Commercialization of Human Feeling*. Berkeley: University of California Press.

Porpora, D. V. (1992). *How Holocausts Happen: The United States in Central America*. Philadelphia: Temple University Press.

Porpora, D. V. (2001). *Landscapes of the Soul: The Loss of Moral Meaning in American Life*. New York: Oxford University.

Porpora, D. V. (2015). *Reconstructing Sociology: The Critical Realist Approach*. New York: Cambridge University Press.

Porpora, D. V. (2020). Populism, Citizenship, and Post-truth Politics. *Journal of Critical Realism* 19(4): 329–340.

Porpora, D. V., Nikolaev, A. G., May, J. H. & Jenkins, A. (2013). *Post-ethical Society: The Iraq War, Abu Ghraib, and the Moral Failure of the Secular*. Chicago: University of Chicago Press.

Porpora, D. V., & Sekalala, S. (2019). Truth, Communication, and Democracy. *International Journal of Communication* (13): 938–955.

Robinson, J. A. T. (2002). *Honest to God*. Westminster: John Knox Press.

Sayer, A. (1999). *Realism and Social Science*. New York: Sage.

Sayer, A. (2005). *The Moral Significance of Class*. Cambridge: Cambridge University Press.

Sayer, A. (2011). *Why Things Matter to People: Social Science, Values and Ethical Life*. Cambridge: Cambridge University Press.

Sayer, A. (2015). *Why We Can't Afford the Rich*. Bristol: Policy Press.

Sayer, R. A. (1992). *Method in Social Science: A Realist Approach*. New York: Routledge.

Sayer, R. A. (1995). *Radical Political Economy: Critique and Reformulation*. New York: Blackwell Publishing.

Singer, P. (1980). Utilitarianism and Vegetarianism. *Philosophy & Public Affairs* 9(4): 325–337.

Turner, B. S. (2006). *Vulnerability and Human Rights*. State College: Pennsylvania State University Press.

Chapter 2

Andrew Sayer

Human Nature and Social Critique

Ted Benton

Since his early arguments for going beyond the dichotomy of hermeneutic and positivist social science and his development of a version of critical realism, Andrew Sayer has gone on to make invaluable contributions to our thinking about the relationship between social science, social criticism and the possibility of human flourishing.

I agree with so much of Andrew's argumentation that what follows is perhaps little more than a suggestion that we need a difference of emphasis – or that a different starting point might offer contextual support for some elements in his argument as well as rendering more central some aspects of human nature left out, or marginal in his account.

After presenting powerful arguments against some traditions in critical social science (CSS), most notably Marxism and the version of 'explanatory critique' advocated by the late Roy Bhaskar and Andrew Collier, Andrew went on, in *Why Things Matter to People*, to defend a strong version of CSS against the prevailing relativist, subjectivist tendencies to withdraw from strong normative commitments in social science that had by then become pervasive through the influence of post-modernist/post-structuralist approaches.

Here his position seems to be that all social descriptions are inherently normative, or 'valuey', and that it is a mistake to attempt to achieve a value-free description as if values were distortions – to do so would be to lose all sense of why what was being described was significant. To accept this or that description is to acknowledge the valuations implicit in it. Instead of searching for value-free descriptions, descriptions that entail evaluations should make explicit their basis in some account of human nature and flourishing. Social practice or set of beliefs may be subject to critique on the basis of the injustice, unnecessary suffering, unmet need or restriction of opportunity for flourishing it involves.

Commonly, Andrew argues, social scientists have used terms, such as 'racism', which involve moral judgement but have been reluctant to make explicit their value-perspectives for fear of being judged 'authoritarian',

DOI: 10.4324/9781003247326-4

'ethnocentric' or indefensibly universalistic in their moral standpoint. But this sort of retreat is unnecessary. So long as the standpoint from which a critical evaluation is rendered explicit, it is itself open to criticism and revision in the light of relevant argument and evidence. Conceptions of human well-being, universalistic claims about human nature and associated judgements about suffering and unmet need are not mere matters of opinion:

> The argument so far calls into question the subjectivist view of well-being or flourishing as merely a state of mind ... [W]e can usually give reasons for how we feel in terms of what has been happening to us and the things we care about. So our subjective feelings seem to be about things which are objective in the sense of independent of them.
>
> (Sayer 2011: 134)

However, it does not follow that only one state of social existence can count as flourishing or well-being: moral pluralism is not the same thing as moral relativism. I take this to mean that where there are differences of view about what counts as flourishing, there is room for reasoned discussion and persuasive use of various kinds of evidence.

A defensible practice of CSS, then, would make explicit its view of the conditions for and content of human well-being. This would need to be sufficiently universalistic to include a great diversity of socio-cultural possibilities but also sufficiently substantive to provide a basis for judging some of those possibilities inconsistent with human flourishing. A common term for such a theoretical enterprise is 'philosophical anthropology', and Andrew offers his version in chapter 4 of *Why Things Matter to People*.

So far I go along with the argument, but there are two reservations about the way Andrew goes about this task. The first has to do with the question 'what it is to ask for the nature of something?'. Andrew cites Kate Soper as distinguishing two senses of 'nature' – that is, as everything that exists versus everything other than what is human, social, or cultural. Andrew endorses the first of these, but I think there are other differences of meaning that sometimes get confused in his account of specifically human nature. I distinguish four distinct things that might be meant by the 'nature' of something (or kind of thing or being). First, one might specify what distinguishes it from other (kinds of) things (the sort of characteristic that figures in identification keys for birds or insects). Second, one might be identifying universal, common features across the individuals belonging to a given kind. This would be broader than the first set of features, since it would include also characteristics shared with other kinds. Third, one might be specifying characteristics that are of special significance, features that make it the kind of being that it is ('to err is human', '(s)he's only human', 'the rational animal', etc.). Finally, one might be attempting to specify some underlying feature or condition in virtue of which the being in question is able or liable to manifest the range of behaviours or powers that we can observe or expect. This might be an internal structure, but it might also be a set of conditions external to the individual without which it cannot develop or exercise some or all of the 'key common characteristics' of its kind, or it might be a combination of the two. Andrew seems to move between these understandings of 'nature' in his own philosophical anthropology, though the first and third are most evidently present.

My second reservation has to do with the contrast he makes between our 'biological nature' and our 'cultural nature'. Against biological reductionism, he argues that we are 'not merely biological beings, but social beings who develop through acculturation and vary historically and culturally'. However, it would be a mistake, he argues, to ignore our biological nature, since 'Our cultural being is an emergent property of our biological being, presupposing certain biological conditions, such as the cerebral cortex' (Sayer 2011: 100–101). The opposition to reductionism in either direction and the recognition of human's capacity for culture as rooted in our organic structure are both welcome, but there is a problem about the referent of 'biological nature'. Biology is a scientific discipline (though it might be better to speak of the cluster of related disciplines as the 'life sciences') not a set of attributes (in this case, of humans). It seems that Andrew uses the term here to refer to something like 'organic' or bodily existence, but as a science biology claims a much more extended territory than this and does offer accounts of psychological, social and cultural aspects of living things. These accounts are often contested by human social scientists, but more often are simply rejected as 'reductionist'. The latter is perhaps the dominant response among social scientists, especially those of liberal or leftist moral orientations in virtue of the long history of (mis)appropriation of ideas drawn from the life sciences in aid of socially conservative (racist, sexist, homophobic, etc.) politics.

This is probably why Andrew holds 'biological nature' at arm's length whilst at the same time not wanting to ignore it. However, I will suggest an alternative approach to philosophical anthropology which is much more strongly rooted in (a critical appreciation of) what the life sciences have to offer. This is intellectually justified as, for example, these sciences have much to offer for an account of human nature in the fourth sense I distinguished above and might illuminate our accounts of human nature in the second and third senses – those things that make us human, but also those things we share with other species. There is another set of reasons why this might be a preferred strategy. This has to do with the point of developing an account of human nature that might sustain a version of CSS. As implicit in the initial critical realist version of 'emancipatory critique', the diagnosis of society's ills was centrally concerned with injustices as between social groups, and forms of illegitimate power of some groups over others. These concerns are certainly no less relevant today, with powerful movements such as 'Black Lives Matter' and 'Me Too', as well as the more institutionalised, day-to-day struggles in the workplace, civil society and the domestic sphere to challenge injustice and the infliction of harms of many kinds.

However, I write in the midst of a pandemic in which an entity consisting of a few strands of organic molecules is in process of wreaking sickness, death and economic chaos across the world. It certainly seems right not to ignore 'the biological' – by which I mean organic existence, and the relations among species and their conditions of life. But this is merely one aspect of a growing and multi-faceted crisis in the relations between current human civilisation and the rest of nature – the climate and extinction crises being the most widely recognised. These existential crises both for our species and many others certainly do not displace, or make less important, the questions of social injustice posed by 'traditional' emancipatory critiques. On the contrary, the incidence of the harmful effects of these crises is strongly skewed across different human populations, and policies to address them cannot avoid engaging with prevailing patterns of inequalities of power, wealth and recognition.

Now, let us consider the view of human nature as outlined in *Why Things Matter to People*. First is the human variability. We come in various shapes, sizes, sexualities and so on. It makes no sense to regard any of this natural variation as 'unnatural'. Second, it is important to recognise that we are animals, and not shy away from bodily mechanisms, needs and compulsions. Here Andrew recognises that an account of human nature must include features we share with other species, as well as those that distinguish us (cf my second sense of 'nature of' above), but the connection between embodiment and what we have in common with other animals implies a limitation in that commonality – that is, we are both embodied – but we may share more than that. Third, as beings who come into the world with only very limited capacities, we depend from the beginning on care from others as conditions for our development of all the bodily, psychological and cultural potentials of a fully realised social being. Fourth, as needy and suffering beings, we seek (but may not succeed) to develop capacities to meet our needs, or overcome suffering, but under social and cultural conditions that produce a great variety of different ways of recognising and meeting those needs.

Next, Andrew argues, we are 'reasoning beings'. He gives a rich and complex account of this, far from the 'rational self-interest' model that permeates much of current social and economic thought. The ability to reason is associated with the acquisition of language, and this is a learned capacity. Language or 'discourse' is not merely a means of describing things but enables cooperative interaction with others, and that in turn involves learning how to behave towards them, acquiring an understanding of social norms, and of oneself as a participant in social life. But this is not a merely passive process, as people are able to develop critical capacities and become reflective about the character of the norms they find, and also develop a sense of themselves leading a life to which they can attach a meaning. Andrew includes here work as a practice through which people interact with one another and the environment, and cites Marx as showing that it is through this that we may also become 'historical beings'. Closely linked with reasoning in Andrew's account of it is 'fellow-feeling' – the capacity to recognise or identify with the feelings of others.

All this amounts to the more general claim that we are essentially social beings. From birth (and before) we are dependent on the care of others and come to a sense of ourselves as independent subjects through our interactions with others, who we recognise and who recognise us. Our relations with others – including not just discursive ones, but practical, bodily and emotional ones – are constitutive of our developing self, but through them we become autonomous selves, capable of evaluation and independent action. Here Andrew explicitly disputes the dichotomy of self-interest and altruism. Humans often behave in a self-interested way, but this is not always unethical, nor does it make sense to reduce all human behaviour to the category of self-interest. Humans may act altruistically, but often our commonality with others makes the distinction unclear, and we may be acting both altruistically and egoistically at the same time. Friends simply taking pleasure in one another's company would be an example.

A further aspect of our social being is the necessity to form attachments and commitments. Attachment to care-giver is thought to be essential to the psychological development of children, but with development as a social being, we form attachments and commitments to a great range of objects – other people, places, values, professional standards, political projects, sporting associations, cultural traditions and many others. These become fused with our sense of self, to the extent that we may be hurt when the object of our commitment fails or is damaged, and elated when things go well. This aspect of our social nature calls into question the liberal valuation of autonomy. This cannot mean just doing what we want without reference to others, nor can it mean freely choosing all of the relationships we enter into. Our dependence in childhood on committed and long-term carers illustrates this well, but in adulthood continuing to live and act in adherence to a commitment or personal attachment may be an expression of autonomy whilst at the same time requiring limitations on one's freedom of choice.

The account of the social–relational shaping of personal identities and dispositions given by Andrew yields important insights into virtues, vices and, more generally, the capacities for both benevolent and evil action and diversity in evaluating these. He rightly criticises much moral philosophy (and lay moral judgement) for its focus on the moral character of particular actions – or particular characters. Our social development through engagement with wider social structures and practices shapes us in ways that become habitual, so that we have embodied characteristic dispositions to respond in certain ways to given situations ('habitus'). These dispositions may be brought to consciousness and reflected upon, but for most of us much of the time, they are un-thought and spontaneous regularities. So, working in certain kinds of corporate hierarchy may make us either submissive, deferential and defensive, or domineering, insensitive to the feelings of others and self-satisfied, depending on where we are in the hierarchy. Similarly, different sorts of society may favour cooperative and generous dispositions, whilst others may encourage competitive and self-interested ones. It is important to note that this account is not determinist in the sense that these dispositions are inevitable and unchangeable outcomes, leaving no space for individual agency. On the contrary, it is always possible to reflect on one's behaviour and reassess the value of one's previous socialisation. In fact, some thinkers – most notably the Italian Marxist, Antonio Gramsci – emphasise the sheer diversity of life experiences and social practices through which people live their lives, so that the 'common sense' which they share with others is made up of a complex and often contradictory set of practical and moral predispositions and understandings. At times of personal or social crisis, contradictory urges or dispositions may set in motion conscious reflection on meanings, values and purposes in life. However, Andrew's key point is that instead of focusing exclusively on the moral value of individual action, it is necessary also to direct moral evaluation at the wider social structures, relations and norms through which individual moral dispositions are formed.

In case this account of human nature seems unrealistically benign, ignoring aspects of human nature that are frequently identified as inimical to the sorts of 'progressive' vision of social transformation that proponents of CSS usually subscribe, Andrew writes of the place of 'evil' in human nature:

> A capacity for evil is a striking feature of human nature. It seems likely that even those who have never knowingly harmed anyone are at least familiar with having evil thoughts – perhaps of inflicting pain on people they particularly despise.
>
> (Sayer 2011: 13)

Sometimes evil thoughts and deeds arise from ignorance, or distancing, achieved by a complex division of labour in modern societies. Systematic forms of oppression and harm emerge from power relations within which victims are rendered less than human or 'objectified' by those who would oppress them. Evil can also come as a response to formative experiences of violence or neglect, but Andrew also recognises conscious, deliberate, face-to-face harm:

> Sometimes evil involves inflicting suffering face to face, where the perpetrator knows precisely that the victim is a human subject capable of immense suffering – and often, as in domestic violence, a familiar person.
>
> (ibid)

Recognising and elaborating on these aspects of human nature have been the stuff of conservative thought from Hobbes in the midst of the revolutionary turmoil of mid-17th-century Britain through to social Darwinism and its successor disciplines of sociobiology and evolutionary psychology, as well as some versions of depth psychology. However, a rather different source of conservative thought has been less concerned with inner psychological drives or dispositions, and more with the implications of what we might call the 'human predicament'. Here Thomas Malthus is a key figure.

Malthus (1798) declared himself 'warmed and delighted' by the speculations of utopian writers such as Condorcet and Godwin, and claimed that he 'ardently wished for such improvements' (1970: 69). Sadly, however, there were 'unconquerable difficulties' in the way of achieving them. These difficulties stem from the truth of three propositions – that human population cannot increase without means of subsistence; that where there is means of subsistence, population increases; and that the 'superior power' of population cannot be checked without 'misery and vice'. The superior power of population derives from the different mathematical patterns of growth between population – growing geometrically (exponentially) – and the means of subsistence – growing arithmetically. It follows that the suffering of the lower orders of society is unfortunately unavoidable, whilst attempts to achieve equality can only have the consequence of rendering the misery universal:

> But though the rich by unfair combinations contribute frequently to prolong a season of distress among the poor, yet no possible form of society could prevent the almost constant action of misery on a great part of mankind, if in a state of inequality, and upon all, if all were equal.
>
> (Malthus 1970: 79)

Malthus's *Essay* has been seen as a serious challenge by radical thinkers from Marx and Engels through to contemporary environmental thinkers on the left. Marx and Engels combined two doubtfully consistent lines of attack. Sometimes the claim was that the productive power of the earth, human labour and science were without limit – production could always keep pace with population growth. Alternatively, it was noted that only a third of the earth's surface was yet cultivated, but, in the distant future, if a limit was reached, the education of the people would enable population itself to be brought under control (a reference to Malthus's own subsequent revision of his law of population to allow of 'moral restraint').

Arguably, the second 'realist' strand in their argument is more consistent with the general tendency of historical materialism than the first 'utopian' one. Both Malthus and the founders of historical materialism shared a recognition of the unavoidable dependence of humans upon continuous interaction with their physical and living conditions of life:

Nature is man's *inorganic body* – nature, that is, in so far as it is not itself human body. Man lives on nature – means that nature is his *body*, with which he must remain in continuous interchange if he is not to die. That man's physical and spiritual life is linked to nature means simply that nature is linked to itself, for man is a part of nature.

(Marx & Engels 1987:276)

This early view was developed in the later work, notably in *Capital* (vol 1):

The labour process … is human action with a view to the production of use-values, appropriation of natural substances to human requirements; it is the necessary condition for effecting exchange of matter between man and Nature; it is the everlasting Nature-imposed condition of human existence, and therefore independent of every social phase of that existence, or rather, it is common to every such phase.

(Marx 1961: 183–184)

Despite this strongly naturalistic tendency in the thought of Marx and Engels, Marx himself sometimes worked with a strong 'humanist' opposition between distinctively human and animal natures. This is especially clear in his early exposition of the concept of alienated labour. However, even in the same texts he also recognised the commonalities of humans and animals, describing both as 'active natural beings'. Arguably this line of thought was strengthened by his later recognition of Darwin's *Origin* as the counterpart in the natural sciences of his and Engels's view of human history.

So, drawing on both Darwin (and Wallace) and Marx and Engels, we have grounds for a view of human nature, not as manifested in individuals of the species, albeit recognising their social–relational attributes, but, rather, as beings whose socially combined populations coexist with, depend upon and share kinship with all other forms of life. As provisional outcomes of aeons of the workings of natural selection through innumerable vicissitudes of life conditions, animals, as 'active natural beings', are equipped to serve two main purposes: survival and reproduction. As a species that occupy distinct locations in the immensely complex web of ecological connection, humans share with other species dependence on the integrity of that web, both for survival and flourishing.

So, our alternative account of human nature would begin with three key features that we have in common with other animals: the dominant purposes of survival and reproduction, and dependence on continuous interaction with the physical and living conditions of life.

This approach begins with an account of our nature that treats as fundamental what we share with other species, and only through further discussion arrives at an understanding of what makes us distinct (Benton 1993). A useful concept for this further exploration is that of a 'mode of life'. As a writer of books on natural history, I find myself discussing each species – let's say, a bumblebee – in terms of its appearance, and how it can be distinguished from similar ones. But only after that does the exercise become interesting. What does it feed on? How does it recognise and access its food? How does it deal with the seasons or with inclement weather? What are its predators and parasites? How do the sexes meet up? How does each sex express its preferences and choose its mates? How are the offspring nurtured, and by whom? In the case of a social species such as a bumblebee, this last set of questions has a complex set of answers involving the construction of a nest, forms of communication and social coordination of activity among reproductive and non-reproductive members of specific communities of individuals. Today, any such account of the 'mode of life' of a species is unlikely to end without an account of the prevailing threats to its survival (usually attributable to human activities).

These questions are, perhaps surprisingly, no less appropriate to any plausible consideration of human nature – as 'mode of life'. However, given the open-ended variability of human modes of social life expressed in history and across the planet, it is necessary to search for the sources – and possible limits – to that variability in our evolutionary prehistory. The discipline of palaeoanthropology has made great advances both in sources of evidence and in sophistication of interpretation in recent decades (Stringer & Andrews 2011). We know that the lineages that lead to modern humans diverged from the ancestors of our closest living relatives, the chimpanzees, between 5 and 6 million years ago, that the genus *Homo* emerged between 2 and 3 million years ago, and that our own species (arrogantly and absurdly named *Homo sapiens*) emerged in Africa some 400 thousand years ago. Both apes and hominins left their African homelands to colonise the rest of the world in a series of migrations, so that during the most recent 100 thousand years some five or six species of our genus coexisted in some places and for some periods of time.

These species and also some of the apes had in common several of the features frequently claimed to be unique to modern humans. These include high cognitive and communicative capacities, associated with well-developed and sometimes very variable forms of social life. Both cognitive and communicative skills are associated with the ability to make and use tools and to pass on the relevant craft skills to others in local communities and to successors. Hominins and apes are mostly fruit-eaters, using tools to open nuts, process foods and, for example, in present-day chimp societies, to 'fish' for insect prey. Early humans seem to have evolved in a transition from dense tropical forest to more open habitats that necessitated more extensive foraging, and an associated diversification of diets. Currently favoured is the thesis (previously suggested by Engels!) that bipedalism, which emerged some 2.5 million years ago, was less a response to the needs of locomotion in these more open habitats, and more of modification to free the hands for making artefacts.

These features of early hominin modes of life are clearly related to the evolutionary priority of survival. What about reproduction? The currently

surviving apes have a great variety of forms of social organisation of reproductive behaviour. Gorillas are polygamous and live in family groupings
dominated by a powerful male, whilst chimpanzee's social organisation
centres on bonds between groups of males and bonobos have a matriarchal
form of organisation. Gibbons have strong monogamous pair bonds within
which offspring are reared. We know from anthropology, comparative sociology and from everyday experience that there is no single human mode of
organisation of reproductive activity. However, there are some distinctive
aspects, compared with other primates. One is the extreme and prolonged
dependency of human infants. This is connected to the demands for learning
very complex linguistic, social, cultural linguistic and material–practical skills
early in life – but continued into old age. In so far as human emotional life and
behavioural dispositions are shaped by their genetic inheritance, this feature
of our developmental pattern would lead us to expect an evolved tendency
and ability to form strong and lasting emotional bonds among offspring and
carers, and also among adults who share caring roles in the immediate social
group. Another feature is the relatively small average differences in physical
size and strength between males and females, and lack of bodily equipment
for conflict. This contrasts with the gorillas, whose dominant males are twice
as heavy as females. This suggests an evolutionary history of relatively egalitarian and pacific forms of social life, favouring social cooperation and more-
or-less persistent forms of social organisation in response to the demands of
protection from large predators, and of foraging and hunting (as that eventually formed a part of the mode of life of some hominin groups).

With increases in cognitive, communicative and emotional capacities, the
evolutionary outcome of 'adaptation' is displaced in favour of 'adaptability' –
humans are able to invent new techniques for finding and processing their
food and adopt new ways of ordering their social life in response to climatic
and other environmental exigencies, as well as migrating to new places and
acquiring the skills to survive there. From some 75 thousand years ago, there
is evidence of what we now recognise as artistic creation, although it is arguable that artefacts created long before that showed signs of an aesthetic sensibility beyond mere functionality. There is evidence of symbolic creation in
both modern humans and Neanderthals, in the design of tools as well as
in ritual objects, such as bone or clay sculptures. This suggests from early
in our prehistory the development of investment of meaning and emotional
expression in the making of things. From some 40 thousand years ago, we
have evidence of palaeolithic cave art of great beauty and skill. There is no
consensus about the significance of this, but there are clues. Almost always
the paintings depict animals, often showing keen insights into their behaviour; they appear on the walls of often very large caverns deep inside mountains, and only accessible with difficulty. It seems that the caves were places
where wider populations beyond the small intimate groupings typical of the
period could be brought together on special occasions. This suggests already

a socio-cultural flexibility and ability to coordinate across large spaces and populations. The paintings themselves show great attention to and appreciation of the animals portrayed, suggesting a more-than-instrumental valuing of them – kinship? – possibly even, some suggest, worship?

So far this sketch, mainly derived from palaeoanthropology, confirms each of the elements in Andrew's philosophical anthropology – the centrality of dependence and caring, of the inherently social nature of humans, of fellow-feeling and solidarity, as well as cultural variability and creativity. The ability to form commitments, too, can be associated with long-term caring relations, but my alternative sketch in terms of the concept of 'mode of life' brings out the significance of commitment in relation to other objects and beings, as manifested in craft skills and artworks, as well as to places. It is notable how this is expressed in people's desires for the disposal of their bodies after death: the practices of scattering ashes in a beloved place, or of a body next to the resting place of a partner in life. A commemorative plaque on a seat near where I live reads: 'Sit and stare as I have done for many years, enjoying the delights of Frinton. A place I love'.

This view of humans, not just as embodied beings, closely related to other species, but as 'active natural beings' who depend on continuous metabolism with the rest of nature both for survival and for developing their full human capacities also gives some evolutionary grounding for other human attributes. These include the meaning and emotional significance of bodily interaction with external nature – in fashioning artefacts, creation of artworks and, possibly, physically engaging with wider surroundings: running, walking, climbing, as well as studying and contemplating ('sitting and staring'). These physical capacities and the cognitive skills that go with them are evolved features of our species. A 'love of nature' may not be a secondary cultural acquisition, experienced only when the basic needs for food, drink and shelter have been met. It may be something deeply rooted in our evolutionary prehistory. Similarly with the need for meaningful work and the special delight taken in the development of practical skills:

> Craftsmanship is often equated with precision but I think there is more to it. I feel it is more important to have a long and sympathetic hands-on relationship with materials. A relaxed, humble, ever-curious love of stuff is central to my idea of being an artist.
>
> (Perry 2011: 169)

But this takes us to the promised element in the account of our natural history: threats to our survival. In this context, foremost among those threats derive indirectly from our evolutionary success as species capable of combining socially and developing our cognitive and practical, creative skills to enhance our metabolism with the rest of nature. But how could our competitive advantage over other species have turned into an existential threat to our own and the other species with whom we coexist on earth? Andrew begins an answer to this question, referring to humans as both social and historical beings. The open-ended sociability, cognitive capacities and practical creativity inherent in human communities have given rise, over millennia, to a transition from successfully drawing from nature and transforming materials into means for our survival, to a qualitatively different relation to the rest of nature. This is one in which aspects of external nature are systematically transformed so as to yield more means for our subsistence than they would if left unaltered. The emergence of horticulture, agriculture and the domestication of animals are early phases of that transition and mark the origin of a long-term historical process of a human socio-economic and technical project of mastery of nature. The scale and scope of this have now reached the point of so disrupting the complex web of interdependencies upon which our metabolism with nature is premised, that extinction in the foreseeable future cannot be ruled out. At the same time, our evolutionary history has endowed us with capacities for coordinating and transforming our activities in relation to nature, combined with capacities for deep affective ties with our fellow species and shared spaces.

References

Benton, T. (1993). *Natural Relations*. London & New York: Verso.

Malthus, T. (1970; orig. 1798). *An Essay on the Principle of Population and A Summary View of the Principle of Population*. Harmondsworth: Pelican.

Marx, K. (1961). *Capital*, Volume 1. Moscow: Foreign Languages Publishing House.

Marx, K. & Engels, F. (1987) *Collected Works*, Volume 3. London: Lawrence and Wishart.

Perry, G. (2011). *The Tomb of the Unknown Craftsman*. London: British Museum.

Sayer, A. (2011). *Why Things Matter to People*. Cambridge: Cambridge University Press.

Stringer, C., & Andrews, P. (2011). *The Complete World of Human Evolution*. London: Thames & Hudson.

Chapter 3

Objectivity and Normativity

Justin Cruickshank

Critical Social Science and the Modernist Dualisms

It is an honour to be invited to contribute to this festschrift on Andrew Sayer. In this chapter, I will discuss Andrew's argument that a critical social science (CSS) needed to be based on an ontology of agency – or human being – with normative claims motivated by objective conceptions of well-being and its negation.

Andrew (Sayer 2011) agreed with the postmodern and feminist authors who criticised the modernist dualisms, which are gendered, with the masculine side privileged over the feminine side. The dualisms were: fact–value, is–ought, reason–emotion, science–ideology, science–ethics, positive–normative, objectivity–subjectivity, mind–body (Sayer 2011: 29). The emotions were seen as counter to reason, and reason was seen in instrumental terms, with values being subjective ends that could not be rationally discussed unlike instrumental means (Sayer 2011:40). Nonetheless, despite criticism of the modernist dualisms, Andrew was positive about the Enlightenment, because Enlightenment thinking about society sought to combine objectivity and criticism. Andrew argued that '[o]nly with the great fragmentation of the study of society into disciplines and the divorce of philosophy from social science that occurred in the late nineteenth and early twentieth centuries did it become uncritical or disavow its critical elements' (Sayer 2011: 217. See also Sayer 2000a).

CSS re-emerged in the late 1960s with a revival of interest in Marxism along with interest in feminist and anti-racist politics. However, a lack of reflexivity and self-criticism led to divisions and a concern that normativity was 'potentially authoritarian and ethnocentric' (Sayer 2011: 218). Despite the influence of modern positivism, the postmodern suspicion of normativity and the right-wing political climate, the main problem was with the still-pervasive influence of:

> modernist, liberal ways of thinking [...] which treat values as beyond the scope of reason, and which make social scientists reluctant to discuss

DOI: 10.4324/9781003247326-5

conceptions of the good, or of well-being or of flourishing. For these reasons recent CSS never really established its rationale and now the wider political climate has become less congenial these weaknesses are being exposed.

(Sayer 2011: 219)

Two more recent CSS positions, Habermas' deliberative democracy and Bhaskar's critical realist explanatory critique, were criticised by Andrew for failing fully to break from the influence of these modernist dualisms. Habermas was criticised for having no positive conception about the outcome of dialogic deliberation. Habermas regarded a lack of dialogic deliberation as harmful, but he did not motivate this with an appeal to what objectively facilitated agents' well-being (Sayer 2011: 228). Habermas' discourse ethics:

> remains a way of evading the most important issue: what is good and why? Small wonder, then, that discourse ethics has had so little influence on concrete studies in critical social science. [Discourse ethics ...] is neither necessary nor sufficient for flourishing.
>
> (Sayer 2011: 228)

Bhaskar's (1998) critical realism developed an explanatory critique, with the aim of unmasking ideology and helping people replace unwanted determinants with wanted determinants, that is, helping agents replace structures conditioning agency with negative constraints, for structures taken to provide improved enablements. This was problematic because, as with Habermas' deliberative democracy argument, it furnished no substantive and objective positive definition of well-being. For Andrew:

> the idea that the good can be reached simply by removing 'bads' step by step, without having any conception of the good and how it could be realised in feasible alternative forms of social organisation is naïve.
>
> (Sayer 2011: 227)

Bhaskar's explanatory critique sought to give an objective account of structures combined with a normative response to those structures. However, the normative response turned not on the objective analysis of structures causing objective harm to agents but on agents' lay conceptions of what they took to be wanted and unwanted determinants. In place of this, CSS needed to motivate normative critique by appealing to an objective conception of well-being, or flourishing, and harm.

Andrew (1992, 2000a) agreed with Bhaskar (1998) that modern philosophy and much social science were based on the epistemic fallacy and that ontological questions of what social being is constituted by needed to be addressed as such, rather be redefined in epistemological terms of reference. He also agreed with Bhaskar that social structures are objective entities that condition agency but went on to emphasise the importance of addressing another fallacy, which occurred within many ontological definitions of agency. Andrew drew on Bourdieu (2000) to argue that many conceptions of agency commit the scholastic fallacy, of defining agency in terms of a socially detached contemplative stance, which is more a reflection of academics' privileged social position than of real agency which faces constant social–practical pressures and affective influences. For Andrew:

> Philosophy's preoccupation with reason and autonomy make it particularly liable to ignore or devalue practice, emotion, vulnerability, dependence and embodiment, and to marginalise psychological and sociological considerations. Another kind of scholastic fallacy involves the projection of social science's suspension of evaluation onto the people it studies so their evaluative relation to the world is over looked.
>
> (Sayer 2011: 15)

He went on to argue that '[r]emarkably, the literature on social ontology rarely gets beyond the discussion of structure and agency and fails to recognise humans as needy and vulnerable beings' (Sayer 2011: 140). Within critical realism, Andrew noted, Archer (see, for instance, Archer 2005) and Collier (1999, 2003) developed ontologies of agency that avoided the scholastic fallacy. Archer conceptualised agents in terms of reflexivity and discussed the way agents conceptualised normative ends to pursue and the means to realise those ends, recognising also that agents had affective ties to their commitments and an 'inner conversation' to reflect on them and the possibility of their realisation in particular social contexts. Collier argued that being is of intrinsic worth and that recognition of this should motivate a socialist transcendence of capitalism, because the social relations capitalism generated harmed our being, by turning us into objects to be used instrumentally (Collier 1999, 2003). While he was critical of the way class entailed agents making evaluative judgements about their worth and the worth of others which are harmful to agents' well-being (Sayer 2005), and critical of the way wealth polarisation undermined economic growth by removing demand from the economy (Sayer 2015), Andrew did not hold that capitalism needed to be replaced by socialism.

Overcoming the Scholastic Fallacy

We may say that for Andrew, the scholastic fallacy stemmed from the mode of thinking inaugurated by the modernist dualisms. To overcome the scholastic fallacy and the mode of thinking it stemmed from, Andrew set out to develop an ontology of agency that drew on Aristotle. Two points are salient with regard to Andrew's (Sayer 2011) use of Aristotle. The first is that we need to recognise the importance of *phronesis*/practical reason, or embodied action, in understanding agency. The second is that we need to understand the objective well-being of agents in terms of what Aristotle called flourishing and objective harm in terms of the negation or limitation of such flourishing. Flourishing is obviously not conceptualised in negative utilitarian terms as the absence of harm but as a condition where our being has objective positive existence.

Andrew made a distinction, drawing upon Flyvbjerg (2001), between *phronesis*, meaning practical embodied knowledge, which can also be described as wisdom; *episteme*, meaning analytic knowledge; and *techne*, meaning instrumental rationality (Sayer 2011: 71). Andrew argued that '[t]he very success of theory, science and capitalist technology has encouraged the illusion that abstract theory and formal technical reason can displace phronesis' (Sayer 2011: 96). Normativity is then detached from what it is about and appeared as groundless subjective values, but it should be understood in terms of 'the ongoing flow of continual concrete evaluation' (Sayer 2011: 97). *Phronesis* should not be dismissed by having a conceptualisation of agents based on the modernist tendency to see agency as detached contemplation, as this entailed the scholastic fallacy. We experience a flow of events and in that we draw upon our implicit knowledge, which we have an affective relationship with and, as we deal with others, we are in relations of care that make us undertake evaluative and affective responses that transgress the fact–value dualism (Sayer 2011: 80).

Phronesis may be unreflexive and irrational, considered from Kant's conception of modernity as using your own reason, with reason conceptualised as transcending social and affective bonds, rather than being mediated through them. However, drawing on Dunne (1993), Andrew argued that *phronesis* should include a habit of attentiveness (Sayer 2011: 87). The failure to engage with the fallibility of practical reason:

> could be argued to arise not from the limitations of practical reason as such but from *failures to pursue practical reason properly*, so that instead of continually learning from each new situation, the experienced actor becomes indifferent to their specificity and novelty, and assumes 'she had seen it all'.
>
> (Sayer 2011: 87. Emphasis in original)

Phronesis is fallible and therefore our practical knowledge can improve through people being attentive to the limitations of their practical knowledge.

In defining the flourishing of social beings defined by *phronesis*, that is, in defining flourishing in terms of an ontology of embodied, affective and evaluative agency, we need to recognise that our commitments help constitute us, and the success or failure of these can impact upon our flourishing or harm, respectively (Sayer 2011: 125–127). Our commitments are not just sets of ideas akin to tools that can be picked up and just used for an instrumental purpose, nor are they divided into the positive and the normative, with both being detached from a transcendent subject-agent. In contrast to any subject–object dualism, the knowing subject or agent is constituted by their commitments, which combine the positive and the normative and with which the agent has an affective bond. Further, we have a capacity for becoming, meaning that our being and its potential is socially realised through interaction with others (Sayer 2011: 110). Our relations to others help constitute us, both in terms of recognising the limits to our practical knowledge and in terms of our affective bonds which shape our cognitive processing of knowledge, ideas and their limits (Sayer 2011: 119). We are emotionally invested in many of our commitments, the everyday flow of our practices and their evaluative nature, and the well-being of those close to us. We are also defined by our sense of dignity. Andrew held that it is ironic that some philosophers associate dignity:

> with reason, as the 'highest' of our powers, as opposed to the 'lowly' qualities of the body, in everyday life dignity is signalled in comportment, eye contact and bodily control. The dance of dignity among people in the way they comport themselves in relation to one another reveals much about the peculiar dialectic of the personal and social, subjective and the intersubjective.
>
> (Sayer 2011: 191–192)

In elaborating his conception of flourishing, Andrew also briefly drew on the work on capabilities by Nussbaum's neo-Aristotelian philosophy and also by Sen's political economy. Andrew listed six out of ten of Nussbaum's criteria, which were: life; bodily health; bodily integrity (free movement and safety from attack); practical reason (being able to conceptualise the ends to follow and the ability to plan one's life); affiliation (being able to mix with others of one's choice and be treated with dignity); and control over one's environment, meaning the right to political participation, free speech and assembly, and materially the right to hold property (Sayer 2011: 235).

Abstraction and Authority

For Andrew, '[a]s in medicine, the whole point of social science and ethics is or should be the improvement of well-being' (Sayer 2011: 252). In developing knowledge that should be of use to the improvement of well-being, social scientists, Andrew argued, need to:

> attempt to understand the 'target group's' own interpretation of their condition. This matters more in social science than in medicine, for

well-being in the broader social sense depends heavily on our involvement in the socially constructed practices whose internal meaning is important. The doctor needs to know my symptoms, but whether I understand my liver makes little difference to whether she diagnoses it as healthy or malfunctioning, for my liver functions largely independent of how I understand it. However, my conduct in social life depends very much on how I understand it. We therefore need a more dialogical model that gets at what understanding is.

(Sayer 2011: 250–251)

Nonetheless, the task of 'democratic dialogue' between critical social scientists seeking to understand the meanings of lay agents is not that of Habermasian 'uncoerced agreement' where all agents are equal in the search for a consensus. Rather, social scientists would have 'epistemic authority' in contrast to the 'experiential authority' of lay agents. Lay agents will know their lives best, but a social scientist 'does not have to agree with the interpretations offered by those she studies' (Sayer 2011: 251), because social scientists should have a better understanding of objective well-being and the social factors undermining or promoting this.

Epistemic authority stemmed from the process of abstraction and, specifically, the use of abstraction correctly to define the essential features of agents and the structures that condition them. Critical realist abstraction worked by defining the underlying structural causal mechanisms at work and distinguishing these from empirical patterns (Sayer 1992, 2000a, 2000b, 2001, 2011). So, for example, in analysing gender and class inequalities, one would have to go beyond the contingent empirical manifestations of these phenomena occurring together in capitalist societies, using abstraction to define the underlying essential properties. This would entail defining the essential features of patriarchy and the essential features of capitalism and then arguing that patriarchy and capitalism constituted two structures and that these two structures interacted in contingent ways. Andrew then sought, as we have seen, to complement this critical realist approach to an ontology of structures that condition agency, with an ontology of agency that escaped the scholastic fallacy and the modernist dualisms it stemmed from, by defining agents in terms of practical reason and the ubiquity of affective and evaluative responses in the flow of ongoing agency.

Using the terms cited by Andrew from Flyvberg (2001), I would say that for Andrew, professionals can rely on both the technical abstractions that constitute *episteme* and *phronesis*. Using the example of medical practice, Andrew argued that '[f]ast, competent action requires the actor to develop appropriate *embodied* dispositions, forms of sensitivity, awareness and response, so that, for example, the nurse does not have to stop and think which action comes next when assessing a patient' (Sayer 2011: 71. Emphasis in original). The experienced nurse's embodied and evaluative agency is able to draw on the abstractions of *episteme*, in the form of the technical body of medical knowledge learned during instruction, and apply these by having an intuitive understanding of the specifics being encountered in the course of day-to-day practice. Whereas a novice would have their decision-making slowed down by having to work out how to apply the formal knowledge of their technical training to different specifics not directly prepared for, the experienced nurse would have an intuitive understanding of how quickly to define a problem and resolve it. Practical reason complemented the nurse's technical knowledge and enabled the nurse to define their being as an effective professional helping people in a meaningful job.

While the *phronesis* in the example above concerned the fast application of *episteme*, the process of changing our constitutive commitments and thus our being, through *phronesis*, as embodied affective agency, would be likely to be a slow process. This is acknowledged by Andrew who argued that the process of change with embodied and affective practical reason could be very slow indeed. As he put it:

> Having become consciously and sincerely anti-racist [a previous racist person] may feel ashamed about the persistence of [...] unreformed reflexes, but *it can take many years of repeated experience and practice to reshape these completely*. The process involves not just acknowledging errors of thought and action, but becoming a different person with different habits of thought.
>
> (Sayer 2011: 78–79; emphasis added)

Our commitments are important to us and are part of us, which is why Andrew held that our flourishing depends on their success, so any change to these may well be a difficult and thus slow process. In this process, dialogue with others and reflection in the form of active listening to them could, over time, lead to an unsettling of previously taken-for-granted commitments, and the more deeply held those commitments were the more difficult it would be to swap confirmation bias for an understanding of alternative ways of thinking and feeling – and thus being.

Referring back to the example above, we may say that the nurse felt their job to be meaningful and so their being was constituted to some extent by their professional knowledge (*episteme* and its practical realisation) and the emotional ties to using that knowledge to help people. Therefore, any change to their being, for example, recognising that a well-established habit of action was now contestable and potentially in need of change, may be slow to occur, while the application of existing knowledge may be fast. In other words, the first type of *phronesis* would be a means to the end of fast decision making (to promote patient well-being efficiently), and the second type of *phronesis* would refer to the constitutive beliefs and emotions that served to orient agency, which would be likely to be slow to change.

The recognition of fallibilism is likely to be problematic given these two approaches to *phronesis*. With the first type of *phronesis*, fast decision making focused on the efficient application of knowledge rather than the revision of knowledge. There is thus the danger of cutting the problem to fit the experience of the professional here. To this, Andrew would argue that fallibility needs to be remembered. How this recognition may be put into effect would, I think, be unclear though given the professional may interpret what is said within their extensive experience. The patient's reports on their experience could be read in the light of the nurse's extensive body of experience. Moreover, if we consider that the second type of *phronesis* implied a slow change to commitments that were constitutive of being, then changing a well-established habit of action which was seen as partly constitutive of one's being as a skilled and effective nurse may be emotionally difficult. Such a change entails recognising that a previously positive way of acting which helped generate a positive sense of self was actually not so positive after all and that recognition may not be quick to occur.

Academic Knowledge and the Problem of Changing Constitutive Commitments

I now want to consider social scientists' knowledge production and dissemination. For Andrew (2000c), the search for objective knowledge to motivate robust normative arguments needed not only to be based on a correct ontological definition of agency (and structures) that furnished abstractions and that defined the essential features of social being but also on a postdisciplinary approach to knowledge production. In developing a CSS, we needed to adapt the conceptual tools to suit the problem, otherwise, there is a risk that objectivity will be undermined, by cutting the problem to fit the tools, to some extent. Therefore, for Andrew, research should recapture the spirit of the Enlightenment not only in linking objectivity to normative criticism but also in the avoidance of demarcating knowledge into artificial hermetic disciplinary silos.

However, the tacit ontology of academic agency presumed here is one that could commit the scholastic fallacy. This is because it was presumed that changing intellectual commitments can be fast, with academics quickly overcoming disciplinary socialisation and commitments, to follow 'ideas and connections wherever they lead' (Sayer 2000c: 89), with explanatory problems shaping the tools used when, using Andrew's conception of being, constitutive commitments will be likely to be changed slowly. Changing our being is likely to be slow and that means the definition of and attempt to solve academic-intellectual problems is likely to be shaped by the intellectual disciplinary/sub-disciplinary commitments that play a constitutive role in at least partly defining academic agents. It could be objected that academic commitments are not significantly constitutive, but in many cases academics, like the nurse in the example above, would be likely to define themselves in relation to their professional knowledge. It is not common for people to change their mind quickly in a discursive exchange in print or verbally at a conference. Rather than recognise fallibilism and act on it by changing position or significantly reworking a position, a position is often adhered to when faced with criticism, with change to academic positions being a slow process indeed. In this case, academics often see themselves as having both epistemic and experiential authority, because the experience of being an academic would be the experience of living with constitutive commitments that underpinned research and often at least some teaching. One would not want to have one's commitments and experience at least partly negated. The second type of *phronesis*, which entailed a slow change to our being, would be linked to the first type of *phronesis*, with academics constituted by different commitments engaging in fast exchange, in the sense that arguments would not entail the practical recognition of fallibilism and the use of this to start the slow process of change to one's being but would be exchanged with the outcome often reinforcing constitutive commitments. Academics would have the practical intellectual – embodied knack of responding to criticisms from opposing positions to the (sub-disciplinary) position that formed part of their constitutive commitments by seeking dialogue-stopping rejoinders that rejected the intellectual authority of the criticism.

I now want to turn from inter-academic dialogue to dialogue between critical social scientists and lay agents. On the above account, academic agents would have epistemic authority stemming from having knowledge based on *episteme*, with that *episteme* being constituted by abstractions that correctly defined structures and agents, and empirical research into how particular structures objectively harm well-being and what ought to change to facilitate well-being. They would also have experiential authority in terms of living in accord with their constitutive commitments and seeing them realised successfully in professional research. The experiential authority could also include the fast inter-academic dialogue, where constitutive commitments were reinforced. Lay agents would lack epistemic authority because they lacked a knowledge of the abstractions that correctly defined the essential features of the structures conditioning their agency and agency itself, that is, they lacked knowledge of the abstractions that constituted *episteme*. Further, their experience of the social world, given a lack of knowledge based on abstraction, may rely on making inferences based on observing the empirical 'surface', in which case lay knowledge may commit the epistemic fallacy, with this exemplified in any 'associational thinking' (Sayer 2000b) that took the correlation of events to entail causal relations. Their experiential authority may not be authoritative concerning the interplay of structures and agency, but it would be authoritative in the sense that it would render information of the lived experience of the effects of structures on agents, even if not seen in terms of those abstractions by lay agents themselves. Given this, the critical social scientist may draw on their experience to use as examples to bolster their knowledge based on abstractions and empirical research based on those abstractions.

For CSS to improve well-being though, dialogue between academics and lay agents has to assist change by applying social scientific knowledge rather than gathering new social scientific knowledge, and this presents a problem because there would be little basis for any genuine dialogue. Instead, the critical social scientist would need to impart their objective knowledge, and the objective normative critique it motivated to help improve the objective well-being of lay agents.

In such a situation, people may feel undermined by an expert seeking to change their agency, to motivate more critical and engaged political agency, by changing their constitutive commitments using a language and ideas that were unfamiliar and thus uncomfortable to engage with. In addition to the problem that constitutive commitments may be slow to change anyway, the attempt by the expert academic to impart their CSS-based knowledge of abstractions may entail a sense of alienation from the supposedly dialogic process. Academics could try to approach such a situation by using the first type of *phronesis* to develop a knack for translating and disseminating academic knowledge to lay audiences. Here the language used and the concrete examples given may be accessible and appealing to people who are unfamiliar with any social science argot. This may overcome any alienation caused by the use of a technical or technical sounding argot, but such a knack though would not be able to facilitate fast dialogic change, given that a change in people's constitutive commitments was required and these may well take time to change. For even if academics had the knack of translating technical language into accessible and interesting language, based on examples that appealed to the audience, it may well be difficult for people to change their most deeply held constitutive commitments quickly, given their emotional ties to them. The more likely best outcome may well be a form of cognitive–affective dissonance that had a short life as the older and more comfortable ways of thinking and feeling – and thus being – were returned to. Audiences can watch Michael Moore's documentaries that expose the iniquities of capitalism and politics and be moved by these but then return to acting and thinking as before, perhaps with a modicum of dissonance. Even if people reject the notion that 'there is no alternative', radically changing their constitutive commitments to become a different being is unlikely to be a fast process.

Therefore, a slow dialogic process may be needed, unfolding over months or longer. However, the problem would be that the supposed dialogue would be one way, with the academic expert seeking to change laypeople, using knowledge based on abstractions translated into lay language. Such a one-sided approach to dialogue is in tension with two of Nussbaum's criteria, namely practical reason (being able to conceptualise the ends to follow) and affiliation (being treated with dignity) (Sayer 2011: 235). A supposed dialogue that was in effect monologic, conducted by an expert seeking to change people by using appealing language, would entail a potential loss of dignity because lay agents would have no meaningful input into the transformational process. Politics relates to ontology and a transformational political change requires a change in being. However, if that entailed one group seeking to change another, the outcome may be that the latter is reduced to the status of an object to be used instrumentally, by an expert elite using dialogue solely as a means to an end and not as a process that allowed others to liberate themselves by re-orienting their constitutive commitments.

Education, Dissatisfaction and Change

One way, I suggest, to deal with this problem concerning critical socio-political knowledge dissemination is to turn to co-operative universities. A number of these now exist in the UK and have academics volunteering their time and knowledge working with lay agents who do not pay any fee. There are no degrees awarded at the end of the study, but lay agent-students have the opportunity to engage in the process that Collini (2012) called 'dissatisfaction'. For Collini, recent neoliberal attempts to impose market 'reforms' on higher education, with higher education being presented as a human capital product and students being presented as customers that need to be 'satisfied' with the product consumed, fundamentally misunderstood what higher education ought to seek to do. Instead of defining students as rational choice instrumentally rational utility maximisers with fixed 'preferences', who know beforehand what a good product is, students ought to find higher education a transformational process. Higher education ought to be a transformational process because existing beliefs and values – their constitutive commitments – would be challenged in an unsettling process that entailed dissatisfaction, in the sense that the process of being exposed to new ways of seeing and evaluating the world is uncomfortable. This is a slow process that develops over the three years and which can entail the being of the student changing. I will leave aside discussion of to what extent this happens in mainstream higher education and refer instead to student lay agents at co-operative universities being potentially able to experience this transformational, dissatisfying process, not least because they are motivated by a desire to learn new ways of seeing the world. In this process, academics could teach their critical perspective alongside a range of other perspectives and adopt the dialogic approach advocated by Freire, with this entailing students playing a role in the formation of the curricula.

For Freire (1996), we can say that the form of education was as important as the content. What this meant is that a dialogic approach to education, rather than a monologic approach, was as important as the content of what is being taught. A monologic form entailed what Freire termed 'the banking approach', whereby an authority figure 'deposited' fixed facts beyond question into passive learners' heads. This implicitly instructs learners passively to accept authority. Further, it caused harm by denying the process of becoming, whereby learners were free to develop and redevelop their constitutive commitments, and sought instead to use monologic authority to require people to adapt to the demands of authority. Agents became alienated from their true being in a process that entailed objective ontological harm. Consequently, if the content of education shifted from, say, a conservative approach to history and society, to a revolutionary approach, people would not be liberated, if the form remained the 'banking approach', with a revolutionary elite taking a monologic approach, because lay agents would still be objects adapting themselves to the demands of monologic authority, rather than subjects shaping their own becoming. For Freire, liberation was not something that could be done to someone but something that must be achieved by the agent themselves. Freire recognised that this could be uncomfortable – or dissatisfying – because it required us fundamentally to change what I have termed here as our constitutive commitments. This uncomfortable – indeed, potentially and emotionally painful – process of changing the ideas and values that constitute our being was likely to be a slow process. Agents were thus not seen as objects to be liberated by an epistemic authority in the form of an expert, authoritative elite, furnishing educational content that agents should adapt themselves to. Instead, agents would engage in a more dialogic approach to education with the teachers, with the teachers acting as guides rather than authority sources.

This is not to undermine the concept of expertise, but it is to say that a rational approach to expertise has to be dialogic rather than monologic. Here I want to turn briefly to the work of Gadamer. Gadamer (2013) argued that the Enlightenment had mistakenly taken any authority claim in knowledge to be erroneous, in reaction to clericalism. However, while accepting knowledge claims on the basis of the authority of the source of (putative) knowledge was erroneous, we could not escape authority in the form of the prevailing traditions which provide the constitutive commitments that defined us. As these traditions constituted our being, they had authority. Nonetheless, it was possible to have a rational approach to such authority by recognising that our constitutive commitments provided horizons that were by their nature limited – that is, by recognising our condition of finitude. This in turn could motivate a dialogic exchange that ultimately led to the changing of constitutive commitments and thus a change in being.

As regards expertise, Gadamer position was that, to use Fryberg's and Andrew's terminology here, it was not just the technical knowledge or *episteme* embodied in experts' professional training that defined them as successful competent and rational experts, but *phronesis* too, with phronesis entailing not just the experience to know how to apply technical knowledge quickly but, more importantly, when to withdraw. To return to medicine to give an example, we can draw on Gadamer's *The Enigma of Health* (1996). Here Gadamer argued that the successful practice of medicine was both an art and a science. It required the physician to know the scientific body of technical knowledge and to be able to apply this using judgements that were outside science and based on a practical skill to know when to withdraw intervention and to allow the body to return to equilibrium by itself. The 'master of their art' had authority but this was not based on a totalising sense of control over the situation, but on knowing how best to apply scientific knowledge and, as important, when to cease applying that (Gadamer 1996: 21–22). In other words, it concerned an appreciation of finitude – finitude enables rather than undermines professional capability. In this process, the physician would enter dialogue with the patient, so as to best assess when to withdraw treatment. Successful care relies on establishing a 'common ground' of mutual understanding, and this needed genuine dialogue. Indeed, dialogue needed to 'be seen as part of the treatment itself' (Gadamer 1996: 127). The physician, as a master of their art, would not need to demonstrate their epistemic authority in a monologic way and would instead embody their authority in their response to their condition of finitude. Professional decision making could not be fully 'rationalised', meaning that while technology can assist medical diagnoses and treatment, it can never replace the need of the practitioner to make judgements based more on 'art' than science, that is, on the doctor's practical knowledge and its ability to let them know how to improve situations by recognising the limits of their intervention.

This fits in with Gadamer's (1992) broader discussion of the role of experts in an increasingly bureaucratised and instrumentally rationalised world, which held that any rational engagement with the authority of experts had to be dialogic and not rely on lay agents expecting experts to have the expertise and authority stemming from that to engage monologically. A purely rationalised technocracy where experts legislated monologically on all domains would be one with an irrational approach to authority, because expertise would overreach itself and lay agents would not rationally hold ideas and commitments, as those ideas and commitments were passively consumed. In other words, a rational response to expert authority cannot entail the banking approach but instead required a dialogic approach where *phronesis* enabled experts to know the limits of their expertise.

Conclusion

In conclusion, I would say that I am in broad agreement with Andrew's conception of being and the task of a CSS. When it comes to the use of social scientific knowledge to help further well-being, I think Andrew's conception of expert–lay dialogue benefits from some reconceptualisation. To increase well-being, I would argue that agents have to liberate themselves rather than be liberated by an expert. This is because the latter entailed a potential loss of dignity and encouraged agents to adapt to monologic authority. This not only causes objective harm, by negating agents' ability to flourish by defining and redefining their constitutive commitments, that is, their ability to actively define the open-ended process of becoming. It is also in tension with what, drawing on Gadamer, we could call a rational approach to authority. The needed increase in well-being can result from lay agents engaging in the co-production of critical knowledge necessary to motivate transformational political agency. This is not to reject the concept of expertise and argue for a 'folk epistemology'. Rather, it is to argue for a dialogic engagement between lay agents and expert academics, with the latter recognising the finitude of their being and the concomitant need to not define all problems and other agents within the terms of reference that constitute their professional being.

References

Archer, M. S. (2005). *Being Human: The Problem of Agency*. Cambridge: Cambridge University Press.

Bhaskar, R. (1998). *The Possibility of Naturalism: A Philosophical Critique of the Contemporary Human Sciences*, Third edition. London: Routledge.

Bourdieu, P. (2000). *Pascalian Meditations*. Cambridge: Polity Press.

Collier, A. (1999). *Being and Worth*. London: Routledge.

Collier, A. (2003). *In Defence of Objectivity and Other Essays: On Reason, Existentialism and Politics*. Abingdon: Routledge.

Collini, S. (2012). *What are Universities for?* London: Penguin.

Dunn, J. (1993). *Back to Rough Ground: Practical Judgment and the Lure of Technique*. Indiana: University of Notre Dame Press.

Flyvbjerg, B. (2001). *Making Social Science Matter*. Cambridge: Cambridge University Press.

Freire, P. (1996 [1970]). *Pedagogy of the Oppressed*. London: Penguin.

Gadamer, H-G. (1992). The Limitation of the Expert. In D. Misgeld & G. Nicholson (eds) *Hans-Georg Gadamer on Education, Poetry and History: Applied Hermeneutics*. New York: State University of New York Press.

Gadamer, H-G. (1996 [1977]). *The Enigma of Health*. Cambridge: Polity.

Gadamer, H-G. (2013 [1975]). *Truth and Method*. London: Bloomsbury.

Sayer, A. (1992). *Method in Social Science: A Realist Approach*, Second edition. London: Routledge.

Sayer, A. (2000a). *Realism and Social Science*. London: Sage.

Sayer, A. (2000b). System, Lifeworld and Gender: Associational versus Counterfactual Thinking. *Sociology* 34(4): 707–725.

Sayer, A. (2000c). For Postdisciplinary Studies: Sociology and the Curse of Disciplinary Parochialism and Imperialism. In J. Eldridge, J. MacInnes, S. Scott, C, Warhurst & A. Witz (eds), pp. 83–91, *For Sociology: Legacy and Prospects*. Durham: Sociology Press.

Sayer, A. (2001). Reply to Holmwood. *Sociology* 35(4): 967–984.

Sayer, A. (2005). *The Moral Significance of Class*. Cambridge: Cambridge University Press.

Sayer, A. (2011). *Why Things Matter to People: Social Science, Values and Ethical Life*. Cambridge: Cambridge University Press.

Sayer, A. (2015). *Why we can't afford the Rich*. Bristol: Policy Press.

Chapter 4

Abstract and Concrete
Some (More) Groundwork

Steve Fleetwood

Introduction

I am delighted to have the opportunity to contribute a chapter in this collection in honour of Andrew Sayer. As an undergraduate in the 1980s, his work introduced me to the philosophy of social science in ways that strongly influenced my intellectual trajectory. A decade or so later, we became colleagues and friends at Lancaster University, enjoying many days cycling and hill walking in Lancashire and the Lake District.[1]

It was Sayer's paper 'Abstraction: A Realist Interpretation' (1981) that first sparked an interest in this issue. He recognised the importance of the terms 'abstract' and 'concrete', before setting about the *groundwork* of clarifying these terms in his usual careful and lucid style. He continued this task in his two books (Sayer 1984, 1992) referring to abstraction as 'an important but under-analysed way of conceptualising objects'. Little has been done to correct this under-analysis since then, largely because of the widespread belief that we all know what the terms 'abstract' and 'concrete' mean, so why bother re-inventing the wheel? Sayer and Rosen respond to this belief:

> In many accounts of science abstraction is assumed to be so obviously necessary that little is said about how it should be done. It is a powerful tool and hence a dangerous one if carelessly used.
>
> (Sayer 1992: 86)

> The abstract/concrete distinction has a curious status in contemporary philosophy. It is widely agreed that the distinction is of fundamental importance. And yet there is no standard account of how it should be drawn.
>
> (Rosen 2020)

The aim of this chapter is, therefore, to do some (more) groundwork clarifying the terms 'abstract' and 'concrete', hopefully, with something like Sayer's level of care and lucidity.

DOI: 10.4324/9781003247326-6

Format

The section 'Some Dictionary and Encyclopaedia Entries' briefly discusses dictionary and encyclopaedia entries for the terms 'abstract' and 'concrete'. The section 'Terminology' introduces some terminologies that will become necessary to investigate these terms as the chapter unfolds. The section 'The Abstract and the Concrete' investigates the ways the terms 'abstract' and 'concrete' are used in social science. The section 'Etymology versus Contemporary Use' looks at the etymology of the term 'abstract', revealing a tension between its origins and the way it is used in contemporary social science: abstraction as *extraction* and as *exclusion*. The section 'Abstraction: Extraction or Exclusion?' deals with this tension by paying attention to the *process–product* distinction, before distinguishing between *internal* and *external* abstraction. The section 'Unsatisfactory Abstractions' deals with unsatisfactory abstractions. The conclusion suggests two further areas that might be explored in the future, namely *isolation* and *Systematic Dialectics*.

Some Dictionary and Encyclopaedia Entries

A glance at the various dictionary and encyclopaedia entries[2] for the terms 'abstract' and 'concrete' reveal three things: (i) these terms have several meanings; (ii) many of these meanings are relevant for metaphysics, but not for social science; and (iii) some of these meanings have leeched into social science where they can be misleading. The following definition is a fairly typical one for social science:

> A general definition of *abstraction* is the process of removing characteristics from some entity to reduce it to some set of essential properties. This process of abstraction often requires the mental or conceptual manipulation of observable objects, facts, and events to reduce to essential properties and create a deeper or more complex description of a phenomenon or a set of phenomena. Consequently, *abstract* is often contrasted with *concrete* because abstract categories are not only more generalised in nature than other categories (due to the distillation of essential properties), but they often refer to representations of objects and events that are not located in time or space.
>
> (Damico 2019: 1)

Terminology

The term 'abstraction' can be used as a *verb*, as in 'abstracting', and refers to the action, process or *practice*[3] of abstracting as in 'she abstracts', 'she is abstracting', 'she has abstracted' or in the past participle form as in 'consumers were abstracted from producers'. It can be used as a *noun*, as in *the* abstraction, *an* abstraction or 'the consumer is an abstraction' where it refers to the result, outcome or *product* of the practice – i.e. the product of the practice of abstracting is an abstraction. It is common to refer to '*the* abstract' and '*the* concrete' as generic terms to refer to a class of abstract and concrete entities, respectively.[4] It can also be used as an *adjective* to give information about a noun as in 'the concept is abstract', meaning it excludes much or extracts little. The term 'abstract' can be used to mean 'difficult to understand', 'abstruse', 'vague' or 'removed from reality'. It can also be used to mean thinking *abstractly*, especially in thinking mathematically or formally – for example, 'In modern economics … models are frequently specified in a mathematical and highly abstract form' (Elliot 1991: xvii). I will not be using these meanings.

I use the term 'entities' in a generic and neutral way, and synonymously with objects, phenomena, things and stuff. The term 'objects' is more common, but I prefer the term 'entities' because the former is more suggestive of material stuff, a suggestion I want to avoid.

Sometimes I will refer to entities in terms of an entity's elements and aspects or elements/aspects for short. For example, an entity like a production system consists of entities (e.g. workers) and their aspects (e.g. skills). I understand entities to include *events* such as a change in a wage rate and *states of affairs* such as occurrences, episodes or states of being such as being female or being unemployed.

Let me now turn to the slippery term 'real' and make two introductory comments.[5] First, I employ the '*causal criterion for existence*', whereby an entity is understood to be *real* if it is *causally efficacious* – i.e. if it can make a difference.[6] Second, some entities (e.g. stars) exist autonomously, or *independently of human action* – i.e. without human beings knowing about them, observing them, cognising them, conceptualising them, creating them, constructing them or altering them in any way. Other entities (e.g. norms) *cannot* so exist because human beings create them. Nevertheless, although 'social phenomena cannot exist independently of actors or subjects they usually do exist independently of the particular individual who is studying them' (Sayer 1992: 49).

Entities are real in different ways or '*modes*', of which I believe there are four. These four modes of reality are *materially, conceptually, socially and artefactually real*. Materially real entities exist independently *of human thinking and acting*, but conceptually, socially and artefactually real entities do not.

(a) *Materially real* entities include galaxies, stars, planet Earth, electrons, photons, oceans, mountains, forests and 'flesh and blood' people.[7]

(b) *Conceptually (or ideally) real* include conceptual (i.e. immaterial) entities such as stereotypes, thoughts, beliefs, words, discourses, semiotised entities (e.g. signs, symbols), texts, meanings, understandings, ideologies and outright lies.[8] Conceptually real entities, i.e. conceptions, can be held by individuals or by communities, but the latter are the focus of my attention.

(c) *Socially real* entities include immaterial entities such as economic systems, states, organisations, workers, employers, class relations, laws and rules. What gives entities the label 'social' and allows us to refer to them as 'socially real' is the fact that they are what they are in virtue of being part of a society. Stars, for example, are not *socially* real.

(d) *Artefactually real* entities are a synthesis of materially, conceptually and socially real entities and include machines, computers, *i*phones and cosmetics. In certain contexts, some apparently materially real entities are better classified as artefactually real – i.e. *managed* forests and, arguably, weather systems.[9]

Allow me to elaborate. First, the distinction between conceptually, socially and artefactually real (but not materially real) entities should not be interpreted as three 'silos' but as three different interlinked dimensions to social life.

Second, if the reader is wondering what is *not* real (i.e. unreal), note that unicorns and infinitely lived agents are *not real* – although *conceptions* of unicorns and infinitely lived agents are real: they are conceptually real.

Third, let me deal with a common source of confusion. As social scientists, we often need a way of distinguishing between the entities we are investigating and conceptions of these entities. Take consumers. On the one hand, the term 'consumers' is a reference to flesh and blood shoppers pushing shopping trolleys around a supermarket, or 'depositing' items in a 'shopping basket' online. On the other hand, the term 'consumers' is a reference to a conception of these flesh and blood shoppers. In order not to, inadvertently, mix up these two meanings of the term consumers, social scientists often follow the *convention* of referring to flesh and blood shoppers as real. Now, as competent language users, we are rarely misled by this conventional use of the term real. When, for example, I say to my wife 'I am going shopping', she knows I do not mean 'I am going shopping *in thought*' or 'I am *conceptually* going shopping'. But, as social scientists, and especially when dealing with terms like abstract and concrete, we are often misled by this convention. Consider the ontological distinction between materially, socially and artefactually real entities like (a) planet Earth, workers and *i*phones on the one hand and (b) *conceptions* (e.g. *thoughts*) of planet Earth, workers and *i*phones. We often refer to (say) planet Earth as real, but this leaves the tricky issues of how to refer to *conceptions* of planet Earth. Sayer follows convention and invokes the terms 'real objects' and 'thought objects'.

A factual statement like 'the Earth is spherical' is not the same as the thing to which it refers. One is a 'thought object', the other is a 'real object', something that exists regardless of whether we happen to know it

> ... Thus properly qualified, the thought object/real object distinction still applies to social science.
>
> (Sayer 1992: 47 and 49)

Unfortunately, this phraseology has a negative unintended consequence. It implies (or at least does nothing to prevent) the interpretation that 'thought objects' (i.e. conceptions) are *not* 'real objects'. Sayer, of course, knows that thought objects *are* real objects. Indeed, it underlies his *insistence* that social phenomena are *concept dependent*, i.e. dependent upon 'ideas, beliefs, concepts and knowledge held by people in society'. He suggests that his account 'may seem too obvious to warrant such a laborious treatment' (ibid: 28–35 *passim*). Nevertheless, counterposing 'thought objects' to 'real objects' has this unintended consequence. Notice that in my lexicon, the Earth is *materially* real, and conceptions (i.e. thoughts) about the Earth are *conceptually* real. In this way, I avoid giving the misleading impression that the Earth is real, but conceptions of it are not real.

Fourth, for Sayer (1992: 87) 'the abstract and the concrete should not be aligned with the distinction between thought and reality'. Whilst I believe this to be entirely correct, it does not sit well with his previous phraseology apropos 'real objects and thought objects'. As I will explain in the section 'The Abstract and the Concrete', abstractions are conceptions, abstractions are thoughts, and abstract objects or entities are thought objects or entities. Unfortunately, the moment we invoke the terms 'thought objects' and 'real objects', we give the impression that abstract objects are not real objects. In this case, and *contra* Sayer's intentions, abstractions become 'aligned' with thoughts, and the latter become (somehow) not real.

Finally, whilst the phrase 'four modes of reality' is mine, I suspect that many social scientists accept something like this distinction, perhaps not explicitly and perhaps using different phraseology. Social scientists routinely differentiate between the 'natural world' (e.g. stars and flesh and blood people) and the 'social world' (e.g. economies and people as consumers). They also routinely differentiate between sex (i.e. materially real) and gender (i.e. socially real), between lumps of bauxite (i.e. materially real) and aluminium pans (i.e. artefactually real), and between stars (i.e. materially real) and ideas about stars (i.e. conceptually real).[10]

The Abstract and the Concrete

In metaphysics, to abstract is often taken to mean 'consider as a general object or idea without regard to matter', 'withdrawn or separated from material objects or practical matters' and 'opposed to concrete' – as noted in the section 'Some Dictionary and Encyclopaedia Entries'. This conception appears in the notion that concrete entities are *real* because they are *concrete*, meaning *material, physical or tangible*, and abstract entities are *unreal* because they are *non-concrete* meaning *immaterial, non-physical, intangible,*[11] existing only in thought, as conceptions. In metaphysics, paradigmatic examples of abstract entities are triangles and numbers, and paradigmatic examples of concrete entities are triangular cheese packs and *three* cats. These metaphysical notions have leeched into social science via the presumption that abstract entities are unreal and immaterial, and concrete entities are real and material. After all, if the abstract is unreal (i.e. triangles) then, presumably, the concrete is *real* (i.e. triangular objects) otherwise why counterpose them? This presumption is a mistake, encouraged by careless use of the terms 'real', 'unreal', 'abstract' and 'concrete'.

The Abstract[12]

Abstraction can be understood as *doing something (α) to something (β) in order to produce something else (γ)*. In order to figure out exactly what these 'somethings' are, I consider an example from economics, involving abstraction and consumers and then highlight three problems.

> Abstraction can be understood as *carrying out* the practice of abstracting *(α)* on consumers *(β)* in order to produce abstractions *(γ)*.

First, if we think of consumers as flesh and blood shoppers, it is clear to see that consumers (the 'somethings' denoted β) are not the kind of entities that can be subjected to the practice of exclusion and extraction – i.e. the 'somethings' denoted α. What would it mean to abstract consumers: excluding the trolley's wheels or the shoppers' hands? This would, of course, be a *category mistake*. If economists do not mean this and, clearly, they do not, then what do they mean? What kind of entities can (legitimately) be subjected to the practice of abstraction? My answer is *conceptions*. Consumers cannot be subject to the practice of abstracting, but *conceptions* of consumers can. It is conceptions that are subjected to the practice of abstracting.

Humphreys is alert to this problem. He starts with a comment from Cartwright:

> For Aristotle we begin with a concrete particular complete with all its properties. We then strip away (in our imagination) all that is irrelevant to the concerns of the moment to focus on some single property or set of properties, 'as if they were separate' ... For Aristotle, at least in principle, all the properties that science will study are there in the objects to begin with.

He then adds:

> [W]e start with a concrete particular and then mentally remove many of its properties. In the past, this idea of having thought processes operating

on real systems has not been easy to understand ... Yet if we get the abstract object by literally subtracting features from a concrete object (i.e. starting with a full complement of properties and mentally removing some of them) why do we not always know what to add back during the concretisation process, thus making the concretisation process the inverse of abstraction?

(Humphreys 1995: 158–159)

I agree entirely that what is involved in abstraction is stripping stuff away in our imagination, mentally removing stuff, and abstractions are thought processes operating on real systems. Indeed, abstraction is a process taking place in humans' cognitive systems.[13] I also agree with his identification of a likely source of the problem, namely:

not keeping a sharp separation between concrete systems, symbolic representations of these systems, and our mental operations on those symbolic (or other) representations ... These are very different categories of entities.

(Humphreys 1995: 158–159)

Second, the practice of abstracting delivers a result, output, or *product*, typically, referred to as 'abstractions', 'abstract consumers', 'consumers in the abstract' or 'abstract objects' as Humphrey might put it – i.e. the 'something else' denoted *(γ)* above. The question is: what kind of products (objects or entities) are these *abstract* products (objects or entities)? My answer is *conceptions*. These products cannot be flesh and blood consumers with this or that part/property excluded or extracted, but the products can be *conceptions* of consumers with this or that part/property excluded or extracted. *The products of abstracting are altered conceptions.*

Third, most readers will know of two ideas: (i) abstractions can be understood in terms of *levels* of abstraction – for example, higher or lower levels of abstraction; and (ii) the methodological *movement* from higher to lower levels of abstraction. But, consumers (as flesh and blood shoppers) cannot be characterised as having, or moving between, levels of abstraction. What kind of entities can be characterised in terms of levels of abstraction? My answer is *conceptions*. Conceptions can be characterised in terms of levels of abstraction.

Introducing Conceptions

My answer, to all three questions above, is *conceptions*, a term that I will use interchangeably with *concepts*. What, then, are conceptions? I understand conceptions to be thoughts, ideas, construals, notions, schemas, representations or understandings, located in humans' cognitive systems.

I understand *conceptualisation* as a process taking place in humans' cognitive systems.

Unfortunately, the relations between conceptions and conceptualisation and abstractions and abstracting are not well understood either in social science or in cognitive science. Some brief comments *apropos* for the latter may be helpful.[14] Cognitive science deals, primarily, with what I will call 'pre-analytical' conceptions and abstractions – i.e. the unconscious conceptions and abstractions that competent adults create in order to engage in any and every kind of interaction with entities that exist independently of themselves. Here we run into a 'chicken and egg' problem: humans cannot have conceptions without abstractions or abstractions without conceptions. Let me explain how I deal with this.

As I see it, human interaction with entities in the external world requires that we form thoughts, ideas, construals, notions, schemas, representations or understandings of these entities, immediately raising the question: what should we call them? As far as I am able to tell, there is no agreed term.

> Because people rely on their senses and do not have direct access to reality, they in fact regulate themselves with respect to construals of objects, rather than the objects themselves. For example, people choose between representations of different cars, not between cars.
>
> (Shapira et al. 2012: 229)

Whilst Shapira et al. plump for 'construals' (although they go on to refer to concepts and abstractions without elaboration) and others plump for 'abstractions', I am going to plump for 'conceptions'. I accept that there is a degree of arbitrariness to my choice, but here is my thinking. The term 'conceptions' implies generality, whilst 'abstractions' implies specificity: abstracting involves, minimally, exclusion or extraction, whereas conceptualisation does not. Moreover, the practice of abstracting is not carried out on itself but on something else: we do not abstract abstractions. The practice of abstracting cars, for example, is not carried out on cars, but on something else, and whilst likely candidates are construals, representations and conceptions, I am going to plump for the latter. Henceforth, wherever possible, I will refer to the product of abstracting as '*abstracted concepts*' – i.e. using the past participle to make it clear that we are dealing with a concept that has been subjected to the practice of abstracting.[15]

Unlike cognitive science, social science does not deal, primarily, in pre-analytical conceptions and abstractions but with what I will call 'analytic' conceptions and abstractions – i.e. the conscious concepts and abstractions that social scientists necessarily create in order to investigate real entities.[16] Imagine a social scientist investigating sex-based discrimination by constructing some kind of a model of it. She will start by doing what any lay person does – i.e. putting her *pre-analytical* concepts (e.g. concepts of men and women[17]) to work. This must be the case, otherwise, she would have no idea that there might even be *sex-based* discrimination. She also starts doing what every lay person does – i.e. engaging in an unconscious process or practice of abstraction. She may, for example, exclude concepts such as the heights of men and women and extract[18] concepts such as their biological sex. So far, so good. At some point, however, she has to step beyond her role as a lay person with pre-analytic concepts and into her role as a social scientist, where she has to actively create *analytical* concepts and abstractions. She may, for example, alter the concept of sex to one of gender, or alter the concept of sex-based differences to gender-based discrimination. In this way, lay persons' pre-analytical conceptions and abstractions are 'working in the background', metaphorically speaking, to underpin the creation of social scientific-analytical concepts and abstractions.

Let us have a closer look at the example of altering the concept of sex to one of gender. This could be interpreted in terms of conception, or more accurately, *re*-conception – i.e. replacing one conception with another. Or it could be interpreted in terms of abstraction – i.e. the exclusion of biological features of men and women, and/or the extraction of socially constructed features of men and women. At present, social scientists do not really know which one of these interpretations is the 'right' one.[19] Nevertheless, let me use an example that might shed some light on this issue.

Imagine that our social scientist (consciously) starts with a conception (sex), engages in a process of re-conceptualisation and ends up with a new conception (gender), which I style as follows:

conception → practice of re-conceptualisation → new conception

Unfortunately, this leaves the practice of re-conceptualisation as a 'black box' when, as a matter of fact, we often have knowledge of the practices occurring inside this 'box'. This is why I exemplified the practices as the exclusion of biological features of men and women, and/or the extraction of socially constructed features of men and women. These practices of exclusion and/or extraction are regarded as constituting abstraction. Let me style this as follows:

abstracted conception[20] → practice of abstraction → altered abstracted conception

The altered abstract conception might be altered in the sense that it excludes less and extracts more than the initial abstract conception.

Notice that this lends itself to the evolution of models as step by step, the abstracted conceptions exclude less and extract more elements/aspects of the entities under investigation. Let me style this as follows:

abstracted conception₁ → practice of abstraction₁ → abstracted
                                                        conception₂

abstracted conception₂ → practice of abstraction₂ → abstracted
                                                        conception₃

abstracted conception₃ → practice of abstraction₃ → abstracted
                                                        conception₄

Notice also that, whilst products are outputs, products/outputs like abstracted conceptions of 'consumers' can become *inputs* into completely different domains of activity whereupon they may have performative effects.[21] For example, the economist's abstracted concept of 'consumers' might encourage many university students to see themselves not as learners but as consumers, causing them to alter their thoughts and actions accordingly.

It should be clear that abstraction is a practice carried out entirely *in* humans' cognitive systems and entirely *on conceptions* of entities, not *on* the entities that are being conceptualised. Put bluntly, we cannot abstract stars from the wider galaxy, and we cannot abstract consumers from the wider economy, but we can abstract *conceptions* of stars and *conceptions* of consumers from *conceptions* of their wider environments. Consumers cannot be abstract or concrete, cannot be abstracted or concretised, cannot be more/less abstract or (using the antonym) more/less concrete. Only *conceptions* of consumers *can* be abstract or concrete, can be abstracted or concretised, can be more/less abstract and can be more/less concrete. Sayer (2000: 19) knows this, writing of the need to 'abstract out the various components or influences *in our heads*' (emphasis added).[22] Marx understood this, referring to the 'reproduction of the concrete *by way of thought* … [T]he method of rising from the abstract to the concrete is only the way in which *thought appropriates the concrete*, reproduces it as *the concrete in the mind*' (Marx 1973: 34). It is not hard to understand 'the concrete *in thought*', as something like 'the concrete conceptualised'.[23]

Finally, let me deal with two misunderstandings. First, although abstractions are conceptualisations, they are not unreal, indeed, they are real: they are conceptually real. We must, therefore, be careful with definitions, rooted in metaphysics, stating or implying that the abstract is *unreal*. Some social scientists are aware of this.

> A final word on the term 'abstract'. It is not meant here to indicate some kind of purely a priori determination … Thus, while we conventionally speak of abstraction as the act of drawing away from the material, the concrete, the real, and towards the intellectual, the 'philosophical', the unreal, this is not its only sense. In fact, *the abstract is not the unreal,* it is the real on its own terms.
>
> (Roffe 2015: 5; italics added)[24]

the things to which these abstractions refer[25] need be no less real than those referred to by more concrete concepts. Hence the abstract and the concrete should not be aligned with the distinction between thought and reality.

(Sayer 1992: 87)

Second, abstractions are not 'highfalutin'. In the section 'Some Dictionary and Encyclopaedia Entries' above, I cited the Merriam-Webster dictionary entry (part 3a) defining abstract as 'dealing with a subject in its abstract aspects: *theoretical, abstract* science'. Sometimes the term abstract is used in this sense, meaning 'highly theoretical', 'removed from reality', 'withdrawn from the practical', 'abstract theory' or even 'highfalutin'. I also mentioned metaphysics and the paradigmatic example of triangles. The term abstract is often used to refer to 'triangles' – i.e. generalisations over a range of triangular entities. Sometimes the term abstract is used in this sense, meaning highly generalised. I will not be using abstraction in this way.

The Concrete

The term concrete appears frequently in social science, almost always without elaboration or further comment, *as if* we all know what it means: unfortunately, we do not. It means different things to different individuals, and across the disciplines. But, without some idea of how the term is used, we can never start to do any groundwork on it? Before offering my interpretation of the term as it appears in social science, let me deal with two issues.

First, my concern is within a specific context, namely wherein the term concrete is used in association with the term abstract and not with other contexts, such as the context of methodology where reference is made to doing 'concrete research' (Sayer 1992: circa 237). Secondly, the term is used, in Marxist theory as follows:

The concrete is concrete because it is the concentration of many determinations, hence unity of the diverse. It appears in the process of thinking, therefore, as a process of concentration, as a result, not as a point of departure, even though it is the point of departure in reality and hence also the point of departure for observation ... and conception.

(Marx 1973: 34; italics added)

Sayer (1992: 87) uses similar phraseology, noting that the 'concept of "concrete objects" draws attention to the fact that objects are usually constituted by a combination of diverse parts or forces'. In another place he notes that 'the objects that social scientists study ... are concrete in the sense that they are the product of multiple components and forces' (Sayer 2000: 19). Unfortunately, there is no agreement on the meaning of Marx's rather cryptic phrase. I take the various incarnations of this phrase to mean something like the following: *concrete objects or entities are said to be concrete because they exist, typically, as complex combinations of different component parts and their properties.* Whilst this draws our attention to an important characteristic of entities, it runs into all the problems apropos the term concrete that I will mention below. I will not elaborate further on this use.

The term concrete and variants like 'the concrete', 'concretisation', 'concrete objects' or 'concrete entities' are frequently used in association with terms like abstract and variants like 'the abstract', 'abstraction', abstract objects' and 'abstract entities'. The term 'concrete entities' has evolved into the 'go-to' term for those who want to differentiate objects or entities from *conceptions, abstract conceptions* or *abstractions* of said objects or entities. For example, referring to *i*phones as 'concrete entities' is done to indicate that we are not dealing with *conceptions* of *i*phones, 'conceptual entities'. Moreover, once abstractions are understood as conceptions, the term 'concrete entities' is used to indicate that we are *not* dealing with abstract entities or abstract conceptions.

The term 'concrete' is not only used in association with the term 'real', the term 'concrete' is often (mis)understood to mean 'real', and the term 'real' is often (mis)understood to mean 'concrete'. By extension, the term 'concrete entities' is often (mis)understood to mean 'real entities', and this manifests itself in terms like 'concretely real objects', 'concretely real entities' and so on.[26]

Like it or not, the term 'concrete' has connotations of materiality – at least in English. Thus, often when the term 'concrete' is used, it is presumed that we are dealing with 'lumps of physical stuff'. The *Wikipedia* definition (endnote 2) is a paradigm case, suggesting that '*Abstract objects* have no physical existence, whereas concrete objects do'. The same goes for Rosen's examples of 'concreta', namely 'stars, protons, electromagnetic fields'.

In short, the term 'concrete entities' is often (mis)understood to mean concretely *real* entities,[27] which are then differentiated from abstract entities, or abstract conceptions *of* concretely *real* entities, on the grounds of their reality.

Now, recall the section 'Terminology' where I discussed 'thought objects' and 'real objects' (I will use the term 'entities') and noted that this phraseology implies (or at least does nothing to prevent) the interpretation that 'thought entities' (i.e. or abstracted conceptions) are *not* 'real entities'. Now, however, we can throw the terms 'concrete' and 'concretely real entities' into the mix. The phraseology of 'concretely *real* entities' and 'abstract entities' implies that *abstract entities* and *abstract conceptions are not real entities.* And this is, of course, a mistake: abstract entities, abstract conceptions are *real*: they are conceptually real. The consequence of this is that, if both abstract entities and concrete entities are real, then we cannot differentiate between them on the grounds of their reality. Nevertheless, despite the fact that entities and abstract conceptions of entities are both real, social scientists often need to differentiate between them. This I do by making two moves.

First, when there is the risk of confusion, I prefix the term 'real' with its appropriate mode – i.e. materially, conceptually, socially and/or artefactually real. For example, when I want to refer to consumers, as opposed to *abstracted conceptions* thereof, I do not refer to '*real* consumers' but to *socially real consumers*. In this way, I can differentiate consumers from abstracted conceptions thereof without implying that the latter is somehow not real or unreal. Incidentally, this also works in (difficult) cases where we are investigating conceptions and so have to deal with conceptions of conceptions.[28] Thus, if necessary, I can refer to a lay person's conceptually real stereotypes in order to differentiate them from (say) a social scientist's conception of a lay person's stereotype without implying that the latter is not real.[29]

The second move is simply to drop the term 'concrete'. Using my lexicon means there is no need to use the term 'concrete entities' as a reference to 'real entities'. Moreover, there is no need to use the term 'concrete' when we need to refer to conceptions being 'more/less' abstract (concrete) or being presented at 'high/low' levels of abstraction (concretion). Indeed, this is the *de facto* position anyway.

Etymology versus Contemporary Use

Exactly *what* practices are involved in abstracting? The aim of this section is to explain this and, in the process, uncover a tension between the history of the term and the way it is used in contemporary social science. Etymologically speaking, the term 'abstract' is derived from terms like to draw away from, to withdraw, to remove from, to detach from, to pull away, pull out of or drag away from (see endnote 2). In contemporary social science and philosophy of science, however, the term 'abstract' is commonly used to mean *omitting* or *excluding*.[30]

> *abstraction* is the process of removing characteristics from some entity to reduce it to some set of essential properties.
>
> (Damico 2019)

> according to the general intuition abstraction is understood to be more or less synonymous to omission of features of systems, which means that something is left out from a description and something else is retained.
>
> (Portides 2018)

> An important feature of my view of abstraction is that … [the scientist] simply focuses on some parts and properties that are relevant for studying the phenomenon of interest … and ignores the rest.
>
> (Elliot-Graves: 22)

There is, then, a tension between the etymological roots of the term and its use in contemporary social science. Indeed, the tension is between abstraction as 'drawing away from' or *'extracting'*, and abstraction as *'excluding'*. How can we deal with this tension?

Abstraction: Extraction or Exclusion?

A moment's reflection suggests that we can think about abstraction either as extraction *qua pulling something(s) out* and as exclusion *qua pushing something(s) away.*

(a) Abstraction as extraction

> To pull A from A, B,... Z is to conduct an operation or carry out practice *on* A. That is, we 'do something' to A but 'do nothing' to B, C,... Z; we are active *apropos* A and passive *apropos* B, C,... Z; A is the *direct product* of the practice; A is obtained by doing something to A. The analogy is drawing a ball from an urn containing many balls – for example, A, B, C,... Z. Note three things:
>
> - one ends up with A, just with A, and not A *and* B, C,... Z.
> - because the process of abstraction = extraction is carried out *on* A, not *on* B, C,... Z, it is *not* difficult to refer to A as 'the abstraction'.
> - this is in keeping with the etymological roots.[31]

It is necessary to recognise this form of abstraction because without so doing we would not be able to make sense of comments about abstraction like the following:

> In order to conduct an analysis of the labour market we need to *abstract the crucial elements of the behaviour of economic agents from the complexity* of labour market outcomes.
>
> (Smith 2009: 2; emphasis added)

> A model ... represents the real world by *abstracting, or taking from* the real world that which will help us understand it.
>
> (Hall & Lieberman 2003: 7 emphasis original)

(b) Abstraction as exclusion

> To push B, C,... Z away from A is to carry out practice on B, C,... Z, *not on* A. That is, we 'do something' to B, C,... Z, but 'do nothing' to A; we are active *apropos* B, C,... Z and passive *apropos* A; A is *the by-product* of the practice, A is obtained by doing something to B, C,... Z. It

is instructive to consider the above analogy (drawing a ball from an urn) carefully because it breaks down in this case. To push the analogy, to see why it breaks down, it would be like *emptying* the urn of all the balls except one – i.e. *excluding* all the balls except one. The term 'emptying' sits well with 'excluding', but not with 'extracting'. Why not? Because one *empties* the urn of, let's say, balls B, C,… Z, but one does not *extract* ball A. Rather, ball A is left as a 'residue' once the urn has been emptied of the other balls, once the other balls have been extracted. Note three things:

- one ends up with A, just with A, and not A *and* B, C,… Z.
- because the process of abstraction is carried out *on* B, C,… Z, not *on* A, it is difficult to refer to A as 'the abstraction' – although it would be less difficult to refer to A as 'the residue' or some such.
- this is in keeping with contemporary social scientific usage.

This raises a question: Are (a) and (b) both *bona fide* cases of abstraction or is one merely a 'look-alike', and if so, which one?

Processes and Their Products

Portides (2018) addresses a similar question when distinguishing between 'processes and their products' – i.e. the distinction between the process or practice of abstracting and its product, namely, an abstraction. This is referred to by Mäki (2009: 30) as 'the process–product ambiguity'. Portides makes a similar distinction:

> according to the general intuition abstraction is understood to be more or less synonymous to omission of features of systems, which means that something is left out from a description and something else is retained … Let us call this the *omission-as-subtraction* view. But the cognitive operation of omission could also be interpreted so as to involve the act of extracting something and discarding the remainder … Let us call the latter the *omission-as-extraction* view. Frequently, in our common vocabulary we refer to omission-as-extraction with the phrase 'abstracting away from'.
>
> (Portides 2018)

Portides and I use different terminology but, I believe, are getting at the same thing. In my lexicon, omission and exclusion are synonymous, so for consistency, I replace the former with the latter. Thus, abstraction can be understood (a) as exclusion-as-subtraction (i.e. exclusion *qua* pushing something(s) away); or (b) as exclusion-as-extraction (i.e. pulling something(s) out). What matters is that if 'the emphasis is put on the product of the cognitive process of omission [*a.k.a.* exclusion] then there is no noticeable difference between the two interpretations' – i.e. between *exclusion*-as-subtraction and as *exclusion*-as-extraction. In other words, abstraction involves two different practices or processes, but the product is the same: abstractions.

This process–product distinction can be understood in terms of the distinction between abstraction as a *verb* and as a *noun*. If one focuses upon the practices (verb), then extraction, qua pulling something(s) out, is a different practice to exclusion *qua* pushing something(s) away. If one focuses upon the product (noun) then the outcome is the same – i.e. one ends up with A, just with A, and not A *and* B, C,... Z.

The practice of abstraction, carried out via exclusion or extraction, has implications for what I refer to (below) as unsatisfactory abstractions. It may be a mistake to refer to an abstraction that *excludes relevant* elements/aspects as *un*satisfactory if it transpires that they can be introduced at a later stage in the analysis – without undermining previously drawn conclusions. It is, however, always a mistake to refer to an abstraction that *extracts irrelevant* elements/aspects as satisfactory because once they are extracted, they become a feature of the analysis and cannot be de-extracted at a later stage in the analysis.

Internal and External Abstraction

Most entities are parts of other entities. A labour market, for example, is part of a 'broader' or 'wider' entity, namely, an economy consisting *inter alia* of markets for goods and services, public and private sector organisations and local, national and supra-national states. It is possible to produce two types of abstractions of a labour market: *external* and *internal* abstractions.[32]

(i) We might carry out the practice of abstracting by explicitly excluding entities in the 'wider' economy – i.e. entities that are *external* to the labour market. The outcome or product might be referred to as an *external* abstraction. We produce an external abstraction by starting with the 'goings on' outside the labour market and excluding them.

(ii) We might carry out the practice of abstracting by implicitly ignoring entities[33] in the 'wider' economy and directing our attention to the 'goings on' inside the labour market – for example, we might exclude workers' gender, race, class or skills. The product might be referred to as an *internal* abstraction. We produce an internal abstraction by starting with the 'goings on' inside the labour market and excluding some of its elements/aspects.

Unsatisfactory Abstractions

Sayer refers to good, bad, rational, chaotic, contentless, empty and one-sided abstractions.

A rational abstraction[34] is one which isolates a significant element of the world which has some unity and autonomous force, such as a structure. A bad abstraction arbitrarily divides the indivisible, thereby, 'carving up' the object of study with little or no regard for its structures ... A fairly uncontroversial example of a bad abstraction or chaotic conception is the concept of 'services' as in 'service employment'; this covers an enormous variety of activities which neither form structures nor interact causally to any significant degree and many lack anything significant in common.

(Sayer 1992: 139)

An abstract concept might be denoted by the symbol p, which in turn might refer to an object P. The danger of taking abstraction to the extreme form of mere notation is that we are easily led to forget P ... so that our [mathematical] manipulations 'take on a life of their own' and we lose our grip on ... those properties of p which determine what it can and cannot do.

(Sayer 1992: 99)

[A]n abstraction isolates in thought a *one-sided*[35] or partial aspect of an object.

(Sayer 1992: 87)

Whilst I agree with Sayer, there are many ways in which abstractions can be said to be bad, deficient, defective, faulty, flawed, insufficient, weak or *unsatisfactory*. In the remainder of this section, however, I want to deal with two matters arising from the above.

First, according to Sayer, 'Abstractions should distinguish incidental from essential characteristics'. I agree and want to add the following point. Whether abstraction is carried out via extraction or exclusion, what is extracted should be *relevant* (or synonyms such as essential, crucial, non-incidental, consequential, non-negligible, significant, non-trivial and important), and what is excluded should be *irrelevant*.[36] Distinguishing relevant from irrelevant entities is, of course, an extremely complicated matter, debate rages and elaborating is beyond the scope of this chapter. Nevertheless, a few brief words are in order.

In contemporary philosophy of science, the issue of (ir)relevance forms part of a debate about pragmatic versus ontological considerations. Pragmatic considerations concern the functions attributed to a model – for example, surrogate or substitute; the use to which a model will be put – for example, inference, interpretation, prediction or explanation; the model's audience; the core beliefs of the discipline; and the meta-theoretical norms of the discipline. Ontological considerations involve 'the way the world is'. As I see it, satisfactory abstractions require social scientists to take both pragmatic *and* ontological considerations into account. As Mäki (2009: 29) puts it: 'Models

... are constrained both ontologically (by their targets) and pragmatically (by the purposes and audiences of the modeller)'. Moreover, relevance has to be argued for and justified, not merely asserted or taken for granted.[37]

Second, the term 'abstraction' is often used synonymously with 'idealisation', in which case, much of what is said about unsatisfactory abstractions appertains to unsatisfactory idealisations and *vice versa*. I cannot do this important matter justice here, but feel it is necessary to say something because, when commenting upon a draft of this chapter, Andrew Sayer questioned my 'wholly pejorative concept of idealising'. This is precisely how I see idealisation. In my view, abstraction and idealisation are *different* practices. In the context of disciplines like economics[38] whilst abstraction can be carried out without introducing distortions to models, idealisation rarely can. Let me start with a few clarifiers.

First, by idealisation I do *not* have in mind conceptualisations such as *possible* future social arrangements – for example, economic systems where high-quality childcare is provided, collectively, to all families. These are entirely acceptable conceptualisations, but it is better to call them 'concrete utopias' or some such. Hodgson (1999) refers to thinking about this kind of utopian system in terms of non-existent, yet possible and desirable systems. By idealisation I *do* have in mind the kind of distortions that mainstream economists frequently deploy such as the following:

> We assume that asset markets are complete, so that employed and unemployed individuals are able to achieve perfect risk sharing, equating the marginal utility of consumption across states.
>
> (Mattesini & Rossi 2009: 1471)

> The economy is populated by ex-ante heterogeneous risk-neutral workers of measure one and firms of a large measure. Each firm has one job. Workers differ in terms of their ability, which is measured by x. Ability is distributed according to the cumulative distribution function $F(\cdot)$.
>
> (Chassamboulli 2013: 219–220)

These are unacceptable conceptualisations because they are of *impossible* social arrangements and are introduced solely for mathematical tractability. Mainstream models based upon idealisations *qua* distortions cannot, or at least should not, be used to derive conclusions that could be true of real economic systems. Moreover, defending such models on the grounds that they are *merely* useful for conducting 'thought experiments' claims significantly reduce their applicability.

Second, whilst the two most common accounts of idealisation are 'Aristotelian' and 'Galilean' idealisation, it is arguable that the former are not idealisations, but abstractions *qua* exclusions, whereas the latter idealisations are *bona fide* idealisations *qua* distortions.[39]

So, let us conclude this section by merely asserting my position, namely that abstraction and idealisation are *different* practices, via comments from two philosophers.

> Jones (2005) has offered a unified treatment of the processes of idealisation and abstraction. The gist of it is that in abstraction some features of the system under study are neglected/omitted (without the system being misrepresented); in idealisation, there is misconceptualisation – the model attributes properties to the system it does not have and/or denies that the system has some properties that it in fact possesses.
>
> (Psillos 2011: 7)

> *Abstracting:* We *abstract* from property *P* of a physical [i.e. or economic] system *x iff:* in our corresponding scientific model, *P* is not included.

> *Idealising*: We *idealise* a property *P* of a physical [i.e. or economic] system *x iff:* in our corresponding model, *P* is not included and *P* is replaced by a different property *Q* which is not exhibited by *x*.
>
> (Ducheyne 2007: 9–10) [40]

Conclusion: What Next?

I want to conclude by making two, brief, suggestions about where research might go in the future.

Abstracting, Idealising and Isolating

One practice widely referred to in philosophy of science, alongside abstraction and idealisation, is *isolation*, as the following comment illustrates:

> I take abstraction to be a matter of omission [*a.k.a.* exclusion], and idealisation a matter of exaggeration [*a.k.a.* distortion] … I regard abstraction and idealisation as the means scientists employ in order to achieve the goal of isolation.
>
> (Hindriks 2013: 529 refs supressed)

One author defines isolation via its outcome, namely an isolation, as follows:

> In an isolation … a set X of entities, is 'sealed off' from the involvement or influence of everything else, a set of Y entities; together X and Y comprise the universe. The isolation of X from Y typically involves a representation of the relationships among elements of X. Let us call X the *isolated field* and Y the *excluded field.*
>
> (Mäki 1992: 321)

This throws up two questions for future research. First, if one isolates a set X of entities, by abstracting *qua* extracting X from Y or by abstracting *qua* excluding everything else in the set Y, does this make isolating synonymous with abstracting? Second, whilst both Hindriks and Mäki (and others) see a role for idealisation alongside isolation and abstraction, what exactly is this role?

Two Approaches to the Move from Abstract to Concrete

The move from the abstract to the concrete can be given a *Systematically Dialectical* (SD)[41] inflection, primarily, by focusing upon what I will call four '*methodological themes*'.

(1) The distinction between the method of *enquiry* and the method of *presentation*. Pursuing the former, we start with a chaotic conception out of which we will have figured out: (i) the nature of the system, totality or organic whole under investigation; (ii) the set of essential categories that constitute this system; and (iii) the correct starting point for the presentation – i.e. the cell-form, concrete abstraction or concrete universal which will, typically, differ from where the enquiry started.
(2) From this starting point, the presentation is unfolded *systematically*, meaning, *dialectically*, as a movement, driven by contradictions in the categories until the whole is presented.
(3) The development of the categories drives the movement between the levels of abstraction, and (if executed correctly) the investigation moves from the abstract to the concrete, via progressively richer or less 'thin' categories.
(4) The overall result is the systematic reproduction of the concrete in thought.[42]

Not everyone who makes reference to the move from the concrete to the abstract and back does so from the perspective of SD. I do not[43] and neither does Sayer. From an SD perspective, I might be asked to take an 'unsystematically non-dialectic' (UND) approach with my suggestions for building a model of labour markets by moving from more to less, abstracted conceptions (Fleetwood 2011, 2014, 2016). Advocates of SD approaches are critical of UND approaches on the grounds that the latter do not adhere to the four methodological themes noted above.[44]

Now, it seems to me that two matters stand in need of clarification at the outset. First, the SD approach seems applicable to one, and only one phenomenon, namely the capitalist socio-economic system as a totality. The snag is not everyone who wants to model a 'relatively small' aspect of the social world (e.g. the Black Lives Matter [BLM] movement) wants to deal with the capitalist socio-economic system as a totality. And this goes for Marxists who understand that the essential forces at work in the capitalist socio-economic system are likely to have a causal impact on most aspects of the social world such as the BLM movement. Thus, we need to know whether it is possible to apply the SD approach to 'relatively small' aspects of the social world. The second matter in need of clarification is an extension of the first, namely to what extent are the SD and UND approaches compatible? Can we take a UND approach to a 'relatively small' aspect of the social world whilst operating with an SD approach more generally?

Notes

1 I would like to thank Andrew for suggesting several extremely useful improvements to earlier drafts.
2 Abstract, www.etymonline.com/search?q=abstract (accessed 8 October 2020). Abstract, www.merriam-webster.com/dictionary/abstract (accessed 26 January 2020). Abstract and concrete, https://en.wikipedia.org/wiki/Abstract_and_concr ete (accessed 1 February 2021). Concrete, www.dictionary.com/browse/concrete (accessed 1 February 2021). The Concise Oxford Dictionary 1999. Rosen (2020).
3 I will use the terms 'process' and 'practice' interchangeably, selecting whichever seems more appropriate.
4 This is rather like using the term 'the tall' to refer to a class of tall people.
5 This draws upon Fleetwood (2004).
6 This is opposed, for example, to empiricist doctrines whereby an entity is real if it is observed.
7 This is a reference to people as material, *qua biological* entities.
8 See Fleetwood (2019a, 2019b).
9 This is why we differentiate, for example, between virgin forests (materially real) and managed forests (artefactually real). Note that all real entities undergo continual evolution and change (i.e. are processual) and can shift between modes of reality – i.e. a virgin forest can become a managed forest.
10 In private correspondence Sayer noted his acceptance of this notion of four modes of reality.
11 Henceforth, I will (mainly) use only the terms 'material' and 'immaterial' to encapsulate the other cognate terms.
12 For me, cognition is not located in the brain, essentially a computer, encoding incoming information as conceptualizations, then issuing instructions to a passive body which executes them. I prefer phenomenologically oriented alternatives wherein, as 'beings-in-the-world', our cognition is *embodied* (i.e. involving the body); *extended, distributed or embedded* (i.e. into or in the external environment); *enacted* or *situated* (i.e. involving practical activities); *anticipatory* (i.e. involving forward looking and pre-prepared); and *dynamic* (i.e. continually adapting to changes in the external environment). See Gallagher (2013, 2015).
13 I have problems with terms like 'concrete systems', 'concrete particulars' and 'concrete objects' for reasons I will mention below. Humphreys has natural science in mind, in which case, there is no problem with thinking about concrete systems or objects as materially real in my lexicon.
14 This is not a dismissal of cognitive science in which I include cognitive psychology. Good social science should be consistent with good cognitive science.

15 I don't want to give the impression that humans could dispense with abstraction and just manage with conception. See, for example, the work of cognitive scientists Yee (2019) and Barsalou et al. (2018) but note that the terms 'abstract' and 'concrete' have different meanings to those found in social science.

16 Clearly, there is no rigid boundary between the pre-analytic and the analytic. There is another unconscious cognitive process that takes place every time groups of humans interact. Ollman (2003: 01) refers to each social class' 'habitual abstractions' that allow members 'to make sense of society from just these mental units'. Whilst I agree, it may be more correct to refer to them as habitual conceptions, I will not be focusing on these conceptions.

17 Pre-analytical conceptions (gestalts) are also used by humans to identify things in the world as something and not a jumble of sense impressions. Thanks to Andrew for reminding me of this.

18 Abstraction can be carried out via *extraction* or via *exclusion*. I will elaborate in the section 'Etymology versus Contemporary Use', but this example gives a reasonably good idea of what these terms mean.

19 Cognitive scientists do not investigate this kind of phenomena.

20 I refer to this conception as an 'abstracted conception' in recognition of the fact that no investigation starts with nothing, so any conceptions are already abstract. This could mean pre-analytical abstractions, or previously existing analytical assumptions.

21 Thanks to Andrew Sayer for reminding me of the importance of this point.

22 Notice that if abstractions are conceptions, they are located, at least initially, in humans' cognitive systems. They can be, and often are, transferred from cognitive systems to artefacts. One might, for example, write one's conception of an economic system, thereby transferring the conception to a piece of paper, or a computer file.

23 See the entry on 'sociological abstraction' that makes the same point with different terminology   Abstraction,   https://en.wikipedia.org/wiki/Abstraction(sociology) (accessed 25 November 2020).

24 The phrase 'real on its own terms' is difficult to interpret.

25 Sayer mentions 'temperature, valency, gender, income elasticity of demand or the circuit of money capital'.

26 This is why terms like 'the entity itself', the 'actually real', the 'objectively real' and even the 'really real' are used. Sometimes, a term like 'objective' is used to mean real, but this implies that 'subjective' means unreal. I follow Sayer's lead in denying that objective and subjective are synonymous with the real and the unreal (Fleetwood 2004: 37–38).

27 With or without the connotations of materiality.

28 This recalls the sociological notion of the 'double hermeneutic', i.e. whereby sociologists seek to understand lay agents' understandings of the social world – i.e. *understandings of understandings*, or meanings of meanings.

29 Imagine a female job-seeker attending a job interview and being conceptualised by the potential employer in stereotypical terms as having a domestic, not a work, orientation. Now, imagine a social scientist conceptualising this stereotype as a mechanism tending to cause gender discrimination. From the social scientist's perspective, the employer's stereotype is conceptually real. From the moment that this social scientist develops this conception, then this conception is also conceptually real, but it is not a stereotype.

30 I prefer the term 'excluding' to 'omitting' because the latter has no obvious antonym, whereas the former does, namely, 'including'.
31 See the entry from www.etymonline.
32 This notion derives from Mäki (2004: 321–322).
33 Notice that in case (i) we would have, implicitly, ignored the political system and the environment.
34 This would be a satisfactory abstraction.
35 From an Hegelian perspective, one-sidedness has an important meaning, namely, as counterposed to the many-sidedness of the totality. I cannot elaborate here but see the conclusion.
36 I will not list the antonyms.
37 See Mäki (2011) and Morgan (2012).
38 And disciplines outside economics that utilize Rational Choice Theory (Archer & Tritter 2000).
39 See Frigg and Hartmann (2020); Morgan (2010: 157); Morgan and Knuuttitla (2010: 5–6, 19 passim); Elliott-Graves and Weisberg (2014: 177); Donato Rodriguez and Zamora Bonilla (2009: 111).
40 These definitions omit Ducheyne's symbolism but otherwise follow his wording.
41 SD stems from a Hegelian reading of Marx and might be characterized as follows:

> At the philosophical level it is a way of working with concepts that keeps them open and fluid, and above all, systematically interconnected. At the methodological level it puts emphasis on the need for a clear order of presentation … Epistemologically it insists on the reflexivity of the subject-object relation. Ontologically, it addresses itself to totalities and thus to their comprehension through systematically interconnected categories, which are more or less sharply distinguished from historically sequenced orderings.
> (Arthur 2004: 5)

42 The ability to successfully present the dialectical unfolding is its own epistemic warrant.
43 Although, I accept many aspects of SD.
44 See Brown (2014) for a critique of UND approaches.

References

Abstract, entry www.etymonline.com/search?q=abstract (accessed 8 October 2020).
Abstract, entry www.merriam-webster.com/dictionary/abstract (accessed 26 January 2020).
Abstraction, entry https://en.wikipedia.org/wiki/Abstraction_(sociology) (accessed 1 February 2021).
Abstract and concrete, entry https://en.wikipedia.org/wiki/Abstract_and_concrete (accessed 1 February 2021).
Archer, M., & Tritter, J. (2000). *Rational Choice Theory: Resisting Colonization*. London: Routledge.
Arthur, C. (2004). *The New Dialectic and Marx's Capital*. Leiden & Boston: Brill.
Barsalou, L. Dutriaux, L. & Scheepers, C. (2018). Moving Beyond the Distinction Between Concrete and Abstract Concepts. *Philosophical Transactions*, B 373: 1–11.

Brown, A. (2014). Approach with Caution: Critical Realism in Social Research. *Work, Employment & Society* 28 (1): 112–123.

Chassamboulli, A. (2013). Labor-Market Volatility in a Matching Model with Worker Heterogeneity and Endogenous Separations. *Labour Economics* 24: 217–229.

Concrete, entry www.dictionary.com/browse/concrete (accessed 1 February 2021).

Damico, J. (2019). Abstraction. In J. Damico & M. Ball (eds), *The SAGE Encyclopedia of Human Communication Sciences and Disorders*. London: Sage.

de Donato Rodríguez, X., & Zamora Bonilla, J. (2009). Credibility, Idealisation, and Model Building: An Inferential Approach. *Erkenntnis* 70 (1): 101–118.

Ducheyne, S. (2007). Abstraction vs. Idealization. *The Reasoner* 1:5 (September): 9–10.

Elliott-Graves, A., & Weisberg, M. (2014). Idealisation. *Philosophy Compass* 9(3): 176–185.

Fleetwood, S. (2004). The Ontology of Organisation and Management Studies. In S. Fleetwood & S. Ackroyd (eds), *Critical Realist Applications in Organisation and Management Studies*. London: Routledge.

Fleetwood, S. (2011). Sketching a Socio-Economic Model of Labour Markets. *Cambridge Journal of Economics* 35(1): 15–38.

Fleetwood, S. (2014). Conceptualising Future Labour Markets. *Journal of Critical Realism* 13(3): 251–258.

Fleetwood, S. (2016). (Mis)understanding Labour Markets. In Murray (ed.), *Labor Markets: Analysis, Regulation and Outcomes*. Nova Science Publishers: New York.

Fleetwood, S. (2019a). Re-visiting Rules and Norms. *Review of Social Economy* 79(4): 607–635.

Fleetwood, S. (2019b). A Definition of Habit For Socio-Economics. *Review of Social Economy* 79(2): 131–165.

Frigg, R. & Hartmann, S. (2020). Models in Science. In Edward N. Zalta (ed.), *The Stanford Encyclopedia of Philosophy* (Spring). https://plato.stanford.edu/archives/spr2020/entries/models-science/.

Gallagher, S. (2013). The Socially Extended Mind. *Cognitive Systems Research* 25 (26): 4–12.

Gallagher, S. (2015). Are Minimal Representations Still Representations?. *International Journal of Philosophical Studies* 16(3): 351–369.

Hall, R., & Lieberman, M. (2nd ed 2003). *Economics: Principles and Applications*. Mason, OH: Thomson/South-Western.

Hindriks, F. (2013). Explanation, Understanding and Unrealistic Models. *Studies in History and Philosophy of Science* 44: 523–531.

Hodgson, G. (1999). *Economics and Utopia: Why the Learning Society Is not the End of History*. London: Routledge.

Humphreys, P. (1995). Abstract and Concrete. *Philosophy and Phenomenological Research* 55(1): 157–161.

Jones, M. (2005). Idealization and abstraction: A framework. In M. Jones & N. Cartwright (eds), pp. 173–217, *Idealization XII: Correcting the Model, Idealization and Abstraction in the Sciences*. New York: Rodopi.

Mäki, U. (1992). On the Method of Isolation in Economics. *Poznan Studies in the Philosophy of the Sciences and Humanities* 26: 319–354.

Maki, U. (2004). Theoretical Isolation and Explanatory Progress: Transaction Cost Economics and the Dynamics of Dispute. *Cambridge Journal of Economics* 28(3): 319–346.

Mäki, U. (2009). Missing the World: Models as Isolations and Credible Surrogate Systems. *Erkenntnis* 70: 29–43.

Mäki, U. (2011). Models and the Locus of their Truth. *Synthese* 180: 47–63.

Marx, K. (1973). *Grundrisse*. London: Penguin Books in association with New Left Review.

Mattesini, F., & Rossi, L. (2009). Optimal Monetary Policy in Economies with Dual Labor Markets. *Journal of Economic Dynamics & Control* 33: 1469–1489.

Morgan, M. (2010). *The World in the Model: How Economists Work and Think*. Cambridge University Press: Cambridge.

Morgan, M. (2012). *The World in the Model: How Economists Work and Think*. Cambridge: Cambridge University Press.

Morgan, M., & Knuuttila, T. (2011). Models and Modelling in Economics. In U. Mäki (ed), *Handbook of the Philosophy of Economics*. Amsterdam: Elsevier BV.

Ollman, B. (2003). *Dance of the Dialectic: Steps in Marx's Method*. University of Illinois Press: Chicago.

Portides, D. (2018). Idealisation and Abstraction in Scientific Modelling *Synthese* 9: 1–23.

Psillos, S. (2011). Living with the Abstract: Realism and Models. *Synthese* 180: 3–17

Roffe, J. (2015). *Abstract Market Theory*. Basingstoke: Palgrave Macmillan.

Rosen, G. (2020). Abstract Objects. In Edward N. Zalta (ed.), *The Stanford Encyclopedia of Philosophy* (Spring Edition) https://plato.stanford.edu/archives/spr2020/entries/abstract-objects/

Sayer, A. (1981). Abstraction: A Realist Interpretation. *Radical Philosophy* 28: 6–15.

Sayer, A. (1984 & 1992). *Method in Social Science*, London: Routledge.

Sayer, A. (2000). *Realism and Social Science*. London: Sage.

Shapira, O. Liberman, N. Trope, Y. & Rim, S-Y. (2012). Levels of Mental Construal. In S. Fiske & N. Macrae (eds), pp. 229–250, *The Sage Handbook of Social Cognition*. London: Sage.

Smith, S. (2009). *Labour Economics*. London: Routledge.

Yee, E. (2019). Abstraction and Concepts: When, How, Where, What and Why?. *Language, Cognition and Neuroscience* 34(10): 1257–1265.

Part II

Dimensions of Moral Economy

Chapter 5

Critical Realism and Moral Economy

Sympathetic Reflections on Andrew Sayer's Work

Bob Jessop

This chapter reflects on Andrew Sayer's contributions to critical realism and their application to critical cultural political economy and moral economy. The latter involves critical realist analyses of class, ethical philosophy, moral economy, critical cultural political economy, the political economy of the rich in capitalist social formations, and so on (Sayer 2005, 2007, 2009, 2011, 2015). These studies are consistent with his view that critical social science should be able to support radical critiques and social emancipation and take account of normative commitments to human flourishing. In this respect, this chapter also identifies how he contributes to critical realism in particular rather than just to critical realism in general. This requires distinguishing between his general reflections on critical realism from its applications in geography, sociology, and political economy and evaluating them both. The chapter concludes with a positive evaluation of Sayer's work on the complex conditions for human flourishing based on his own ethical and moral positions as well as critical realism.

Critical Realism in General

Critical realism is not a general theory. It provides a distinctively philosophical standpoint with strong ontological commitments that have major meta-theoretical implications for theory construction, theory confirmation and theory application (Bhaskar 1998: 132). Its depth ontology posits that the world is stratified into layers and regions that require different concepts, assumptions, and explanatory principles corresponding to their emergent properties. Critical realist explanations should reflect this depth and respect the limits of what can be stated in relation to its definition of the nature of the objects being explained. Andrew Sayer is especially attentive to the open nature of the social world and the interweaving of different domains in its problems and is sensitive to the provisional, incomplete nature of explanations. He also draws systematically on moral and political philosophy in order to develop his own particular reading of critical social science and moral economy.

DOI: 10.4324/9781003247326-8

In particular, critical realism distinguishes real mechanisms, actual events and processes, and empirical observations. The deepest layer comprises the generative structures or causal mechanisms and related properties of a given set of relations. These include tendencies, counter-tendencies, capacities, affordances (i.e., the possibilities of action afforded, or offered by, a given material object or social network), liabilities, and vulnerabilities. These properties may be contingently actualised in specific conjunctures but, because of diverse factors or actors, may remain latent. In other words, the existence of particular naturally necessary powers is contingent rather than necessary and their actualisation is therefore 'contingently necessary' as well as 'necessarily contingent' (Jessop 1982: 228–235; also, Sayer 1992: 107, 117, 142; Sayer 2000: 12, 138, 239; Danermark et al. 2002: 56; Manicas 2006: 31–43). Second, the actual comprises patterns of events or processes that result from the inter-action of a plurality of mechanisms, tendencies and counter-tendencies, in specific conditions. This has implications for the articulation of abstract analyses to reproduce the real-concrete as a concrete-in-thought and exclude the reduction of the concrete to the unmediated realisation of abstract potentials. Abstraction provides a possible beginning to research but not an end (Sayer 1981, 1992: 98; 2000: 19–20). Third, the empirical concerns evidence about the actual, that is, those potentials that are actualised (observations concerning the actual and/or the real, lived experience, observations, and measurements of actual pattern of events). Together the empirical and the actual provoke questions about the nature of the real.

Our knowledge of and/or about the real world is never theoretically inno-cent but starts from a pre-interpreted analytical object. The movement occurs from a research problem defined in more or less simple and, perhaps, one-sided, superficial or, worse, chaotic, terms to an account that is more complex and has greater ontological depth. This does not mean that the complexities of the external world can ever be fully grasped in real time; on the contrary, all accounts, however concrete-complex, still remain partial. Nonetheless, as the spiral of scientific enquiry continues, the explanandum is defined with increasing complexity and concreteness (Danermark et al. 2002). In general, this involves: (1) forming concepts by combining categories from different analytical planes to produce 'hybrid' concepts that are more or less concrete-complex in character and (2) explanations that focus on the contingent interactions among causal mechanisms, tendencies and counter-tendencies, agential forces, and so forth, to produce a given explanandum. This often poses serious forensic problems of causal attribution in the face of complex-concrete objects and many competing explanations.

Sayer on Critical Realism

Sayer's most-cited book is *Method in Social Science: A Realist Approach* (1992), and *Realism and Social Science* (2000) is his second most-cited work.

Both texts critique alternative positions in the natural and social sciences and aim to produce critical realist reflections on explanations in the social sciences. The two books focus on social science ontology and methodology in general terms rather than present his own particular critical realist analyses in detail. Indeed, he is more concerned with distinguishing critical realism in general from opposing positions in the social sciences. The social sciences deal with open systems but lack the advantage of some natural sciences in having relevant closed system sciences on which to draw (1992: 123). The opposing positions include the empiricist and positivist paradigms found in the natural sciences and the relativism of Thomas Kuhn (1970) and Paul Feyerabend (1975), which is rooted in their critiques of the allegedly cumulative advance of natural science. This is reflected in turn in Sayer's critiques of nomothetic approaches in social science that seek to derive universal laws based on false natural science analogies as well as of social constructivism that one-sidedly emphasises interpretation at the expense of the materiality of structures (1997: 466–469; 2000: 6). He also criticises the regularity theory of causation that emphasises constant conjunction rather than the contingent necessity of social relations in open systems. Indeed, abandoning hopes of finding regularities does not mean abandoning explanation (1981, 2000: 5). Rather, explanation depends on identifying abstract causal mechanisms and how they work and then discovering if they were activated and under what conditions (2000: 14). The realist dissociation of causality from regularity does not signal any loss of interest in causal explanation but rather its pursuit in a form appropriate for the study of open systems (2000: 132). In this regard, he also rejects Popperian views of falsification as the criterion of scientific statements (1992: 166–173). Other positions that Sayer rejects are atomism, which posits only external, contingent relations, not internal, necessary relations (1981: 11; 1992: 157); idealist explanations in terms of actors' reasons alone (1992: 66; 2000: 79); and strong essentialism, in which everything has an essence (1992: 162–165).

Sayer argues that critical realism is a philosophy focused mainly on ontology, not epistemology. It is also anti-foundationalist in so far as it does not seek to establish the correct foundations for natural or social science or lay down absolute ethical principles. Instead, it aims primarily to under labour for social science (Sayer 2000: 73, 78) and acknowledges its dependence on the materials/knowledge available to it in society (Bhaskar 1979). This does not prevent it from engaging in epistemological critiques as supplements to realist criticism nor exclude clearly stated normative commitments in its critical applications. Indeed, these are important aspects of the theory of knowledge and crucial to Sayer's ability to critique naïve objectivism and relativism (and conventionalism) (1992: 83–84). Observation is neither theory-neutral nor theory-determined, but theory-laden. Truth is neither absolute nor purely conventional and relative, but a matter of practical adequacy (1992: 83–84).

In *Method in Social Science*, which was written when Sayer was employed as a geographer with broad interdisciplinary interests, he emphasises that social phenomena are concept-dependent. Unlike natural (i.e., non-social objects) objects, they are not impervious to the meanings ascribed to them (1992: 30). Human existence depends heavily on societies' self-understanding that is socially produced, and changes in this self-understanding are coupled with changes in society's objective form. Knowledge can be not only explanatory and descriptive but also evaluative, critical, and emancipatory (1992: 43). Thus, understanding a social phenomenon requires a double contextualisation owing to its situation in a 'double hermeneutic' that requires observers to reflect on their own readings that social agents attribute to their actions and social relations (1992: 60). Indeed, one must reflect critically on how problems are defined, rationally or chaotically, in order to offer practically adequate explanations (1981, 1992, 2000: 19). This implies that (1) answers to empirical questions presuppose answers to questions about the scientific (and other) concepts used in identifying their objects; (2) that in the case of concept-dependent social objects, empirical knowledge presupposes understanding the constitutive concepts; and (3) that any question about concepts must reckon with the (empirical) circumstances in which they are used (1992: 58). Abstraction does not translate directly to the concrete without empirical analysis that studies context, conditions, and agency.

> in addition to conceptualising phenomena, *theories make their strongest claims at the abstract level about necessary or internal relations, and about causal powers, or in other words, about necessity in the world. Where relations between things are contingent, their form must always be an empirical question, that is one which must be answered by observing actual cases.*
> (1992: 143; italics in original, cf. 105)

Realism and Social Science critiques a different set of then-fashionable positions in the social sciences. It addresses post-modernists, who imply relativism, idealism, and rejection of social science ambitions, and post-structuralist positions (2000: 6, 30). Realists seek to identify both necessity (naturally necessary properties) and possibility in the world: 'what things must go together, and what could happen, given the nature of the objects' (2000: 11). This later text proposes a way of combining modified naturalism with recognition of the necessity of interpretive meaning in social life. It seeks to avoid both scientism and 'science-envy' on the one hand and radical rejections of science on the other (2000: 2–3). In this regard, it focuses on causation, contingency, necessity, internal relations, and so forth, and highlights the open nature of social science contexts, their contingency, and context-dependence. Social science explanation requires attentiveness to its stratification, to emergent powers arising from certain relationships, and to how the operation of causal mechanisms depends on the constraining and enabling effects of contexts. Realists should also recognise that, since reasons can be causes, they are not separate from or alternative to causal explanation (2000: 27). Indeed, social scientists' reflexivity is important for developing true or practically adequate accounts of action (2000: 61). In this sense, realists must reject strong social constructionism but can happily accept weak social constructionism. Only some construals have constructive effects and this must be explained in terms of their material conditions as well as discursive effects (2000: 90). Likewise, Sayer critiques the strong essentialist position that everything has an essence but accepts the moderate essentialist position that some things do (2000: 87).

The open nature of social systems and the contingent nature of their reproduction mean that the historical and geographical course of development is always an empirical question. This is why, despite their strong interrelationships, one can still recognise the difference between social theory and concrete (properly geographical and historical) research: they do not do the same job (2000: 127). Analysis can take the form of theorising the nature of such structures in abstraction from concrete situations, or, alternatively, it may be applied empirically to the explanation of concrete circumstances (2000: 141–142). Concrete analysis is concerned with the concrete as a unity of multiple determinations. This requires synthesising a range of social theories, concerned with different aspects of the concrete. The balance between nomological and contextualising explanation must reflect the explanandum rather than be judged a priori, that is, by reference to the structure and constitution of the objects that possess them (2000: 145). This may sometimes require a redescription of the event in terms of its meaning to the actors involved to avoid chaotic conceptions and misplaced explanations (2000: 235).

Critical Realism in Particular

Critical realism has an important 'under labouring' role in the natural and social sciences (Bhaskar 1998: 18; Collier 1989; Lawson 1999; Cruickshank 2003; Sayer 2000: 73, 78). It examines, critiques, refines, and reflects on the ontological, epistemological, methodological, and substantive presuppositions of different philosophical and theoretical traditions, disciplines, schools, and so forth. It also provides meta-theoretical grounds for preferring some approaches, notably, critical realism, over others by providing rigorous criteria of 'judgemental rationality' for choosing among them (cf. Archer et al. 1998: xi). This implies that, while philosophical argument can justify a 'critical realist ontology and epistemology in general' on the basis of a negative or diacritical under labouring role, thereby excluding alternative philosophical positions (such as empiricism, rationalism or idealism), it cannot validate, let alone elaborate, a 'critical realist ontology and epistemology in particular'. For example, in the social sciences, critical realism clarifies the relation of social structure and agency through its transformational model of social action (Bhaskar 1998). But this is consistent with various specific critical realist accounts of this relation (e.g. Archer et al. 1998; Danermark et al. 2002; Lawson 1999, 2009; Cruickshank 2003: 6, 36ff; Elder-Vass 2007: 227). This holds especially for particular critical realist ontological arguments rather than general critical realist arguments. By definition, under labouring cannot supply the substantive concepts and methods needed for a particular research investigation.

This poses the challenge of how to translate general meta-theoretical work into relevant research questions, strategies, studies, and conclusions regarding particular analytical objects, generative structures, actual events, and processes (Danermark et al. 2002; cf. Collier 1994: 208–209). These ontologies must be developed through means adequate to the specific object of enquiry (cf. Bhaskar 1998: 54). This does not occur in a vacuum and is also subject to the spiral movement of continuing and reflexive critical realist enquiry. In short, the challenge is to move from abstract, philosophical, and meta-theoretical reflections on critical realism in general to specific, practical, and theoretically grounded research programmes.

I now consider some particular applications of critical realism in Andrew Sayer's analyses of critical cultural political economy and moral economy. Regarding the critical cultural political economy, he argues that, if cultural political economy is to be worthwhile, it needs to be critical of its object. This requires at least four tasks. First, while the cultural turn has sometimes inverted economic reductionism's dismissive treatment of culture and the lifeworld, it must avoid reducing economic systems to the lifeworld in which they are embedded. It should consider how systems are responsible for economic and cultural effects, whether good or bad. Second, it must explore not only the social and cultural embedding of economic activities but also how the system mechanisms of capital accumulation and uneven development have powerful disembedding and disruptive effects. Third, it needs to reconsider classical political economy, which was always cultural and is still relevant today (2001: 687). Fourth, a critical cultural political economy should include and develop some older views on economy and society, returning to the classical political economy of the 18th and early 19th centuries, and even to Aristotle (2001: 688). Critical cultural-political economists should not reject the idea that the economy is determinant in the last instance in favour of the dogma of culture going all the way down. The relative importance of economy and culture is always an empirical question that will depend on the particular case in which it arises.

Regarding moral economy, Sayer argues that political-economic analysis may claim to be 'critical' if it shows that particular economic processes and forms of organisation are harmful to well-being and/or that actors fail to understand them adequately. In this respect, moral economy can hardly avoid normative implications. Indeed, the positive-normative distinction breaks down in dealing with matters of needs and flourishing and suffering

(2007: 262). In contrast with certain tendencies in sociology and economics, moral economy relates morality to everyday life and the experience of well-being and ill-being without reducing it to a matter of individual subjectivity or social convention (2007: 261). It studies the constitutive moral norms and sentiments that structure and influence economic practices, both formal and informal, including their impact on flourishing and suffering, and how these are reinforced, compromised, or overridden by economic pressures (2007: 264). Another aspect of moral economy considers that economic actions, however motivated, may be legitimated by appeal to how they improve actors' well-being. This can be questioned by asking what happens in practice and assessing the legitimation in this light (2007: 265–268). In short, a critical moral economy approach can highlight how economic practices induce unjust or unethical behaviour, institutions, and outcomes and how this restricts flourishing (2007: 269).

Critical social science engages in 'critique'. This is distinguished from mere criticism because it tries not only to identify false beliefs and the practices that they inform but also asks why those false beliefs are held (2009: 770). To take critique beyond the reduction of illusion, critical social scientists must develop a conception of the human good and flourishing and aim at 'emancipation' from constraint and domination (2009: 774–777, 783). This requires critical evaluation of the complex forms of reasoning that inform moral and political philosophy based on thick ethical concepts that are concerned with the good and the conditions for human flourishing. This reduces the danger of premature judgements about flourishing and suffering by re-engaging social science with moral and political philosophy (2009: 781–782).

Sayer explores these critical insights into cultural political economy and moral economy in his books on *The Moral Significance of Class* (2005) and *Why We Can't Afford the Rich* (2015). Both are concerned with the morally problematic nature of class, with the former addressing the everyday aspects of people's life chances and social mobility and the latter focusing on the ability of the rich to exploit capitalism to advance their interests. In his assessment of the moral significance of class, Sayer develops a qualified ethical naturalism, which relates the good and bad to human needs and the capacities for flourishing and suffering and emphasises that these needs and capacities are always culturally mediated (2005: 218–219). He employs both abstract and concrete, academic and lay concepts of class, and also respects the difference between the politics of distribution and recognition and their interaction. He also elaborates a qualified Bourdieusian analysis of habitus and habitat, forms of capital, to which he adds the importance of emotions, commitments, and ethical dispositions (2005: 51). In this respect, he explores the micropolitics of social struggles over goods and valued circumstances, practices, relationships, and ways of life that affect human flourishing (2005: 96). And he also offers non-reductionist readings of moral and immoral sentiments and their influence on class and other social relations (2005: 140ff). This involves taking lay normativity seriously and how it affects people's egalitarian tendencies, the pursuit of respect and respectability, class pride, and moral boundary drawing. He concludes by calling both for a politics of recognition and a rejuvenated egalitarian politics of distribution that confronts the injustice of class inequalities openly (2005: 232).

In his openly critical text on the rich, which is addressed to lay readers, Sayer examines the sources of wealth extraction (as opposed to wealth creation) and critiques the common justifications for wealth inequalities. He highlights the role of property and money in its accumulation and puts these in their economic, political, and social context. The rich extract wealth by creating indebtedness, hide it in tax havens, engage in conspicuous consumption that harms the poor, provoke financial crises, and generate climate change. He condemns these practices and the neoliberalism that encourages them (2015: passim).

In his text on *Why Things Matter to People*, Sayer elaborates on reflective philosophical anthropology that rejects philosophy's under-socialised view of individuals and addresses social science's often over-socialised view of individual action (2011: 5, 98–99). Here his under labouring role in critical realism is heavily influenced by philosophy, particularly moral philosophy, and aims to overcome social science's difficulty with lay normativity in general, and ethical being in particular (2011: 14). Sayer criticises the widespread use of the fact-value distinction in social science, arguing that values involve a kind of reasoning and that it is dogmatically held values that pose problems, not reasonable ones (2011: 32, 44, 56). Close attention to 'how people evaluate things and decide what matters and why' requires engaging with 'elements such as moral sentiments, capacity for fellow-feeling, virtues and vices, norms and moral reflection and argumentation' and their relation to our sense of harm and flourishing (2011: 19, 20). This calls for critical social scientists to engage in evaluative reasoning, which requires looking beyond instrumental means-end rationality to include the practical reason that is concerned with the embodied and tacit reasons that people draw on in particular situations to address ends rather than means and to decide how to act in light of ethical dimensions and individual character (2011: 61). Thus, individuals and groups take account of 'needs, lack and becoming, suffering and flourishing' (2011: 57). It is important to combine causal and hermeneutic approaches by including reasons and discourses among the range of causes of change (139). We need to develop

> 'a needs-based conception of social being', viewing actors not only as causal agents and as self-interpreting meaning-makers, but as needy and dependent, having an orientation of care and concern about some things, and capable of flourishing or suffering. 'Needs' here is used as a shorthand that also covers lack, want and desire, and includes culturally acquired or emergent needs. Failure to acknowledge human neediness

and vulnerability invites misattributions of causality or responsibility, so that, for example, discourses are treated as capable on their own of motivating people.

(Sayer 2011: 139–140)

Likewise, critical social science should address the impact of unequal power structures and social interests in affecting human flourishing and suffering (2011: 178). This is related to treating others in a dignified way that acknowledges but does not exploit their vulnerability and in turn trusts them not to exploit our vulnerability (2011: 203). In short, critical social science depends on some conception of well-being and ill-being that reflects practical reason and dignity. Sayer suggests that this seems alien to much contemporary social science. Its practitioners are worried not only about essentialism and ethnocentrism but also by the challenges posed by the fact–value, science–ethics, positive–normative dualisms of modernist thought, and by the subjectivisation of values associated with the rise of a liberal society. To overcome this alienation, critical social scientists must acknowledge that their evaluations of practices imply a conception of human flourishing (2011: 245).

Concluding Remarks

Andrew Sayer was an early advocate of critical realism, influenced in part by the work of Roy Bhaskar and Rom Harré, but was more interested in its application to the social sciences and to geographical and historical explanation. His books on critical realism are based on very wide-ranging reading and carefully address the problems of alternative approaches in the social sciences. He is attentive to the problems of abstract reasoning and the need to explain events at the level of meaning as well as material causality and insists on the stratification of the real world. His particular applications of critical realism are shaped by critical concerns with human flourishing and the dialectic of distribution and recognition. Attention to realist analysis of causality is essential to avoid strong essentialism and determinism because only actors who accept that reasons can be causes can explain the contingent necessity and thus intervene in the chains of causation to produce human flourishing (1997: 475). The early works already address the problems of human dignity, human well-being, and vulnerability. But his later particular applications of critical realism are shaped by much greater awareness of the lessons of moral and political philosophy and are concerned with the conditions required for human flourishing and the dialectic of distribution and recognition. These applications are less directly critical realist in focus, but they draw on the lessons in the earlier texts. They are also sensitive to the difficulties posed by conventional readings of the fact-value distinction and worry about the risks of making value judgements. Here Sayer integrates practical reason and lay normativities into his analysis and is concerned with the real mechanisms that produce well-being and ill-being. This translates into recommendations about ethical and moral behaviour based on respecting the dignity and autonomy of others and their specific capacities and vulnerabilities. While he continues to work with critical realist philosophical assumptions, he is now more concerned with developing his 'qualified ethical naturalism' and exploring the complex conditions for human flourishing. This reflects his own ethical and moral positions as well as his engagement with moral philosophers and it enables him to offer reasonable and well-reasoned criticisms of the crisis-prone world order and its effects on everyday life.

Acknowledgements

Thanks are due to Andrew Brown, Norman Fairclough, and Andrew Sayer for discussions on critical realism; and to Mervyn Hartwig, Petter Næss, and David Tyfield for excellent suggestions on the distinction between critical realism in general and particular critical realism.

References

Archer, M., Bhaskar, R., Collier, A., Lawson, T. & Norris, A. (eds) (1998). *Critical Realism: Essential Readings*. London: Routledge.
Bhaskar, R. (1998). *The Possibility of Naturalism*, Third edition. London: Routledge.
Collier, A. (1989). *Scientific Realism and Socialist Thought*. Hemel Hempstead: Harvester Wheatsheaf.
Collier, A. (1994). *Critical Realism: An Introduction to Roy Bhaskar's Philosophy*. London: Verso.
Cruickshank, J. (2003). *Realism and Sociology. Anti-Foundationalism, Ontology, and Social Research*. London: Routledge.
Danermark, B., Ekström, M., Jakobsen, L. & Karlsson, J. C. (2002). *Explaining Society. Critical Realism in the Social Sciences*. London: Routledge.
Elder-Vass, D. (2007). A Method for Social Ontology: Iterating Ontology and Social Research. *Journal of Critical Realism* 6(2): 226–240.
Feyerabend, P. (1975). *Against Method: Outline of an Anarchistic Theory of Knowledge*. London: New Left Books.
Jessop, B. (1982). *The Capitalist State: Marxist Theories and Methods*. Oxford: Martin Robertson.
Kuhn, T. R. (1970). *The Structure of Scientific Revolutions*, Second revised edition. Chicago, IL: University of Chicago Press.
Lawson, T. (1999). Critical Issues in Economics as Realist Social Theory. In S. Fleetwood (ed.), pp. 209–257, *Critical Realism in Economics: Development and Debate*. London: Routledge.
Lawson, T. (2009). Underlabouring for Substantive Theorising: Reply to Davidsen. In E. Fullbrook (ed.), pp. 58–82. *Ontology and Economics: Tony Lawson and his Critics*. London: Routledge.
Manicas, P. T. (2006). *A Realist Philosophy of Social Science: Explanation and Understanding*. Cambridge: Cambridge University Press.

Sayer, A. (1981). Abstraction: A Realist Interpretation. *Radical Philosophy* 28: 6–15.

Sayer, A. (1992). *Method in Social Science: A Realist Approach*, Second edition. London: Routledge.

Sayer, A. (1997). Essentialism, Social Constructionism, and Beyond. *Sociological Review* 45(3): 453–487.

Sayer, A. (2000). *Realism and Social Science*. London: SAGE.

Sayer, A. (2001). For a Critical Cultural Political Economy. *Antipode* 33(4): 687–708.

Sayer, A. (2005). *The Moral Significance of Class*. Cambridge: Cambridge University Press.

Sayer, A. (2007). Moral Economy as Critique. *New Political Economy* 12(2): 261–270.

Sayer, A. (2009). Who's Afraid of Critical Social Science? *Current Sociology* 57(6): 767–786.

Sayer, A. (2011). *Why Things Matter to People: Social Science, Values and Ethical Life*. Cambridge: Cambridge University Press.

Sayer, A. (2015). *Why We Can't Afford the Rich*. Bristol: Policy Press.

Chapter 6

Why (Mundane) Things Matter

From Moral Economy to Foundational Economy

Kevin Morgan

Introduction

One of the most significant relationships in the academy is between doctoral students and their supervisors. When this relationship works well it can be life-enhancing, as well as career-shaping, and I was fortunate to be the beneficiary of such a relationship when I was supervised by Andrew Sayer at Sussex University in the late 1970s. At that time Sussex was distinctive for having inter disciplinary schools rather than discipline-based departments, and this gave staff and students alike the confidence to challenge the desiccated academic division of labour that had stymied the development of the social sciences in the twentieth century.

The institutional and intellectual milieu of Sussex in the 1970s and 1980s helps to explain why Andrew Sayer ranged so widely beyond geography – his original discipline – and embraced a form of postdisciplinary social scientific analysis that had more in common with the ethos of the Scottish Enlightenment than the conventional academy of the time. Indeed, one of the most striking features of his academic career is the impressive number of fields in which he has made substantial contributions: not least in economic geography, radical political economy, realist research methods, social theory and moral philosophy. Far from being separate domains, these fields have been mutually reinforcing in the sense that his work on moral economy, for example, was stimulated by an earlier concern with radical political economy, a field in which he felt the need to find new and better ways to evaluate alternative economic systems. This is what inspired him to search for a more robust form of critique in which the values of human flourishing and suffering would unashamedly be rendered more explicit.

Why Things Matter to People: Values-in-Analysis

One of the books to which I return time and time again is *Why Things Matter to People*, and there are perhaps two reasons for this. First and foremost, it makes a truly compelling and totally convincing case as to why values

DOI: 10.4324/9781003247326-9

are both unavoidable and essential to a critical social science that aims to treat human beings with dignity and respect. But, secondly, it also illustrates the astonishing range of intellectual influences that shaped Andrew's own philosophical outlook, particularly the neo-Aristotelian ethics of Martha Nussbaum, the moral political economy of Adam Smith, the critical realism of Andrew Collier, the capability approach of Amartya Sen, the neuroscience of Antonio Damasio and the ethic of care literature, most closely associated with feminist scholars like Joan Tronto, which went furthest in spanning the divide between normative and positive analysis in his view.

Drawing on all these theoretical perspectives, the book argues that mainstream social science has a problem that it doesn't sufficiently acknowledge, namely that it cannot convincingly explain why things matter to people because of its deeply embedded aversion to normativity. As this is the core argument of the book, it is worth quoting at length:

> In social science, it is common to regard values in emotivist or subjectivist terms, as not being about anything, except perhaps the holder's emotional state of mind. They are often seen as conventional – as merely derived from social norms – rather than as valuations of circumstances and actions. This ... has a detrimental effect both on social science's interpretations of social life, and on its own self-understanding. In the former case, it prevents social scientists from identifying why anything matters to people, and hence what kinds of things motivate them. In the latter case ... sociology and other social sciences have still not adequately come to terms with the reason-laden – or reasonable – character of values, so that there is still an aversion to normativity, that is to offering valuations of social phenomena, since values are seen as a source of bias and a threat to objective thought ... This weakens social science's ability to understand and convey why anything matters to actors, why values and norms have normative force, or why actors or researchers see anything as good or bad.
>
> (Sayer 2011: 24)

In other words, it is not values per se that pose a problem for social science but dogmatically held values. Rather than being beyond or opposed to reason, in this view, values are part and parcel of what moral philosophers refer to as 'ethical reasoning' and the 'intelligence of emotions' (Nussbaum 2001). Ethical reasoning challenges the widely held notion in mainstream social science that positive and normative statements must be inversely related, when in reality they can provide enriched explanations when used in concert.

The divide between normative and positive analysis is shown to be just one example of an entire family of dualisms, the most notorious being the *mind–body* dualism, which has been assailed from many intellectual quarters in recent years. In addition to the critiques from moral philosophers like

Nussbaum, it has also been challenged by a growing corpus of neuroscientific findings that demonstrate the interplay rather than the separation of mind and body because 'feelings have not been given the credit they deserve as motives, monitors, and negotiators of human cultural endeavours' (Damasio 2018: 3; 1994). Other cognitive scientists have put it more bluntly, arguing that no part of the body – including the brain – is functionally separate from or superior to any other part because intelligence is embedded in the flesh, so much so that one leading proponent of embodied cognition pithily says that 'we do not *have* bodies; we *are* bodies' (Claxton 2015: 3).

The interplay of mind and body in ethical reasoning is most apparent in the ethic of care literature, which Andrew deems to be one of the most important developments in moral philosophy in the last century because 'it challenges the under-socialised and disembodied models of human being that have dominated political and moral philosophy' (Sayer 2011: 257). It is no coincidence that the ethic of care literature was pioneered by feminist scholars because, more than any other ethical theory or social movement, feminism foregrounds the quality of personal relationships along with the other forces, public and private, that foster human flourishing/suffering.

Andrew Sayer embraced the moral economy concept because he also wanted to foreground the issue of well-being, by posing the apparently simple but fundamental question: *what are economies for?* (Sayer 2000, 2007). He also believed that the moral economy concept could rejuvenate radical political economy as a critical social science by helping it to overcome its aversion to normativity. Radical political economy had lost its bearings in Andrew's view essentially because ethical issues had been progressively sidelined by an economistic perspective that displaced ethics in favour of economic imperatives. In contrast, the moral economy concept embodied

> norms and sentiments regarding the responsibilities and rights of individuals and institutions with respect to others. These norms and sentiments go beyond matters of justice and equality, to conceptions of the good, for example regarding needs and the ends of economic activity.
>
> (Sayer 2000: 79)

In short, then, the moral economy perspective was embraced because it helped the radical political economy to reclaim an ethical stance that had been abandoned because it was wrongly assumed that normativity (values-in-analysis) was incompatible with critical social science.

From Moral Economy to Foundational Economy: Values-in-Action

While a moral economy perspective enables us to critique systems that perpetuate inequality and suffering, it doesn't in itself help us to fashion alternative worlds that reduce or redress these problems. Therefore, we need to move beyond moral economy as an ethical critique to embrace the *foundational economy* as a political strategy because the latter can translate the values of the former into the kind of policies and practices that are necessary for the provisioning of the 'mundane' goods and services that sustain the well-being of people and planet alike (Morgan 2015, 2020).

The foundational economy (FE) perspective constitutes a radically new concept in the development literature because it focuses not on the fashionable high-tech sectors of the knowledge economy but the 'mundane' sectors that are designed to keep us all safe and civilised – namely health, education, dignified eldercare, food, energy, housing and the like. The FE includes the goods and services which are the social and material infrastructure of civilised life because they provide the daily essentials for all households (Foundational Economy Collective 2018; Heslop et al. 2019).

These include *material services* through pipes and cables, networks and branches distributing water, electricity, gas, telecoms, banking services and food; and the *providential services* of primary and secondary education, health and care for children and adults as well as income maintenance. Foundational goods and services are purchased out of household income or provided free at the point of use out of tax revenues. The state often figures as a direct provider or as funder, with public limited companies and outsourcing conglomerates increasingly delivering foundational services. The requirement for local distribution gives the foundational activity a broad social and spatial footprint because it tends to correlate with and cater to existing population centres. Foundational thinking rests on two key ideas which break with established ways of developmental thinking and challenge taken-for-granted assumptions about the interplay of economy, society and politics:

- Firstly, the well-being of citizens depends less on individual consumption and more on their social consumption of essential goods and services – from water and retail banking to schools and care homes. Individual consumption depends on market income, while foundational consumption depends on social infrastructure and delivery systems of networks and branches which are neither created nor renewed automatically, even as incomes increase;
- Secondly, the distinctive, primary role of public policy should therefore be to secure the supply of basic services for all citizens, not a quantum of economic growth and jobs. If the aim is citizen's well-being and flourishing, then politics at national and subnational levels needs to be refocused on foundational consumption and securing universal minimum access and quality (Foundational Economy Collective 2018).

At a time when even conservative governments feel obliged to speak about 'inclusive growth' to address the problems of so-called 'left-behind' people and places, the FE concept would seem to be a timely contribution to this political agenda given its *employment share* on the one hand and the significance of its *essential services* on the other.

On the employment front, FE sectors collectively constitute between 40 and 50 per cent of jobs in most parts of the UK, though some of these sectors (e.g., eldercare) are notorious for their low pay and poor working conditions. As a place-based development policy, however, the FE signals a radical departure from conventional regional development policies, many of which seek to promote inter-place competition to attract mobile capital from abroad, a zero-sum game because there can only be one winner and many losers in each locational tournament (Morgan & Sayer 1988). In contrast, the FE amounts to a positive sum game in the sense that all regions stand to benefit from investments in material infrastructure and providential services. Indeed, this is what is most distinctive about the FE as a place-based development policy because 'far from being socially and spatially exclusive, it has something to offer everyone everywhere in the sense that it constitutes the infrastructure of everyday life' (Heslop et al. 2019: 6).

As regards the *quality* of employment, the FE needs to be given a much higher political priority because some of its low-paid sectors present us with a societal paradox. The COVID-19 pandemic threw this paradox into sharp relief because, in every country, the list of 'essential workers' – in health, social care, education, food provisioning, transport and the like – was with few exceptions the same as the list of the lowest-paid workers in society. The societal disconnect reveals the paradox of a society in which the lowest status workers play the most important role in keeping society safe and civilised. In other words, the pandemic demonstrated the importance of the foundational as that part of the economy which cannot be shut down, so much so that the list of 'essential workers' in each society provides a common sense and practical definition of what counts as foundational (Foundational Economy Collective 2020).

The significance of its essential services to social well-being is another reason why the FE is critically important to the 'inclusive growth' agenda. Here the FE perspective is closely aligned with the concept of *universal basic service* (UBS) provision, which has been defined and defended in the following way:

> Money spent on basic services – the most fundamental building blocks for life required by every citizen in the 21st century – dramatically reduces the cost of basic living for those on the lowest incomes. Basic services will reduce poverty because they will reduce the cost of a minimum living standard. Even if income levels remain static, it will make accessible a life that includes participation, builds belonging and common purpose and potentially strengthens the cohesion of society as a whole. Focusing on basic services, such as housing, food, communications and transport,

is, we conclude, far more effective at driving down the cost of living than spending the same money on existing services, or on redistribution.

(Institute for Global Prosperity 2017)

The overriding concern of both the FE and UBS perspectives is the provision of intrinsically significant services that meet basic human needs and nourish human capabilities, services that are delivered as part of collective consumption rather than individuated through market income.

But, no matter how intellectually compelling the FE may be, it is also politically challenging. To illustrate the point, I conclude this chapter by focusing on four challenges that highlight the barriers to putting progressive values into practice.

Financing Foundational Activity

In political debates about the FE, one of the first objections that tend to surface – especially in the UK – is the claim that its growth is inevitably constrained by the fact that the Treasury is averse to raising tax income to provide revenue support for providential public services like education, health, social care and so on. Although this is a legitimate objection, it assumes that the fiscal mindset in the UK is set in aspic, when it isn't. Before addressing the growth objection, what first needs to be established is that the FE is primarily to be understood in terms of a *well-being agenda* rather than the conventional growth agenda. As its original authors have clearly stated: 'the "growth and jobs" objective should be demoted, and the primary policy objective of government in the domestic policy arena should be to secure the wellbeing of current and future generations by ensuring adequate foundational provision' (Calafati et al. 2019: 17).

The conservative fiscal mindset of the UK Treasury, far from being set in aspic, has already been shattered by COVID-19, indeed, the resulting pandemic has triggered the biggest economic recession in 300 years, and a conservative government has been forced to jettison its neoliberal credo to boost public expenditure to unprecedented levels to assuage the crisis. The pandemic has also spawned an acute mental health crisis, and it is likely that this will require permanently higher levels of public expenditure on health and social care in the future to cope with the debilitating effects on well-being.

At the core of the conservative fiscal mindset in the UK Treasury is the Green Book, which contains the cost-benefit analysis (CBA) methodology for deciding whether public investment projects pass the value for money test. The CBA methodology uses market prices, and critics have shown that this 'gives rise to a "Matthew Effect" whereby further infrastructure investment occurs in places that are already productive' (Coyle & Sensier 2018: 2). Since this CBA methodology runs counter to the new political agenda of 'inclusive growth' the Green Book is being revised to remove the algorithmic bias against public investment in poorer regions. Reinforcing this process will be the growing influence of devolved polities as devolution to cities and regions proceeds apace, creating a more polycentric political system in which the conservative fiscal prejudices of a centralised and imperious Treasury will no longer go unchallenged. However, if this polycentric political system is to make a systemic difference, it will need to pay more attention to (a) tax reform to put foundational activity on a more secure fiscal footing and (b) a new set of metrics to assess what 'good' looks like in the FE. Some foundational theorists have made a useful start on the metrics front by proposing *residual household income* as the first measure of foundational liveability, a metric that subtracts essentials like housing and transport from disposable income (Calafati et al. 2019). But the conventional metric of GDP per capita will not be easily displaced from its throne without a more concerted effort from the well-being alliance (Morgan 2021).

Procuring Foundational Activity

Along with the powers to tax and regulate, public procurement – the power of purchase – is arguably the third most powerful policy instrument to effect behavioural change in economy and society. Procurement is the single biggest component of UK government expenditure: in 2017/2018, total government procurement expenditure was £300bn (when academies are included). This means that roughly one in every three pounds that the public sector spends is spent on procurement: by comparison, £264bn is spent on grants, which includes all welfare benefit payments, and £184bn is spent on pay for government employees (Institute for Government 2018).

Procurement has become a panacea in all political circles, especially in progressive centre-left circles, where the power of purchase is extolled for its transformative potential. Despite the promise, however, the practice of embedding progressive values into public contracts has proved to be easier said than done, and this is most apparent in a sphere that is often deemed to be the litmus test of sustainability – the challenge of serving sustainable school food. The nadir of school catering in the UK occurred under successive Thatcher governments, which abolished nutritional standards, deskilled the workforce and, most perversely, allowed low cost to masquerade as 'best value' in procurement contracts (Morgan & Sonnino 2008).

If the most egregious examples of this low-cost catering regime were removed by the Blair governments, the austerity budgets inflicted on the local government after 2010 have imposed new pressures on the school catering service, making it difficult to serve locally produced nutritious school food. Even beacons of good practice in school catering – like Oldham Borough Council – are struggling to stay afloat. The secrets of Oldham's award-winning school catering service were attributed to the 'people at the helm' of the service – the professional commitment of the catering manager, the skills and enthusiasm of the catering team and the sustained political support of local politicians. But despite its impressive achievements, Oldham's school catering service remains in a financially fragile state, like its counterparts throughout the UK, highlighting the structural limits of progressive localism. The key issue for progressive school food reformers is a clash of values: school caterers are expected to provide what is essentially a *well-being* service while being forced to operate as a *commercial* venture (Morgan 2020).

Governing Foundational Activity

The governance of foundational activity raises issues about the locus of political power and the nature of civic engagement. The locus of political power will loom larger and larger in the UK as the centralised state system comes under mounting pressure to decentralise power and influence in response to the demands of devolved polities in the nations, cities and regions of the UK. A more polycentric political system is likely to be far more receptive to the need to support local experimentation in the FE, and this may involve new forms of public ownership, hybrid forms of management in which municipalities work in concert with private or civic enterprise, and social licensing to generate more public value (Foundational Economy Collective 2018).

Civic engagement is an equally important challenge because the FE is partly predicated on the idea of *active citizenship* where citizens are portrayed as co-producers of the services which they use. But this raises more questions than answers – such as whether all citizens are equally able and willing to play such a role? Since the evidence of active citizenship is not particularly encouraging,

> we need to devote much more thought to what kind of governance structures – local juries, citizen assemblies and the like – can be fashioned to ensure that participation is fostered rather than frustrated by the formal and informal institutions that govern our everyday lives, and to consider how these become socially embedded.
>
> (Heslop et al. 2019: 11)

Greening Foundational Activity

Early versions of the FE were criticised because they didn't 'say much about how foundational economic policies can be combined with green policies that rapidly decarbonise the production and consumption of goods and services' (Sayer 2019: 44). To compensate for these elisions, more recent versions of the FE have benefited from the 'eco-social' arguments embodied in *Heat, Need and Human Greed*, where Ian Gough offers a cogent analysis of the critical contradiction in many high carbon-intensive societies between securing emission reductions and ensuring an equitable distribution of real income.

This is especially the case with respect to domestic energy and food because these two sectors – quintessential foundational sectors – also happen to be high emission sectors. Gough's prescription is that the carbon composition of consumption urgently needs to be addressed because social policy can no longer be concerned purely with equity and distributive issues: 'In the age of the Anthropocene, social policy must be about changing patterns of consumption as well as redistributing incomes' (Gough 2017: 170).

FE theorists have responded to the criticisms of what they now call FE 1.0 by developing a more ecologically robust conception (FE 2.0). The challenge of FE 2.0, they argue, 'is about making the link between nature and social welfare and delivering ways of providing the latter without harming the former' (Calafati et al. 2020: 8). The need to calibrate the values of social justice and ecological integrity in a progressive transition narrative is precisely what the Green New Deal and the Sustainable Development Goals are designed to achieve. Crafting a sustainability narrative is one thing, but crafting a coalition of change to give it practical effect is something else entirely.

Conclusions

This chapter has underlined the significance of *Why Things Matter to People* because it so clearly demonstrates that values are an essential component of a critical social science that treats human (and non-human) life with dignity and respect. Far from being a threat to critical social science, in other words, normative analysis is shown to have an enriching effect when values are properly understood to be within the scope of reason. The practical implications of the book are equally profound because, without a robust ethical basis for their analysis, engaged social scientists will find it difficult to justify their public stances – for example, why they may prefer renewables to fossil fuels, fresh as opposed to processed food in school meals and dignified eldercare to the 'time and task' model that dominates UK home care today.

Andrew Sayer has applied these arguments to many fields. Among other things he has used the concept of moral economy to help radical political economy to come to terms with normativity, thereby helping it to rediscover its ethical bearings. He rightly feared that radical political economy had become too economistic, a positively perverse position to be in because it mirrored the under-socialised view of human beings in the neoliberal economics to which it was avowedly opposed.

But as well as confirming the arguments in the book, the chapter also tries to advance the debate beyond moral economy because, of itself, ethical critique cannot help us to fashion the alternative worlds that are necessary to reduce human suffering and create the conditions for human flourishing. The concept of FE helps us to do just because it focuses attention on the concrete policies and practices that are needed to promote social justice and ecological integrity in the mundane goods and services that are critically important for human well-being. Rather than being a criticism of moral economy, how-ever, the FE concept should be understood as an extension of it because, by drawing on the ethical case for well-being, it aims to give practical expression to the rights and responsibilities we have to each other as citizens. But the chapter concludes with a sobering reminder that the FE concept – which has something to offer everyone everywhere – needs to be politically endorsed by a new coalition of change if it is to become part of the warp and weft of everyday life.

References

Calafati, L., Froud, J., Johal, S. & Williams, K. (2019). Building Foundational Britain: From Paradigm Shift to New Political Practice? *Renewal: A Journal of Social Democracy* 27(2): 13–23.

Calafati, L., Froud, J., Haslam, C., Johal, S. & Williams, K. (2020). *Serious About Green? Building a Welsh Wood Economy Through Co-Ordination.* Report by Foundational Economy Research Ltd for WoodKnowledge Wales.

Claxton, G. (2015). *Intelligence in the Flesh: Why Your Mind Needs Your Body Much More Than It Thinks.* New Haven CT: Yale University Press.

Coyle, D., & Sensier, M. (2018). *The Imperial Treasury: Appraisal Methodology and Regional Economic Performance in the UK.* Bennett Institute for Public Policy working paper no: 02/2018, University of Cambridge.

Damasio, A. (1994). *Descartes' Error: Emotion, Reason, and the Human Brain.* New York: Putnam Publishing.

Damasio, A. (2018). *The Strange Order of Things: Life, Feeling and the Making of Cultures.* New York: Pantheon Books.

Foundational Economy Collective (2018). *Foundational Economy: The Infrastructure of Everyday Life.* Manchester: Manchester University Press.

Foundational Economy Collective (2020). *What Comes after the Pandemic? A Ten-Point Platform for Foundational Renewal,* https://foundationaleconomy.com/

Gough, I. (2017). *Heat, Greed and Human Need: Climate Change, Capitalism and Sustainable Wellbeing.* Cheltenham: Edward Elgar.

Heslop, J., Morgan, K. & Tomaney J. (2019). Debating the Foundational Economy, *Renewal, A Journal of Social Democracy* 27(2): 5–12.

Institute for Global Prosperity (2017). *Social Prosperity for the Future: A Proposal for Universal Basic Services.* Institute for Global Prosperity, UCL, London.

Institute for Government (2018). *Government Procurement: The Scale and Nature of Contracting in the UK.* London: IfG.

Morgan, K. (2015). The Moral Economy of Food. *Geoforum* 65: 294–296.

Morgan, K. (2020). Foodscapes of Hope: The Foundational Economy of Food. In F. Barbera & I. Rees Jones (eds), pp. 229–248, *The Foundational Economy and Citizenship: Comparative Perspectives on Civil Repair.* London: Routledge.

Morgan, K. (2021). After the Pandemic: Experimental Governance and the Foundational Economy. *Symphonya: Emerging Issues in Management* 1: 50–55.

Morgan, K., & Sayer, A. (1988). *Microcircuits of Capital: Sunrise Industry and Uneven Development.* Cambridge: Polity Press.

Morgan, K., & Sonnino, R. (2008). *The School Food Revolution: Public Food and the Challenge of Sustainable Development*. London: Earthscan.

Nussbaum, M. (2001). *Upheavals of Thought: The Intelligence of Emotions*. Cambridge: Cambridge University Press.

Sayer, A. (2000). Moral Economy and Political Economy. *Studies in Political Economy* 61(1): 79–103.

Sayer, A. (2007). Moral Economy as Critique. *New Political Economy* 12(2): 261–270.

Sayer, A. (2011). *Why Things Matter to People: Social Science, Values and Ethical Life*. Cambridge: Cambridge University Press.

Sayer, A. (2019). Moral Economy, the Foundational Economy and Decarbonisation. *Renewal: A Journal of Social Democracy* 27(2): 40–46.

Chapter 7

Moral Economy

A Framework and a Manifesto

Dave Elder-Vass

Andrew Sayer has employed the multi-faceted concept of *moral economy* in a long series of papers since the turn of the twenty-first century (Sayer 2000, 2003, 2004, 2007, 2015a, 2018). For Sayer, our economy *is* a moral economy, but the term moral economy also refers to an approach to studying it and an approach to its critique. I will argue that it should also be seen as a central organising theme of his work more generally. On the one hand, it provides the framework for his re-introduction of lay normativity into explanations of economic behaviour (and indeed social behaviour in general). On the other, it is the basis of his ethical manifesto for critical social science and in particular for the advocacy of alternative economic solutions. This chapter will begin by explaining the three aspects of the concept as he employs it and their relation to his wider oeuvre, then offer some evaluations of its contribution loosely oriented to these three aspects.

The Economy as a Moral Economy

In the first sense in which Sayer employs it, the term *moral economy* embodies an important theoretical claim about *all* economies. It implies that economies are not alienated spaces in which impersonal isolated individuals act purely calculatively to maximise their own individual interests, as in the notion of *homo economicus* that is central to mainstream neoclassical economics (Sayer 2007: 264). Rather, all economic action is simultaneously social action that is chosen by evaluative actors with personal needs and emotional connections – actors who are affected by the webs of relationships and normative commitments that all social actors are embedded in and thus by a whole host of cultural and historic factors.

This builds on the work of Edward Thompson (Thompson 1971), in particular his argument that 'The moral economy embodies norms and sentiments regarding the responsibilities and rights of individuals and institutions with respect to others' (Sayer 2000: 79). Thompson expressed this argument in the context of explaining food riots in eighteenth-century England, where he argued that there was a customary expectation amongst both working people

DOI: 10.4324/9781003247326-10

and elites that in return for their contributions, the working poor were entitled to be able to purchase subsistence foods at a viable price. Thompson, however, tended to see the moral economy as being replaced by modern market economies, whereas Sayer stresses that the moral and/or normative dimension does not disappear in the market economy or under capitalism.

This is partly because the market never becomes the whole economy, even under advanced capitalism: Sayer identifies the economy with *all* provisioning activity, regardless of whether it is done to produce commodities or not (Sayer 2004: 2; 2018: 23). Work outside the cash economy is directed more immediately towards providing what we need to live and to flourish (Sayer 2018: 23). But even within the market economy, he argues that many exchanges involve 'thicker transactions and relationships involving cooperation, enduring responsibilities or specialist expertise' (Sayer 2004: 9). Paid work, most obviously, does not simply involve an exchange of labour for money but rather ongoing cooperation, relationships, and obligations with one's fellow workers (Sayer 2004: 10). Even an activity like shopping is not conducted purely in the spirit of utility maximisation but is often guided by our caring relationships to other family members (Sayer 2003: 353). Putting it more systemically, 'all economic institutions are founded on norms defining rights and responsibilities that have legitimations (whether reasonable or unreasonable), require some moral behaviour of actors, and generate effects that have ethical implications' (Sayer 2007: 261).

Moral Economy as a Mode of Enquiry

In its second aspect, moral economy (by analogy with political economy) is an approach to studying, describing and explaining the economy. It 'studies the moral norms and sentiments that structure and influence economic practices, both formal and informal, and the way in which these are reinforced, compromised or overridden by economic pressures' (Sayer 2007: 262). It is thus an approach to enquiry that takes the first aspect of moral economy seriously, positioning normativity as an essential focus for the study of the economy in general. However, it also treats normativity very differently than mainstream sociology, which tends to see it as rules backed by social sanctions that produce social order. This, he says, is 'an alienated conception of the moral dimension of social life, for it omits what matters to us and why morality should have any internal force' (Sayer 2004: 3–4). We often act morally 'regardless of whether there are any penalties for not doing so, because we feel that it is right or conducive to well-being, and because to do otherwise would cause some sort of harm to people' (Sayer 2004: 4). We are not merely socialised into normative understandings and behaviours. Rather, we are active, reasoning participants in our normative commitments, influenced not only by our culture but also by our nature as needy beings with desires and commitments, including commitments to the care of others.

This approach feeds directly into Sayer's major works on class (Sayer 2005) and on lay normativity (Sayer 2011). He argues that our class position affects our capacity to flourish or suffer, not only through material mechanisms but also because we may feel pride or shame as a consequence of how we are judged through prevailing normative attitudes to our class. In both books, he argues that our moral sentiments are embodied and emotional, but they are not irrational – we can reason morally, and our emotions are themselves part and parcel of our system of ethical reasoning. Sociology often fails to see the personal, emotive, and reasoning faces of lay normativity and thus to see that people's values matter to them because they are intimately bound up with their well-being. They are *about* how to achieve well-being, but they also *contribute* to our success or failure in achieving well-being. In its fatuous search for an 'objectivity' based on refusing to engage with evaluative issues, sociology has become alienated from questions of well-being and thus produces an alienating account of normativity and class (Sayer 2005). Ironically, it also fails to see what *is* objective about normativity; it is not merely the pursuit of culturally arbitrary norms but is oriented to objective sources of flourishing and suffering. Because we can flourish or suffer, we are evaluative beings who must assess what is good for us and those we care for. Moral economy, then, is a mode of enquiry that recognises and respects questions of care, well-being, and moral judgement that have traditionally been marginalised by the social sciences.

Moral Economy as Critique

It is also a mode of enquiry that itself takes an evaluative stance towards its subject since social scientists, like everyone else, are evaluative beings with ethics of care and commitment based on the desire to flourish and to support the flourishing of those to whom we feel a duty of care. As a result, 'in paying close attention to how economic arrangements affect well-being, [we] can hardly avoid normative implications' (Sayer 2007: 262). With a few exceptions such as the feminist ethics of care literature and the capabilities approach (Sayer 2007: 267), this represents a break with existing perspectives on the economy. On the one hand, mainstream social science disowns evaluative questions, but on the other hand critical social science has also been guilty, in what Richards calls 'a great historical error' that Sayer is devoted to correcting in this third face of moral economy, of effacing the normative basis of its evaluations (Richards 2020).

In a sense, this is Sayer's response to the challenges he posed in an earlier paper, which argued that critical social science largely fails to acknowledge the normative dimension of critique (Sayer 1997: 476). Even critical realism is criticised for giving 'a complacent account of CSS [critical social science] in which ought follows straightforwardly from is' (Sayer 1997: 473) – a reference to Roy Bhaskar's concept of explanatory critique which suggests that we can derive critical conclusions from purely factual premises (Bhaskar 1986: 177). For Sayer, criticism can only be based on an ethical stance driven by our understanding of what is required for us and those we care about to flourish. Such understandings are influenced by our cultural contexts, but they also depend on basic features of human being: our physical and emotional needs, which arise from our 'trans-cultural capacities for suffering and flourishing', even though the way those needs are realised is socially shaped (Sayer 2000: 81–82).

Sayer argues that radical political economy is guilty of 'the long-standing neglect of its critical standpoints' in the sense that it takes those standpoints (such as opposition to capitalism or market forms of economy) for granted without examining their basis in normative judgements (Sayer 2007: 261). This chimes in with criticisms of the Marxist tradition that accuse it of denying its own normative basis, thus becoming incapable of recognising when it contributed to actions that conflicted with that basis (notably Geras 1985). There is also a strong parallel with Erik Olin Wright's argument for concrete utopias in that he suggests that critique also depends on being able to demonstrate the possibility of meeting human needs better (Sayer 2000: 81; Wright 2010).

This third aspect of moral economy is implemented by examining and assessing the legitimations of economic institutions and practices (Sayer 2007: 268), as Sayer does, for example, in his book *Why We Can't Afford the Rich* (which he positions explicitly as a study of moral economy) (Sayer 2007: 268; 2015b: 18–22). The book challenges the economic relations that allow rentiers to extract unearned income while productive workers may be left unable to meet their basic needs. Moral economic evaluations, however, need not always be negative, as we see in his paper on consumer culture and moral economy (Sayer 2003). Without entirely rejecting critiques of consumer culture, he suggests that some are too negative about commodification because they fail to take account of the ways in which commodities are recontextualised by their purchasers in the context of their relationships (Sayer 2003: 344, 353–354).

The Influence of Moral Economy

The concept of moral economy is increasingly influential, and Sayer's influence on it is increasingly acknowledged, although it is typically seen as secondary to that of Thompson and Karl Polanyi. This is ironic, since there are clear differences between their perspectives, and at least some authors invoking Thompson and Polanyi employ a concept of moral economy that is much closer to Sayer's.

Both Thompson and James Scott, whose work on modern peasant villages is also influential, see the moral economy in much narrower terms: not as the normative shaping of the economy in general but rather as a very specific set of moral expectations (Booth 1994: 654). In particular, they identify it with the right to subsistence for the poor and a corresponding duty of redistribution for the wealthy. While these moral standards have a substantial influence in the contexts studied by Thompson and Scott, they regard them as culturally particular and argue that they are extinguished by the rise of a pervasive market that 'has escaped the control of the community' (Booth 1994: 657). Thompson explicitly resisted attempts to widen the concept of moral economy, arguing that this 'would lead to a loss of focus' (Götz 2015: 154). As Thompson puts it, 'The breakthrough of the new political economy of the free market was also the breakdown of the old moral economy of provision' (Thompson 1971: 136). In this respect, their account maps onto the work of Karl Polanyi, who sees the rise of modernity as a great transformation in which the economy becomes disembedded from wider social traditions and norms, taking on a life of its own that is no longer subject to these constraints but instead driven by an individualistic optimising logic (Booth 1994; Polanyi 2001).

For Sayer, however, and other critics of these versions of the concept, the market economy is also and necessarily a moral economy: all economies depend on legitimacy and on moralised practices. The great transformation changes the moral environment, but it does not abolish lay normativity or the dependence of economic activity on it. The market economy is just as embedded as the pre-modern economy in both an institutional structure and a set of moral beliefs (Booth 1994: 661). This perspective, rather than Thompson's, is therefore implicit in all work that seeks to apply the concept of moral economy in the context of contemporary market-based economic forms.

Sayer's contribution has been recognised and integrated by a number of scholars. Sharon Bolton and Knut Laaser, for example, welcome Sayer's re-introduction of lay morality and 'people as ethical and evaluative beings' to the study of work (Bolton & Laaser 2013: 515). They also revisit a well-known earlier paper of Bolton's that 'portrayed cabin crew as deeply moral and insightful beings whose social commitments to each other and to passengers were guided by moral dispositions and evaluations in the light of the concern for their own and others' well-being' (Bolton & Boyd 2003; Bolton & Laaser 2013: 518). They retrospectively recast the argument in terms of moral economy, arguing that the concept strengthens the framework of the argument (Bolton & Laaser 2013: 518).

If Bolton's contribution emphasises moral economy as contributing to a better understanding of economic activity at the micro-level, my own work on the digital economy has also employed it with more of a meso orientation (Elder-Vass 2015, 2016). For example, open-source software creation depends on a radically different set of normative commitments than commodity forms of software, notably labour, as a voluntary activity undertaken for pleasure within a relatively non-hierarchical organisational structure as opposed to wage labour managed for profit; and a product that is freely available to anyone who decides to use it as opposed to a commodity. Having said that, open-source software is embedded not only in this gift-oriented moral economy but also in the normative orientations of the market economy and has become the site of an intriguing hybridisation of the two (Elder-Vass 2015).

What Does Moral Economy Contribute to Explanatory Work?

These applications, however, and Bolton and Laaser's discussion, in particular, raise a question: if a study that was conducted without the framework of moral economy can be recast in its terms, what is the concept of moral economy actually contributing to the explanation developed in the study? Bolton and Laaser have an answer: 'A moral economy approach strengthens the existing conceptual frame by offering analytical connective tissue that more fully binds together the different strands of the cabin crews' experience of work' (Bolton & Laaser 2013: 518). This does not seem to suggest an increase in explanatory power or the identification of any further causal elements, but rather an increase in coherence of the set of explanations taken as a whole, perhaps in the sense that we may now see the different normative elements of the original account as all being examples of the same *kind* of explanation. The framework provides a kind of validation of the particular elements of the explanation by recognition of their relation to the general form of moral economy.

We could also argue that the moral economy, as Sayer understands it, corresponds to a general class of causal mechanisms and their influence: those mechanisms in which ethical commitments oriented to human needs and capabilities and implemented by evaluative actors influence economic practices. To take a moral economy approach is to recognise that all economies depend on such mechanisms and to employ accounts of such mechanisms in economic explanations. It thus sensitises us to the presence of certain kinds of mechanisms, but it does not in itself define specific mechanisms or structures. Thus (like critical realist philosophical ontology, but at a somewhat more concrete level) it remains a framework that needs to be filled out with specifics, and indeed could be filled out in many different ways.

This also helps to explain the division between Sayer's perspective and Thompson's. Thompson's moral economy thesis identified a specific set of causal mechanisms, relating to the moral sense of entitlement to subsistence and the way in which workers reacted when they felt this had been breached. His concern about generalising the concept of moral economy arose from his desire to maintain the focus on this specific explanation. As Götz has argued, this narrows the meaning of the concept relative both to earlier historical usages and to the sense of generality implicit in the term itself (Götz 2015). Still, Thompson's version has an obvious explanatory payoff that more abstract versions of the concept must do without. For these more abstract versions, an explanatory enquiry conducted in the moral economy mode will always have to identify specific normative forces to do its explanatory work.

How Does Moral Economy Contribute to Critique?

Sayer's commitment to basing critique on explicit ethics is an enormous step forward from the crypto-normativity of traditional leftist and post-structuralist critiques (Sayer 2012). 'Critical social science', as he says, 'needs to acknowledge its often hidden or repressed premise – that its evaluations of practices imply a conception of human flourishing' (Sayer 2011: 245). Surfacing that premise requires critics to explain how the objects of their critique impede human flourishing, and how those obstacles could be removed in a way that would improve things, rather than relying on vague allusions and tenuous assumptions about possible alternatives. It also requires that we recognise the positive contributions to flourishing made by existing institutions alongside the harms they create and thus leads to a more careful and caring radical politics rather than an irresponsible politics that disregards its possible consequences.

Again, though, there are limits to what moral economy can do for us in this space. Tying moral economy to an ethics based on human flourishing is attractive but Sayer does not provide us with a firm meta-ethical justification for doing so nor does this principle lead directly to specific ethical conclusions. It may seem self-evident that human flourishing is a good thing, but on the one hand, it is not clear that it is the *only* good thing and, on the other, there may be many different understandings of what produces flourishing in a given case. Some might argue, for example, that we should also be concerned with the flourishing of other animals, or even with the flourishing of the planet or the universe as a whole. I tend to agree with prioritising human flourishing, but we need to be able to justify that priority and more meta-ethical work are required to do that (Elder-Vass 2010).

Nor does moral economy provide us with tools to solve the practical ethical questions that arise when people have different needs and different beliefs about how to encourage flourishing. As in the explanatory argument, moral economy functions here as a framework that needs to be filled out with more specific claims about what contributes to human flourishing. Sayer, for example, bases much of his critique of the rich on the distinction between earned and unearned income, seeing the former as contributing to human flourishing and the latter as not (Sayer 2015a: 293). No doubt this corresponds to a strong moral instinct for fairness – that people's incomes should reflect their contributions to society – but it is all too easy to overplay any single moral principle when there are so many different angles on human flourishing that we need to consider. He overplays this one, I suggest, when he uses it to oppose a Universal Basic Income (Sayer 2018: 29–30), because there are also many flourishing-based reasons for *supporting* it. One might argue, for example, that we all should have the right to subsist without being demeaned and potentially excluded by a disciplinary state administering conditional benefits. Or that when much of the work available is alienating and exploitative, we should provide people with the dignity of being able to refuse it. The more general point, though, is that a commitment to human flourishing, while thoroughly desirable, is not in itself enough to provide an unambiguous basis for critique. This is not an argument, however, *against* Sayer's moral economy, only a caution against asking the concept to do more work than it is capable of.

Conclusion

Sayer's work on the moral economy is a major contribution to reforming CSS. The idea that our economy *is* a moral economy cuts the ground from under economics that detaches its rationalistic model of the economy from any trace of humanity or sociality. The idea that we should study it by examining the norms and sentiments that influence the actions of evaluative ethical actors *restores* humanity and sociality to our understanding of the economy. And the idea that critical social scientists are also ethical actors who should be explicit about the nature of their evaluations is a demand for critique to advance into a responsible adulthood in which we explain the reasons for our calls for change and think seriously about how things could actually be improved for people. Moral economy as a concept does not in itself provide us with explanations or justifications. These still need to be developed on a case-by-case basis, taking account of many different mechanisms and contributions to flourishing, and there will always be scope for debate about the best way to do that. But moral economy provides us with a framework that helps us to develop more realistic social explanations of what happens in the economy and more human evaluations of what *should* happen. It is simultaneously more realistic and more humanistic than prevailing social science – just what one would expect from Andrew Sayer.

References

Bhaskar, R. (1986). *Scientific Realism and Human Emancipation*. London: Verso.
Bolton, S., & Boyd, C. (2003). Trolley Dolly or Skilled Emotion Manager? Moving on from Hochschild's Managed Heart. *Work, Employment and Society* 17(2): 289–308.
Bolton, S., & Laaser, K. (2013). Work, Employment and Society through the Lens of Moral Economy. *Work, Employment and Society* 27(3): 508–525.
Booth, W. J. (1994). On the Idea of the Moral Economy. *The American Political Science Review* 88(3): 653–667.
Elder-Vass, D. (2010). Realist Critique without Ethical Naturalism or Moral Realism. *Journal of Critical Realism* 9(1): 33–58.

Elder-Vass, D. (2015). The Moral Economy of Digital Gifts. *International Journal of Social Quality* 5(1): 35–50.

Elder-Vass, D. (2016). *Profit and Gift in the Digital Economy*. Cambridge: Cambridge University Press.

Geras, N. (1985). The Controversy about Marx and Justice. *New Left Review* 150: 47–85.

Götz, N. (2015). 'Moral Economy': Its Conceptual History and Analytical Prospects. *Journal of Global Ethics* 11(2): 147–162.

Polanyi, K. (2001). *The Great Transformation*. Boston MA: Beacon.

Richards, H. (2020). Moral Economy and Emancipation. *Journal of Critical Realism* 19(2): 146–158.

Sayer, A. (1997). Critical Realism and the Limits to Critical Social Science. *Journal for the Theory of Social Behaviour* 27(4): 473–488.

Sayer, A. (2000). Moral Economy and Political Economy. *Studies in Political Economy* 61(1): 79–103.

Sayer, A. (2003). (De)commodification, Consumer Culture, and Moral Economy. *Environment and Planning D: Society and Space* 21: 341–357.

Sayer, A. (2004). Moral Economy. Retrieved from www.lancs.ac.uk/fass/sociology/papers/sayer-moral-economy.pdf

Sayer, A. (2005). *The Moral Significance of Class*. Cambridge: Cambridge University Press.

Sayer, A. (2007). Moral Economy as Critique. *New Political Economy* 12(2): 261–270.

Sayer, A. (2011). *Why Things Matter to People*. Cambridge: Cambridge University Press.

Sayer, A. (2012). Power, Causality and Normativity: A Critical Realist Critique of Foucault. *Journal of Political Power* 5(2): 179–194.

Sayer, A. (2015a). Time for Moral Economy. *Geoforum* 65: 291–293.

Sayer, A. (2015b). *Why We Can't Afford the Rich*. Bristol: Policy Press.

Sayer, A. (2018). Welfare and Moral Economy. *Ethics and Social Welfare* 12(1): 20–33.

Thompson, E. P. (1971). The Moral Economy of the English Crowd in the Eighteenth Century. *Past & Present* 50: 76–136.

Wright, E. O. (2010). *Envisioning Real Utopias*. London: Verso.

Chapter 8

Putting Resistance Back in Moral Economy

Balihar Sanghera and Elmira Satybaldieva

Sayer's (2000, 2004, 2007) moral economy perspective is theoretically stronger and more robust than the classic texts on moral and embedded economies (e.g. Thompson 1971, 1991; Scott 1976; Polanyi 1944). He draws on scholars from Adam Smith to Martha Nussbaum to articulate his unique approach on moral economy. While there is much to learn and value from reading and re-reading his work, resistance features much less compared to the classic texts. He largely focuses on resignation and acquiescence. By contrast, Thompson, Scott and Polanyi view riots, protests, everyday forms of resistance and countermovements as necessary for preserving and remaking moral economies. This chapter examines how resistance and activism can be more central to Sayer's moral economy perspective.

Arnold (2001: fn. 5) poses the question whether resistance is an important foundation for a moral economy. For traditional moral economists, economic incorporation of pre- or non-market people can produce moral resentment and anger at injustice, leading to collective action. In response to economic liberalism, social and political movements can emerge to protect society from the damaging effects of the commodification of land, money and labour (Fraser 2013). Bernstein (2007) remarks that political struggles are necessary for any hope of realising the promise of a progressive moral economy.

Sayer's position on resistance is ambivalent. While he recognises that social suffering can be a source of resistance, his moral economy perspective is largely silent on the topic.[1] He emphasises social actors' resignation, complicity and accommodation to unjust economic relations. In situations of limited resources and alternatives, subordinate groups are more likely to accept and normalise existing economic arrangements than to resist and rebel against them.

The significance of resistance and collective action is not merely an empirical question. It is important to examine and evaluate how protests and activism can shape economic institutions and practices to develop and nurture people's capabilities and well-being.

This chapter consists of five sections. The first section examines how Sayer has advanced the moral economy scholarship. In the second section, attention

DOI: 10.4324/9781003247326-11

is given to how Thompson, Scott and Polanyi discuss the nature of collective action. Section three explores how the role of resistance can be expanded in Sayer's moral economy perspective. In section four, we offer some research on resistance to rentierism in Central Asia. Finally, some concluding remarks will be offered.

Sayer's Moral Economy Perspective

As several contributors in this book have already noted, Sayer has significantly advanced the moral economy scholarship. His attention to people's moral sentiments, concerns, evaluations and human flourishing means that economic practices and relations are not merely shaped by customs, traditions, norms and values that are external or contingent to them. Rather economic relations are necessarily constituted by people's commitments, feelings, dispositions and judgements about things they have reason to value.

This moral dimension of economic practices is largely missing in Thompson's, Scott's and Polanyi's accounts. It partly explains why they tend towards a dichotomous view of societies between moral/embedded and market/disembedded economies. Although they examine how traditional rights, norms and values legitimised and shaped pre-capitalist societies, scant attention is given to the different forms of moral justification, legitimation and rationalisation in capitalist societies.

Booth (1994) argues that all economies are moral economies. In *Why We Can't Afford the Rich*, Sayer (2015) explains that contemporary capitalists and rentiers often seek to portray their wealth as deserving and 'earned' and use philanthropy to deflect any criticisms of dubious gains. Property rights, discourses and norms justify, regularise and normalise unequal outcomes on the basis of *inter alia* the rule of law, market freedom and choice, moral individualism, the sanctity of contracts and honouring one's obligations.

Property rights and relations are particularly significant because they legitimise and regularise rent, or 'unearned income', based on the mere ownership and control of existing scarce assets (Tawney 1921). Sayer argues that power often plays a significant role in forming economic arrangements, with justifications serving as ex-post rationalisations or as legitimations of vested interests. This makes it all the more important to critically assess justifications, and not to imagine that economic relations are outcomes of democratic moral deliberations or mutual interests.

Crucially, Sayer's moral economy perspective involves an ethical critique of economic institutions and practices. He does not merely analyse how normative factors shape or are shaped by economic activities and forces; he evaluates the consequences on people's well-being and the environment. In recognising how economic activities affect human flourishing, social analysis cannot avoid normative implications. Evaluative judgements are necessary to understand the effects of economic activities on human well-being. They also strengthen rather than weaken objectivity. As Sayer (2018) notes, if descriptions of economies do not understand what things make people flourish or suffer, they are then deficient descriptions of human existence.

His critique of economic activities comes from a qualified ethical naturalism standpoint (Sayer 2003). Evaluative judgements of good and bad relate to human needs and capacities for flourishing or suffering. Evaluations are not merely subjective opinions, because they concern objective matters that exist independently of what particular observers happen to think, and are about things that people have reason to value and care about.

Sayer's ethical standpoint can accommodate a wide variety of cultural ways of satisfying human needs and nurturing well-being, without falling into the trap of moral relativism (Nussbaum 2006). It also acknowledges that people's understandings of good and bad practices can be fallible. Otherwise, there is no difference between understandings and what they are about or of producing wishful thinking and a strong form of social constructionism.

Sayer's view of moral economy is broader than that of Thompson, Scott and Polanyi. The latter largely restrict the scope of moral economic analysis and critique to market coordination. Their critique of the rise of capitalism centres on the dominance of exchange value over use value and the damaging effects of commodifying land, money and labour. Sayer's approach is more inclusive, in that his moral economic analysis and critique extend to non-market forms of provisioning (such as households, planning and networks), and tackle a range of normative questions – from issues of equality and distribution to contribution, care and human capabilities.

Moral Economists on Collective Action

Thompson, Scott and Polanyi extensively discuss resistance and activism in their classic texts. In their moral economic analyses, entitlements and responsibilities constitute pre-capitalist relations and practices, and restricted access to essential resources can generate confrontations over rights, customs and values, leading to revolts, defiance and protests. While worsening economic conditions for subordinate groups are necessary for resistance to occur, they are not sufficient. Collective actions are modified by political culture, expectations, traditions and reason.

In investigating food riots in 18th-century England, Thompson rejects mechanistic interpretations that actual deprivation resulted in direct action, or increases in food prices led to popular uprisings. Rather riots occurred because traditional norms and customs were not respected, and social rights and obligations were not met. Social grievances operated within a popular consensus as to what were legitimate and illegitimate economic practices.

Food riots were class conflicts over entitlements to necessities. As Thompson (1991: 259) explains, 'Food prices were not merely one point of conflict between working and property-owning classes over the material control of an economy, but were linked to class-specific notions of social rights and responsibilities'. Uprisings were supported by the wider consensus of the community that was so strong that it often overrode rioters' fears and deference. Sometimes the authorities reacted against markets to endorse a popular consensus of paternalism that buttressed their political legitimacy and power.

Given the infrequency of riots and rebellions, Scott argues that it is more important to understand everyday forms of resistance, that is 'the prosaic but constant struggle between the peasantry and those who seek to extract labour, food, taxes, rents and interest from them' (1985: 29). Everyday resistance often stops short of direct, open and collective confrontation with powerful elites and authorities. The weak employ ordinary 'weapons', including foot-dragging, dissimulation, evasion, encroachment, slander and sabotage. These forms of class struggle require little or no coordination.

Scott explains that everyday resistance is common because there are several obstacles to open resistance. First, opposition is likely to be less explosive if changes to economic practices are experienced gradually, rather than suddenly. Second, the very complexity of class structure in which different socio-economic groups compete against each other can militate against collective action. Third, 'exit' rather than 'voice' may be the preferred and pragmatic response to economic hardship. Fourth, coercive and repressive tactics by elites and authorities can inhibit open and defiant actions. Fifth, the dull compulsion of economic relations may mean that subordinate groups have little choice but to adjust to their oppressive circumstances, rather than redress them.

In his analysis of market societies, Polanyi examines broader social and political movements. Market societies are constituted by two opposing forces: the free market movement and the protective countermovement, which can emerge to resist the former's disembedding and destructive effects. In particular, the commodification of fictitious goods can prompt safeguards and regulations.

> Undoubtedly, labour, land and money markets are essential to a market economy. But no society could stand the effects of such a system of crude fictions even for the shortest stretch of time unless its human and natural substance as well as its business organisation was protected against the ravages of this satanic mill.
>
> (Polanyi 1944: 76–77)

Polanyi's 'double movement' helps to make sense of capitalism and the development of the welfare state. While working class movements can be a key part of the protective countermovement, rival class interests, especially capitalists, can also demand protection from market uncertainty and instability. Responses to economic dispossession, destruction, precarity and inequality do not merely reflect class struggles over rights and responsibilities, they articulate competing economic and political projects and hegemonic visions. Although Polanyi is sympathetic to the protective countermovement, it can take dangerous forms. It matters whether resistance is conducted in the name of fascism, communism, social democracy or democratic socialism.

Sayer on Compliance and Resistance

As already noted, Sayer (2000, 2004, 2007) makes some distinct claims about what to study and how. He points out that the concept of moral economy has often been too closely associated with resistance to markets. As his moral economy perspective extends to other forms of provisioning and broader normative questions, market resistance becomes less central. While he recognises that subordinate groups can defy economic domination, his analysis tends towards their acceptance and accommodation to existing structures. But his work on lay morality suggests how social activism can be integral to his moral economy perspective.

Sayer (2016) argues that acceptance and submission are less a product of conscious consent or force of ideas than a tacit and practical belief that becomes self-evident and common sense in the context of lack of alternatives. As Bourdieu (1977: 164) writes,

> Every established order tends to produce … the naturalisation of its own arbitrariness. Of all the mechanisms tending to produce this effect, the most important and the best concealed is undoubtedly the dialectic of the objective chances and the agents' aspirations, out of which arises the *sense of limits*, commonly called the *sense of reality*.

Once economic institutions and practices have become established, normative questions about their features tend to be forgotten, and the politics of acquiescence and accommodation prevails. Their continued existence scarcely requires public moral deliberations or justifications, having become depoliticised and naturalised, and treated as 'facts of life'. Established economic arrangements are viewed as how things are and what people deserve, as in the 'belief in a just world'. '[Moral justifications] primarily serve as rationalisations of the already established' (Sayer 2016: 46).

But occasionally established constitutive moral economic rights and norms can be questioned and politicised. People's dissatisfaction can be expressed through hidden and open resistance. Though powerful groups tend to fend off criticisms and suppress protests, trying to secure the necessary acceptance for the established institutions and practices. They offer reasons (however weak or flawed) that legitimise the existing liberal property regime, justify unequal social relationships and delegitimise opposing forces and alternative arrangements (Sayer 2015; Fairclough & Fairclough 2012).

In his work on lay morality, Sayer (2011) discusses how people are evaluative beings, whose relation to the world is one of concern. They continually have to monitor and evaluate how the things they care about are faring, and what to do next. While intended and unintended consequences are important in evaluating and justifying economic institutions, people can also appeal to other criteria, such as need, desert and justice. But their moral evaluations can be limited by economic pressure to survive in a competitive environment. Short-term financial concerns can be prioritised over long-term social ones.

In recognising the importance of reflexivity and evaluative judgements, Sayer (2005) criticises Bourdieu for his tendency towards sociological determinism and reductionism. People cannot simply adjust to any habitat, irrespective of its impact on their well-being. While class dispositions, sentiments and moralities can endorse or accommodate social inequalities, people also possess notions of fairness, justice, equality and dignity that lead them to oppose demeaning and damaging practices. They resist because of their normative commitments. What emerges is a complex set of ethical and unethical feelings, dispositions and values, resulting in inconsistent and imperfect practices against domination.

Olson and Sayer (2009) remark that studies on resistance tend to investigate the political complexities of resistance, rather than evaluating its normative complexities. For instance, critical social science usually analyses protesters' and activists' goals, strategies, actions, discourses and conflicts in the context of their social and political structures, opportunities and resources, but it often overlooks the normative implications. It commonly privileges the oppressed without explaining what oppression is and why it is wrong. Some 'radical' movements can have alternative imaginaries that are of questionable normative values.

Instead of idealising resistance or romanticising activists, critical scholarship should evaluate them in terms of human flourishing. While recognising the potential benefits of resistance in asserting alternative views of how the world ought to be, Sayer (2020) explains that activists' own well-being can be damaged, because commitments to the cause can come at the cost of spending less time with their family and friends. Tessman (2005) argues that resisters tend to develop 'burdened virtues', which are problematic traits that arise from the constant demand of fighting injustice. For example, resisters may be weighed down by perpetual anger to maintain their resolve against oppressors, or discomfort and remorse for committing certain base acts because of tragic dilemmas.

While Polanyi's work on the double movement is important, Sayer (2004) argues that his analysis of economic responsibilities is limited. In the Polanyian account, capitalism reduces individual and collective responsibilities for others, because markets are no longer embedded in society, self-interest and individualism are rewarded, and collectivism is penalised. The rise of welfare states counters individualisation by developing significant responsibilities for others (e.g. social protection programmes). This account, however, fails to examine how capitalism can extend and intensify responsibilities for others.

Drawing on Adam Smith's (1976 [1759]) *The Theory of Moral Sentiments*, Sayer (2004) offers another account of economic responsibilities. Individuals have a capacity for sympathy or fellow-feeling, allowing them to fallibly understand, evaluate and respond to others' situations and conduct. Everyday interactions depend on this capacity. While people can reasonably imagine and feel others' circumstances and act in ethical ways, social and physical distance can corrupt their judgements and actions. This is a 'bottom-up' analysis of morality that recognises social actors' contradictory, inconsistent and imperfect evaluations (Sayer 2005).

Individuals are not only economically interdependent as a result of divisions of labour within, between and outside of enterprises, they are also psychologically dependent on others. They are sensitive to others' emotions, needs, reasonings and experiences, and they require others' recognition and approval. Though Sayer (2004) notes that interpersonal relations will be insufficient to adequately regulate economic relations in modern societies. Moral failings and unintended consequences of individual actions require more formal and institutional types of regulation, which have been a feature of modern capitalism.

Sayer also draws on Williams (2008) to relate economic responsibilities to capitalism. Responsibility is one of the central virtues of modern liberal societies. As people lack the fixed reference points that religion, authority, nature and customs provided them in pre-modern societies, they have to respond to a plurality of normative demands, and this requires the virtue of responsibility. Modern institutions, such as private corporations, public sector organisations and charities, have delimited the plurality of demands by allocating particular responsibilities to individuals, as well as defining their own tasks and concerns. Institutional roles and relations largely define spheres of responsibility and accountability.

The institutional fabric creates a moral division of labour, which is a complex scheme of cooperation that restricts and intensifies responsibilities. The division of responsibilities is also reflexive and responsive to competition, innovation, change and unmet responsibilities (Williams 2008). While roles can clarify responsibilities, they do not exhaust them. Organisational biases, gaps and flaws result in normative demands being neglected, unenforced and unnoticed. Attempts to change institutions can come from above and below through social actors' actions within and outside of formal political structures (e.g. state directives and local petitions). In particular, social movements can demand greater responsibility and accountability, asking for new economic access, rights and status to be created and endorsed, as well as old ones to be protected (Fraser 2013).

In articulating how morality relates to economic responsibilities and divisions of labour, Sayer (2004) argues that moral regulation is internal to economic relations, rather than external to them as in the Polanyian account of capitalism. Modern economies generate sophisticated moral divisions of labour that create individual and collective responsibilities. People can respond to situations of social suffering and unmet needs by making normative demands of public, private and voluntary institutions. Social activism can play a significant role in calling for changes to spheres of responsibility and moral divisions of labour.

Resistance need not be limited to opposing markets or countering the commodification of land, money and labour, though the latter is important. Social struggles can involve assigning blame and causality for harm and lack of flourishing, renegotiating economic responsibilities, and remaking moral divisions of labour. In this way, Polanyi's double movement can be modified to show how capitalism and resistance are closely related.

Rentierism in Central Asia: Harms and Resistance

After gaining independence in 1991, many post-Soviet countries implemented extensive economic reforms to become capitalist economies. International financial institutions, such as the International Monetary Fund and the World Bank, were instrumental in pushing governments to adopt the Washington Consensus model. Property rights were transformed to legitimise rent, usury and capital gains (Sanghera & Satybaldieva 2021). Scarce and valuable assets were transferred from public to private ownership and control. As the rule of law prevailed, state regulation was weakened, favouring the interests of capital, trade and finance over those of labour, consumers and the environment.

The neoliberal commodification of money, land, natural resources and labour in Central Asia created a new economic system. Rent extraction was promoted and expanded, and sources of unearned income were justified and legitimised. 'Investment' was channelled into several major economic sectors, including natural resources, banking and real estate, enabling 'investors' (or rentiers) to extract income by mere virtue of having property rights to scarce assets, rather than producing goods and services.

The consequences of rent extraction have been harmful to economic development, people's well-being, the environment and democracy. Rentier activities enabled the propertied class to amass income and wealth at the expense of propertyless groups. Social inequalities and poverty increased, and many households struggled to make ends meet. In Kyrgyzstan, Tajikistan and Uzbekistan, countless individuals had to migrate overseas, sending remittances back home. In some cases, young children were left in the care of their relatives for several years, straining familial ties.

Under the guise of gender empowerment and poverty alleviation, financial and development agencies encouraged women in Kyrgyzstan, Tajikistan and Kazakhstan to borrow money at usurious interest rates to establish microenterprises. Often operating in a highly competitive environment, most borrowers struggled to repay their loans. Troubled borrowers usually experienced social shame and marital conflicts, because lenders humiliated them in public for delaying repayments and lacking honour, or dispossessed them of assets to foreclose the loan.

Housing has been unaffordable for most young working class families, partly because new apartment complexes were constructed for the rich to make speculative gains, and state mortgage schemes tended to target middle class families with high savings. Unable to pay high rent, many families established informal settlements on the outskirts of major cities in Kazakhstan and Kyrgyzstan. They lacked electricity, clean water and sewage, and were often denied formal access to health care, education and voting.

Transnational corporations have plundered resource-rich Central Asian countries through predatory drilling and mining. They have damaged local ecosystems, polluted rivers and glaciers and increased carbon dioxide emissions from fossil fuels. The extractive industries have also fostered criminogenic and undemocratic conditions in the region. Foreign investors signed lucrative agreements with plutocratic regimes, and have consistently violated environmental and health codes. International investment agreements and arbitration courts have tended to protect investors' property rights in the face of local democratic calls for tighter environmental regulation and a fairer share of the revenue.

While acknowledging social inequalities and discontents in Central Asia, economic elites, the judiciary and international financial institutions have justified and legitimised neoliberal property and rent relations on the basis of economic freedom, formal equality, market choice and the rule of law (Sanghera & Satybaldieva 2021). The majority of the population has normalised and accepted the dominant economic relations, believing there is no alternative to the 'free market'. But marginalised and poor groups have demanded greater responsibility and protection, subjecting economic relations to critical evaluations and interventions.

In the early 2000s, local and national anti-debt movements emerged over the harmful effects of the neoliberal commodification of money in Kazakhstan and Kyrgyzstan. They problematised and denaturalised debt relations and railed against usurious interest rates, financial malpractices and extrajudicial repossessions. The movement activists engaged in a reflexive process of interpreting and evaluating their situation and attributing blame for their suffering (Crossley 2002). They moved from individualising and localising debt relations to politicising and internationalising them. They held predatory lenders, lax state controls and global capital, not borrowers' moral character and integrity, responsible for increasing indebtedness and hardship. They also graduated from attacking local branches of microfinance institutions to protesting in front of central banks and international financial institutions.

For over three decades in Kazakhstan and Kyrgyzstan, many rural migrants and propertyless residents have resisted the commodification of land and its negative impact on their lives. In addition to quietly encroaching on land to build adobe homes, they formed grassroots movements to stop mass evictions, protect their homes from demolition, politicise the lack of affordable housing, lobby for free land for housing, and demand legalisation and improvements to informal settlements. Their relationship with political regimes has been complex. Depending on the balance of social forces, state authorities either have embraced and tolerated informal settlements for political reasons, or have sought to evict them, aiming to modernise the city and extract higher land rent.

Several independent labour and environmental movements quickly arose to tackle exploitative working conditions and destructive ecological practices in Kazakhstan's and Kyrgyzstan's extractive industries. They demanded greater corporate responsibility and accountability for people's safety and well-being. Most of the population sympathised and shared the movements' concerns and supported their strikes and protests. The movement leaders were able to develop alliances with other social forces that threatened the political regimes' legitimacy. As Kazakhstan's labour movement became more politicised, the state used repressive tools to crush dissent and ensure compliance. In Kyrgyzstan, the popular nationalist backlash against neoliberal extractivism reached its apogee in October 2020 with the country's third political uprising since gaining independence.

While all these social movements responded to harms generated by the neoliberal commodification of money, land and labour, they did not necessarily achieve protective measures or significantly change spheres of responsibility. The relationship between political regimes and countermovements was complex and multidirectional (Goodwin 2018). The states had the capacity to accommodate, dilute and repress movements' demands. By privileging investor rights, they often limited democratic forces and grassroots resistance in favour of transnational and domestic capital (Gill 2008).

Conclusion

This chapter has examined how resistance appears in Sayer's moral economy perspective. Resistance is less foundational in his work than in the classic texts, partly because of his shift from markets and resistance to them to other forms of provisioning and broader normative questions. His position on resistance to unjust economic relations is nuanced. Although social suffering and injustice can produce resistance and social activism, he argues that complicity, resignation and normalisation are more likely. He urges critical scholars not merely to explain the political complexities of resistance but evaluate its aims, strategies and effects, and recognise its moral complexities.

We have suggested that resistance and activism can be expanded in Sayer's moral economy perspective. His work on lay morality discusses how people are evaluative beings, who continually have to assess how things they care about are faring. People have moral agency and reflexivity in navigating their way through the social world, as Archer (2007) notes. Individuals can and do pursue goals and concerns related to social change and justice through active participation in professional, social, political and charitable organisations and movements.

Sayer draws on Adam Smith and Garrath Williams to offer an account of capitalism that relates morality to economic responsibilities. Given the nature of divisions of labour in modern societies, economic responsibilities for others are unavoidable. People can respond to others' unmet needs, social suffering and injustice by making normative demands of public, private and voluntary institutions for greater responsibility. Social struggles often involve people's access to or protection from markets and enterprises, expansion or restrictions of rights and care, and recognition or denial of status and identity.

The nature and extent of resistance is also an empirical question. Our research on rentier capitalism in Central Asia identified how marginalised and poor groups established grassroots movements to counter the harmful and damaging effects of neoliberal property and rent relations. The movements called for greater corporate and state responsibilities to ensure flourishing for all. Their achievements were variable, partly because of the unequal relationship between political regimes and countermovements.

By putting resistance back into moral economy, studies can give a richer account of how people experience and evaluate economic domination. Attention to resistance recognises a part of people's lives that is of significance to them and others. Moral economic analyses and critiques that incorporate resistance can acknowledge people's evaluative and transformative powers, however inconsistent and imperfect their actions may be. Wright (2010: 10) writes, '[A]ny emancipatory social science faces three basic tasks: elaborating a systematic diagnosis and critique of the world as it exists; envisioning viable alternatives; and understanding the obstacles, possibilities, and dilemmas of transformation'. Researching resistance and collective action is crucial for a progressive moral economy, explaining what social powers exist or are lacking to get from the world as it is to what it ought to be.

Note

1 For instance, the word 'resistance' only appears twice in his 2007 article *Moral Economy as Critique*, both times in a footnote about the association between moral economy and resistance. Terms such as 'protest', 'activism' and 'collective action' are not present.

References

Archer, M. (2007). *Making our Way through the World: Human Reflexivity and Social Mobility*. Cambridge: Cambridge University Press.

Arnold, T. (2001). Rethinking moral economy. *American Political Science Review* 95(1): 85–95.

Bernstein, H. (2007). Capitalism and moral economy: land questions in Sub-Saharan Africa. Paper for Conference on Poverty and Capital, Global Poverty Research Group and Brooks World Poverty Institute, University of Manchester, 2–4 July.

Booth, W. (1994). On the Idea of the Moral Economy. *American Political Science Review* 88(3): 653–667.

Bourdieu, P. (1977). *Outline of a Theory of Practice*. Cambridge: Cambridge University Press.Crossley, N. (2002). *Making Sense of Social Movements*. Buckingham: Open University Press.

Fairclough, I., & Fairclough, N. (2012). *Political Discourse Analysis: A Method for Advanced Students*. London: Routledge.

Fraser, N. (2013). A Triple Movement? Parsing the Politics of Crisis After Polanyi. *New Left Review* 81 (May–June): 119–132.

Gill, S. (2008). *Power and Resistance in the New World Order*, Second edition. London: Palgrave.

Goodwin, G. (2018). Rethinking the Double Movement: Expanding the Frontiers of Polanyian Analysis in the Global South. *Development and Change* 49(5): 1268–1290.

Nussbaum, M. (2006). *Frontiers of Justice: Disability, Nationality and Species Membership*. Cambridge, MA: Belknap.

Olson, E., & Sayer, A. (2009). Radical Geography and its Critical Standpoints: Embracing the Normative. *Antipode* 41(1): 180–198.

Polanyi, K. (1944). *The Great Transformation: Economic and Political Origins of Our Time*. New York: Rinehart.

Sanghera, B., & Satybaldieva, E. (2021). *Rentier Capitalism and Its Discontents: Power, Morality and Resistance in Central Asia*. London: Palgrave Macmillan.

Sayer, A. (2000). Moral Economy and Political Economy. *Studies in Political Economy* 61(1): 79–103.

Sayer, A. (2003). Restoring the moral dimension in social scientific accounts: a qualified ethical naturalist approach. Discussion paper, Department of Sociology, Lancaster University, www.lancaster.ac.uk/fass/resources/sociology-online-papers/papers/sayer-restoring-the-moral-dimension.pdf

Sayer, A. (2004). Moral economy. Discussion paper, Department of Sociology, Lancaster University, www.lancaster.ac.uk/fass/resources/sociology-online-papers/papers/sayer-moral-economy.pdf

Sayer, A. (2005). *The Moral Significance of Class*. Cambridge: Cambridge University Press.

Sayer, A. (2007). Moral Economy as Critique. *New Political Economy* 12(2): 261–270.

Sayer, A. (2011). *Why Things Matter to People: Social Science, Values and Ethical Life*. Cambridge: Cambridge University Press.

Sayer, A. (2015). *Why We Can't Afford the Rich*. Bristol: Policy Press.

Sayer, A. (2016). Moral Economy, Unearned Income and Legalized Corruption. In D. Whyte & J. Wiegratz (eds), pp. 44–56, *Neoliberalism and the Moral Economy of Fraud*. London: Routledge.

Sayer, A. (2018). Pierre Bourdieu: Ally or Foe of Discourse Analysis? In R. Wodak & B. Forchtner (eds), pp. 109–121, *The Routledge Handbook on Language and Politics*. Abingdon: Routledge.

Sayer, A. (2020). Critiquing – and Rescuing – 'Character'. *Sociology* 54(3): 460–481.

Scott, J. (1976). *The Moral Economy of the Peasant: Rebellion and Subsistence in Southeast Asia*. New Haven: Yale University Press.

Scott, J. (1985). *Weapons of the Weak: Everyday Forms of Peasant Resistance*. New Haven: Yale University Press.

Smith, A. (1976 [1759]). *The Theory of Moral Sentiments*. Indianapolis: Liberty Fund.

Tawney, R. H. (1921). *The Acquisitive Society*. London: G. Bell and Sons.

Tessman, L. (2005). *Burdened Virtues: Virtue Ethics for Liberatory Struggles*. Oxford: Oxford University Press.

Thompson, E. P. (1971). The Moral Economy of the English Crowd in the Eighteen Century. *Past and Present* 50 (February): 76–136.

Thompson, E. P. (1991). The Moral Economy Reviewed. In E P. Thompson, pp.258–351, *Customs in Common*. London: Penguin Books.

Williams, G. (2008). Responsibility as a Virtue. *Ethical Theory and Moral Practice* 11(4): 455–470.

Wright, E. O. (2010). *Envisioning Real Utopias*. London: Verso.

Part III

Applications in Political Economy

Chapter 9

Andrew Sayer on Inequality, Climate Emergency and Ecological Breakdown

Can We Afford the Rich?

Jamie Morgan

Andrew Sayer's work has covered most of the significant social science subjects and societal issues of our time. These include positivism, empiricism and post-structuralism's adverse consequences for explanation, justification and truth claims (Sayer 1992, 2000); alternatives to the baleful influence of mainstream economics that also avoids the pitfalls of some versions of Marxism (Sayer 1995); the role of class as a source of and response to moral sentiment in a world whose ideational frameworks increasingly obscure the relevance of class (Sayer 2005); and the central role normativity plays in human existence and the contribution a fact-value, reason-emotion, mind-body and is-ought sensitive social science rooted in 'qualified' ethical naturalism can play in orienting a progressive ethics of care (Sayer 2004, 2007a, 2011, 2019).[1] Anyone who has read Sayer's work will also know that the transition between subjects and issues is underpinned by critical realist philosophy and by an evolving 'moral economy' inter disciplinary perspective – *not* a pejorative 'moralising' but rather a recognition that both explanation and normative-ideational justification are important for what is imposed upon us, what we choose to do, what we merely acquiesce to and ultimately how we live in comparison to how we might (Sayer 2007b; Götz 2015). This continuity also represents an intellectual journey of a kind that is increasingly rare in the world of academia – Andrew's deep commitment to leaving the planet better than he found it – though given the observed tendencies in the world, much of this has been against the grain of the times.[2]

Sayer's 2015 book *Why We Can't Afford the Rich* brings all of these previous themes together (Sayer 2015). It is an exploration of how extreme wealth and income inequality have been produced and legitimated and why inequality is not just morally objectionable; it is falsely posed and actively harmful to the well-being of the majority and to the survival of our species and many others. The book thus shares features (and in some cases data)[3] with the work of Jamie Galbraith, Thomas Piketty, Anthony Atkinson, Emmanuel Saez and Gabriel Zucman, as well as Robert Wade, Jason Hickel, Danny Dorling and Kate Pickett and Richard Wilkinson (the latter of whom provides the

DOI: 10.4324/9781003247326-13

Foreword). Matters have only worsened since *Why We can't Afford the Rich* was published and so its relevance has only increased. The COVID-19 global pandemic has exposed deep structural fragilities in societies and economies. Many of the most wealthy have simply become wealthier, and we have now entered a period of recognised 'Climate Emergency' and ecological break-down, where the need for drastic urgent action has finally been acknowledged, albeit without proper widespread recognition yet of what this might mean or require. Sayer (along with his long-time colleague and friend John O'Neill, e.g. O'Neill 2007) is quite clear that it is the commitment to compound growth inherent to capitalism that risks our future, and it is the current political, cul-tural and institutional frameworks of contemporary capitalism (whatever its other benefits) that exacerbate both inequality and climatological and eco-logical harms. As Richard Wilkinson states, 'Sayer's important piece-by-piece unpicking of the economic justifications of the rich is an important political act' (Wilkinson 2015: p. ix). With this in mind it is worth reprising, elabor-ating on and slightly updating Sayer's argument with a focus on its climato-logical and ecological implications. Space is at a premium, which means it is impossible to do justice to the diversity and quality of argument, so as a first point I would recommend you simply read the book. For our purposes, how-ever, it is the climatological and ecological implications of unattainable and unsustainable ways of living that are significant.

Sayer's 'Twist in the Tail'

Over the course of twenty chapters in *Why We can't Afford the Rich*, Sayer establishes that modern capitalism (neoliberalism broadly conceived) is a pathological system that, whatever its benefits (and Sayer recognises that there are many and also notes 'markets' are not intrinsically detrimental when confined to appropriate contexts and where carefully constructed, regulated and overseen), has produced numerous avoidable harms. Having first set out key constituents of neoliberalism and writing in 2015 in the global North and in the wake of the global financial crisis, he draws particular attention to aus-terity policies, which implicitly require the many to 'pay' for the damage done by a trajectory of policy that generated overwhelming gains to a minority.[4] General consequences have included falling welfare spending, cuts to ser-vices, low and stagnant wages, unemployment in many places, but also fur-ther increases to dependence on forms of flexible work with generally lower security, wage levels and terms and conditions: forms of 'sub-contracted' 'self-employment', 'platform' employment, zero-hour contracts and so on (exacerbating a situation of overwork for some, underwork for others and mental and physical ill health for many – as, e.g., Angus Deaton's work has highlighted). At the same time, though responses to the global financial crisis directed significant criticism at both mainstream economics and the 'masters of the universe' in finance, neither has fundamentally changed. The former remains rooted in forms of quantitative methods that sit awkwardly with explanation and analysis of economic systems as historical, cultural, socio-normative sets of practices where power is a key issue. The latter has experienced a whole slew of new regulations and guidelines, but all of these have been focused on improving the financial resilience of a financialised system (e.g. various forms of enhanced retained capital to absorb losses under Basel III, ringfencing and changes to exchange-traded central counterparty derivatives), which presupposes crises will occur. Finance continues to promote private debt-dependence, financial asset creation and trading and the process is now referred to as 'financial deepening'. The legitimating subtext of this concept is that finance stands behind productive investment and the flow of capital, which are the lifeblood of contemporary economies and thus vital to those economies and to growth and development – an argument that continues to distract from much of what the system actually does and how the system is really constructed (and Andrew was not in a position to say much about this in 2015, but the Financial Stability Board has played a significant coordinating role at the global level in recent years).

In any case, Sayer argues that one must be careful how one seeks to solve the problems of the system that led to extreme inequality and that has continued to evolve since the global financial crisis because that system is also a growth system and involves an underlying set of tendencies that have led to climate and ecological crisis. There is, therefore, a 'diabolical double crisis' to contend with:

> Given that the rise of the rich and the related slowdown in the growth of ordinary people's wages and salaries have, together, stalled the global economy, slowing the growth of demand and restricting opportunities for profitable productive investment, we should cut off or tax the rich's sources of unearned income and redistribute wealth downwards [as well as facilitate more equal wealth and income across society, which eventually reduces the need to redistribute]. This would boost demand and allow economic growth to resume ... In other words, redistribution plus growth [it seems at first sight] is the answer ... [But] *such a policy would accelerate global warming, indeed it would make runaway global warming and its dire consequences inevitable* ... We are therefore in a *diabolical double crisis.*
>
> (Sayer 2015: 327; italics in original)

A Growth System and Why We Can't Afford the Rich

To be clear, when addressing the 'diabolical double crisis', Sayer is combining two key issues. First contemporary capitalism is a *growth* system (and Sayer notes that state-based command economies were also growth systems). A growth system targets continual increases in GDP, even though there are also numerous other targets and metrics (e.g. Daly 2015; Dale 2012). GDP is a measure of 'exchange value' (the aggregated value of measured output in a given a year), and this is not quite the same as the sum of material resources and energy use. However, whilst there is some evidence of localised 'relative decoupling' of economic activity from material resource and energy use (measured using metrics such as output per $GDP for specific categories such as carbon emissions), there is no evidence that collectively economies are achieving or can achieve 'absolute decoupling' or that they are able to 'dematerialise' (e.g. Hickel & Kallis 2019; Parrique et al. 2019). As ecological economists have argued for years (and mainstream economics has either ignored or distorted), economic activity is a system of material and energy use with thermodynamic consequences, entropy and waste creation (e.g. Spash 2017). Its scale and intensity matter for the Earth system (our ecological and climate systems), and our societies and economies are embedded in and are ultimately dependent on that Earth system. Industrial economies and their consumption heavy contemporary variant inevitably come up against limits imposed by the Earth.

So, a growth system is one that targets continual increases in the scale of activity and so continually expands the problem of resource and energy use that has to be solved. Moreover, as this growth system spreads geographically (development based on industrialised and consumption-directed growth), the associated problems also spread. There may be some technological changes leading to energy production from non-carbon sources, but, in general, contemporary capitalism remains carbon-dependent, and the problem of resource and energy use is not reducible only to the problem of carbon. As Sayer emphasises, a growth system, therefore, is cumulatively and collectively unsustainable because bio-physical limits are eventually exceeded, and as thresholds or tipping points are breached dangerous climate change and ecological breakdown result.

Second, Sayer is suggesting that the 'rich' are incompatible with a sustainable future (where sustainable means a survivable situation that protects and supports the well-being of the many). This, of course, provokes the question 'who are the rich?', and Sayer is clear that this is a contextual question. From the point of view of continual accumulation of greater proportions of annual economic value and from the point of view of power and influence, he suggests this is the 'very rich' – those in or close to the '1%'; and within this grouping there are also further distinctions focused on even fewer people (and their control of vast fortunes and significant corporations or other assets – which some refer to as plutocracy, kleptocracy, etc.).

Though Sayer does not quite put it this way, there are several reasons why the existence of the very rich is incompatible with a sustainable future. The starting point is that a sustainable future seems to require more effective management of 'throughput', that is, material and energy use and their thermodynamic, entropy and waste consequences, and this must be matched to the capacity of the Earth's various systems to absorb, reproduce and renew.[5] This, in turn, seems to require a managed approach to 'steady-state' economic activity, and given that current levels of economic activity already exceed the Earth's capacity in numerous climate and ecological categories, this further implies significantly less and more carefully conducted material and energy use in pursuit of economic activity, that is, a *smaller* aggregated global economy. As such, a category of the 'very rich' seems incompatible with this future because:

1   The very rich captures a significant proportion of economic value, and this would be a larger proportion of smaller economies leaving less for the majority.
2   The very rich tend to capture an increasing relative share of economic value (accumulating great wealth) and this exacerbates 1, which seems incompatible with a steady-state situation.
3   Although unable to consume all the income that they receive, the 'very rich' sit at the top of a system of superfluous consumption and designed obsolescence, which ties growth to the continual creation of 'wants' in the form of ever-proliferating products and services. Their existence is a legitimating symbol of that system (a source of fascination, distraction and aspiration), though they consume a fraction of their income or wealth within that system is still disproportionate (and so also is their climate and ecological 'footprint' via jets, homes, yachts and islands) and their fortunes are fed by growth in that system – so their fortunes are tied to the reproduction of a growth system (irrespective of their personal politics or proclamations), and their particular activity may take the form of impediments to change, delays and so on and be harmful because of their given interests in the current system – e.g. as CEO of a fossil fuel corporation.
4   Given that the very rich are unable to consume their great incomes and their wealth is mainly held as financial assets, it follows that their great incomes and growing wealth feed a financialised system (becoming a source of speculative investment in financial assets chasing 'yield') and thus serves to reproduce the power and interests of that system. This, in turn, undermines or distorts attempts to solve ecological and climate problems, since it leads to perverse ideational framework effects. For example, leading to the primacy of economic analysis of ecological and climate policy (our first question becomes how does a prohibition or an investment affect the economy – what is its 'return' – rather than first asking do we need to do this in order to save the planet and save ourselves?). Once we start viewing climate and ecological problems as first sources of economic opportunity, a basic tension is built into how we address those problems – a primary focus on social redesign and urgently moving to stop doing some problematic things is undermined and a

techno-optimistic 'greening of growth' starts to take precedence, despite the lack of evidence that this is feasible.

The main conclusion is that processes which produce extreme inequality lead to the existence of the 'very rich', the very rich are a source of institutional resistance to a smaller steady-state future, and their incomes and wealth seem institutionally incompatible with such a smaller steady society. This seems to hold irrespective of the public declarations by some of the very rich that they are climate concerned and irrespective of their philanthropy.

Who Are (Maybe You Are) the Rich

Though Sayer is primarily concerned by the existence of the 'very rich' and opposes them for many reasons based on the moral economy – not just climate and ecological ones – his concern with the 'diabolical double crisis' means our significant sense of who the 'rich' are cannot rest with the 'very rich'. Despite decades of increasing global trade as a proportion of globally aggregated GDP (a metric that indicates more exchange of goods and services around the world as a proportion of total economic activity, i.e. a key aspect of contemporary 'globalisation' along with a rise in the proportion of transactions that are intra-firm rather than inter-firm due to the growth of multinational enterprises) and despite the claimed achievements of the Millennium Development Goals (notably the achievement of Goal 1 Target 1 focused on extreme poverty)[6] and the ongoing activity surrounding the subsequent Sustainable Development Goals (SDGs), the world remains extremely unequal in terms of income and wealth and of associated responsibility for climate and ecological effects.

Much, however, has been made of the World Bank and Branko Milanovic's 'elephant curve' data in recent years. The curve depicts relative growth in income across all income groups for the globe (i.e. not broken down into countries and regions). Its elephant shape – a hump for the body coinciding with those in the poorest 10% to 70% and U shape for the trunk rising sharply for the top 1% or 2% – indicates the major relative gains, since the late 1980s, have been to the relatively poor and very rich, since advanced capitalist country working classes and middle classes are towards the top of the global distribution but are not at the very top. This, of course, represents some of the downsides of globalisation for some groups who have suffered from deindustrialisation and changes to working practices under neoliberalism (leading to our current more fractious politics) but is also slightly misleading. It obscures the difference that place makes, and it depends on relative changes to income *not* absolute changes in income or wealth.

As any numerate person knows a given number is a larger percentage of a smaller total than it is of a larger one. For example, 1 is 10% of 10 but only 1% of 100. So, relative income gains to the bottom end of a distribution can actually mask smaller absolute increases in comparison to further up the distribution. As the work of Robert Wade and Jason Hickel makes clear, the poor may be getting slightly better off, but they are not catching up in any meaningful sense.[7] And this is especially so once one allows for the overwhelming effects created by China and looks at the rest of the world outside the core of the global North. Observationally, one need only try to list the countries that, for the last 40 years, have decisively transitioned in status from poor to wealthy modern economies, as we typically understand this term (Japan, South Korea, Taiwan, Singapore, etc.). It is not many and does not yet even decisively include China, despite its aggregate GDP and despite its geopolitical influence (and the number of billionaires). As Hickel makes clear, the global North and global South distinction (how some places are structurally made poor, what we take from them in debt transfers, etc.) still matters, and this is reflected in various kinds of data:

> In 1960 the per-capita income in the richest country was 31.8 times higher than in the poorest country; by 2010, it was 118 times higher, and the absolute gap between the two had more than doubled. We see a similar divergence if we look at the gap between developed and developing regions ... since 1960 the gap between the per-capita GDP of the US and that of Latin America has grown by 206%; the gap between the US and SSA [sub-Saharan Africa] has grown by 207%; the gap between the US and the Middle East and North Africa has grown by 155% and the gap between the US and South Asia has grown by 196%. From this perspective, global inequality has roughly tripled during the period [1960–2014].
>
> (Hickel 2017: 2217)

Once one starts to think about the place, then a whole set of issues are relevant in the context of climate and ecological issues. Relatively few countries and corporations in the world are responsible for the vast majority of carbon emissions and material and energy use.[8] Unsurprisingly there is a close association between GDP of a country and material and energy use; so to be a member of a global North society is to be towards the upper part of the hierarchy and distribution of economies that produce the majority of problems – whatever one's own politics and practices may be and (for the majority) however poor or put upon you may feel within the context of your own country (which is by no means to condone or downplay the problems that exist and how they are experienced).

There are, of course, qualifications to any general claims that might follow from the above. It is, for example, slightly misleading to attribute climate and ecological change merely to the existence of people as the significant factor (the Anthropocene – though the term does have specific meaning), since it is economic systems that play the decisive role, and decisions for these systems (rather than living under them) are taken by relatively few (Jason Moore, e.g., refers to this as the 'Capitalocene', Moore 2015).[9] Moreover, though contemporary globalisation has facilitated the spread of industrialisation and consumption (as the *development* model) much of the carbon emissions and a great deal of the ecological damage done are undertaken for the global North even when emanating from outside the global North – there are, of course, two ways of calculating for emissions accounting, production (where they are produced) and consumption (who they are produced for).

As most readers will be aware, many global North economies have achieved some degree of relative decoupling and have reduced emissions against some benchmark (such as the 1990 level inscribed by the Kyoto protocols) on a production basis but have often done considerably less well on a consumption basis (as imports have grown).[10] The planet, of course, does not care where emissions occur and so transfers are something climate change is ultimately blind to – and it is the continuation of a growth system that further exacerbates problems. Moreover, it is for climate and ecological purposes that the past, present and future are intimately related. The interventions in the Earth systems risk transition changes and feedback loop effects, once tipping points are reached.[11] This is a historic issue since reaching some point follows from *cumulative* effects – responsibility, therefore, cannot simply be attributed to the last source (location) to contribute (most notably today China). Carbon dioxide emissions, for example, can stay in the atmosphere for more than one hundred years, so our current climate (its warming and erratic weather) is partly based on activity that occurred when there were few industrialised countries and over the intervening period those industrialised countries (the UK, USA, Germany, etc.) have built up a climate debt to the world – invoking obligations because of responsibility.[12] This, of course, does not abnegate responsibility from current major sources of climate and ecological effects. China may well have become a 'successful' economic powerhouse based on its role as a source of low-cost manufacture for export and low value-added assembly for re-export – emissions produced for other places – and it may well now be engaged in massive investment in next-generation green technologies (to capture markets), but it also has its own internal engines of climate and ecological destruction that cannot be reduced to its external role (see Smith 2020).

In any case, though qualifications need to be made and nuance is important, the underlying issue remains that for climate and ecological purposes the rich is a far broader base of people than it is for other issues. Moreover, the issue is not just 'who are the rich' but rather the unintended consequences of the system that leads to inequality as we observe it (an industrialised, consumption-based growth system). Climate change and ecological breakdown have a global reach (especially the former), so the local metric that matters is the sum total of impact per person with a view to staying within planetary boundaries that allow for manageable throughput (and subject to all of the considerations that management implies). From this point of view, 'the rich' are all of those whose income and wealth provide them with a disproportionate share of impacts (material and energy use), which keeps us all on the wrong side of 'really sustainable'.[13] This, of course, presupposes more fundamental principles of equality and fairness that imply a just future requires a convergence around this metric, and this, in turn, implies a reduction in impacts created by or for a minority (which is still far above the 1% and the fraction of the 1% that constitute the very rich) of the world's population.

It is an uncomfortable fact then that 'who are the rich' for climate and ecological purposes is far greater than the sum of the 'very rich'. But it is also the case, as Sayer makes clear, that the primary problem is the system of economy that this broader category is embedded in. And changes to this system of economy which allow for *less* economic activity are not necessarily harmful to those of the 'rich' (or of the rest of their society) whose lives of work and consumption would be altered. Nor would it necessarily be to the detriment of 'developing' countries who currently mainly grow by exporting to them. As such, whilst the 'right' thing to do may not be the only thing that could be done, it may well be the most reasonable, desirable and long-term survivable of options. We will return to this in the conclusion. It is sufficient to suggest for the moment that the current situation where we assert (rather than establish unequivocally) that the majority world benefits by growing whilst dependent on the minority wealthy world's *growth* is slow civilisational suicide. The problem, however, is that this seems to be the suicide we are choosing (even if many are unaware of quite what is happening). And this does not seem to have fundamentally changed since *Why We Can't Afford the Rich* was published in 2015. This is despite recognition of 'Climate Emergency', the introduction of the Paris Agreement and a growing number of initiatives and commitments to tackle climate change. The COVID-19 pandemic has provided yet another component to our current problems, and tragic though the death count may be, it is the structural vulnerabilities that it exposed and how we respond to them that might matter more in the longer term.[14] The immediate impact has been to exacerbate extreme inequality, and governments currently must choose between some version of 'getting growth going by any means necessary' as the obvious response to the economic devastation wreaked by the pandemic in many countries and recognising and acting upon their climate and ecological responsibilities. The apparent middle ground takes the form of variations such as 'Green New Deal' and green industrial strategy ('building back better'). But this idea of win-win seems deeply flawed if its emphasis is on the growth aspect of 'green growth' (through infrastructure and technology with no necessary restriction on the total scale of activity) rather than more cautious social redesign and more fundamental economic transformation (e.g. Spash 2021a, 2021b; Lamb et al. 2020; Morgan 2020b).

A Short Five Years: A Worsening Climate and Ecological Situation, the Pandemic and Exacerbated Inequality

At the time of writing in late 2020, Sayer's *Why We Can't Afford the Rich* had been in print for around five years. During that time, the underlying tendency for the very rich to become richer and for extreme wealth inequality to grow had continued. There are numerous statistical sources and different ways to decompose these statistics to present different kinds of facts and trends, and we do not have the space here to consider them all. For indicative purposes, however, the best known is probably Oxfam's periodic publication of wealth and income statistics – contrasting the very rich with the bottom half of the world's population (see Oxfam 2019, 2020). Sayer (2015: 7) highlights the 2014 Oxfam report that states the richest 85 people on the planet have wealth equivalent to the bottom half (then 3.5 billion) and the richest 1% of the world's population own 46% of the wealth ($110 trillion or 65 times the total wealth of the bottom half).[15] The subsequent reports indicate in 2018 it required just the top 43 richest people to create equivalence to the bottom half of the world's population and in 2019 just 26. Applying evocative metaphors, the required number of the very rich in relation to the bottom half of the world's population has thus transitioned from occupancy of a double-decker bus to a bus and now a minibus. This is, of course, a fraction of the very rich. According to David Ruccio and drawing on Wealth-X data, there were 2,825 billionaires in 2019 (an increase of 8.5% in 2018), with a combined wealth of $9.4 trillion (an increase of 10.3% in 2018).[16] According to both Statista and Bloomberg, the pandemic of 2020 has made several of the richest even richer (as we have turned increasingly to online activity, which they dominate – and only two of the ten richest saw their wealth decline) – see Figure 9.1.[17]

So, the very rich have become wealthier in the last five years and existent climate and ecological trends have continued. This, of course, also means that cumulative effects leading us closer to significant changes to natural systems and to tipping points and breakdowns in them have also continued and Earth system analysts and climate and ecological scientists have become increasingly strident in drawing attention to this since Sayer's work was published – 'hothouse Earth' (Steffen et al. 2015, 2018; Hansen et al. 2017; Lenton et al. 2019; Wunderling et al. 2021). The world has, however, begun to respond and there has been growing recognition that 'business as usual' (a term that has been in use for a long time by the UNEP, IPCC and at UNFCCC events or 'conference of the parties' [COP] meetings, to refer to continuation with past practices) is untenable and that radical change is required. The Paris Agreement at COP21 in 2015 was widely hailed as a breakthrough. Article 2 commits signatories to develop targets for 'nationally determined contributions' (NDCs) and to work towards keeping global warming to 2°C with an aspiration to limit it to 1.5°C. Paris is intended to come into full effect in 2020, but in late 2018

U.S. Billionaires Gained $1 Trillion Since The Pandemic Started

Change in the wealth of U.S. billionaires since the beginning of the pandemic

■ March 18   ■ November 24   ● % growth (Mar 18-Nov 24)

Top five U.S. billionaires

Billionaire	March 18	November 24	% growth
Jeff Bezos	$113.0b	$182.4b	61.4%
Elon Musk	$24.6b	$126.2b	413.0%
Bill Gates	$98.0b	$119.4b	21.8%
Mark Zuckerberg	$54.7b	$101.7b	85.9%
Warren Buffett	$67.5b	$88.3b	30.8%

Total U.S. billionaire wealth: $2,947.5b → $3,956.2b, 34.2%

Source: Institute For Policy Studies

statista 🅩

Figure 9.1 US Billionaires' wealth since the pandemic.

the IPCC published its *Global Warming of 1.5°C* report, which was quickly followed by the UNEP's ninth annual 'emissions gap' report (IPCC 2018; UNEP 2018). According to both, the world was in serious danger of quickly exceeding the carbon budgets that Paris depends on and doing so to such a degree that global warming might be far in excess by 2°C (a figure that itself may not be particularly 'safe') over the rest of the century and into the next.

There is, of course, a degree of variation in estimates for both emissions and their consequences (based on different measurements and modelled sensitivities), but the consensus position has been that the lower end of 3,000+ Gigatonnes (Gt) CO_2 comprises the global budget for 2°C and we have already emitted more than 2,000. As the UNEP's ten-year assessment analysis notes, over the last decade the rate of increase in global emissions of CO_2 and equivalents (CO_{2e}) has reduced, but total annual emissions have *not* fallen (and more significantly fallen decisively; Christensen & Olhoff 2019). According to the UNEP, global emissions were 53.5 $GtCO_{2e}$ in 2017 and 55.3

$GtCO_{2e}$ in 2018 and both were record levels. According to the tenth emissions gap report published in 2019, based on current NDCs (at that time) and 'implementation deficits', emissions could rise to 59 $GtCO_2$ by 2030 (UNEP 2019). The remaining budget for 2°C is significantly less than 1,000 $GtCO_2$ and for 1.5°C has been estimated between 238 and 349 $GtCO_2$. Estimates are constantly being revised but the underlying message is clear, we are likely to exceed targeted carbon budgets in few short years.[18] Moreover, we are already beginning to experience effects with just 1.2°C average warming since the beginning of the industrial revolution: increasingly erratic weather and more extreme weather events, heatwaves, sudden freezes, cumulative problems of flooding and drought and thus 'Climate Emergency'. And as the 'Alliance of World Scientists' states, climate change is just one of the consequences of our economic activity, and we are currently at risk of 'ecocide' (Ripple et al. 2020).

So, it is against the background of these trends that there have been growing calls for urgent action. Following Paris, the 2018 interventions by the IPCC and UNEP then resulted in calls for reductions in emissions on the 2017 level of around 45–55% by 2030 and a transition to net-zero by mid-century (45% on the 2010 level, IPCC 2018: 12). Since then a steady stream of governments has committed to net-zero and even those who are still reluctant to make this commitment have signalled significant new commitments (notably China). However, commitments are not policies, policies are not implementations, and implementations do not necessarily solve the problem *if* policy is subverted (deliberately or accidentally), ill-founded, not feasible or insufficient (and these are not the same). NDCs are a bottom-up approach which assumes that an uncoordinated ratcheting in country emissions reductions will ultimately achieve what is required globally. However, much of the formulation of NDCs depends on versions of 'net' reductions whose technical complexity belie the fact they are not immediate real reductions and there is an overwhelming assumption that currently unscaled, untried beyond the laboratory and currently non-existent technologies (and again these are not the same) are how NDCs will be achieved – so targeted quantities are based on what may never happen or on what may not be possible or that may not be possible fast enough or that may require the use of carbon resources used in large volumes to generate the energy and produce the 'green' substitutes 1:1 (and problems have been identified in terms of carbon capture, widespread scaling up of decarbonised electrification using battery technologies for land and sea transport, aviation, massive shifts in land use, etc.).

There is a subtle difference between scepticism in the face of potential changes, where the main impediment is will, and realism whose critique suggests too much of the 'plan' depends on wishful thinking – fiction dressed up as facts in waiting. Moreover, policy currently presupposes a growth system with all that this entails. And the elephant in the room remains inequality and points 1–4 regarding why we can't afford the rich still pertain. A recent report by Oxfam and Stockholm Environment Institute states that between 1995 and 2015:

> The richest 10% of the world's population (c.630 million people) were responsible for 52% of the cumulative carbon emissions – depleting the global carbon budget by nearly a third (31%) in those 25 years alone; The poorest 50% (c.3.1 billion people) were responsible for just 7% of cumulative emissions, and used just 4% of the available carbon budget; The richest 1% (c.63 million people) alone were responsible for 15% of cumulative emissions, and 9% of the carbon budget – twice as much as the poorest half of the world's population.
>
> (Gore 2020: 2)

To be clear, the above does no more than suggesting Sayer's concerns remain relevant and if anything the issues have become more acute. It does not and cannot, in a few short sections, capture the breadth or nuance of the evidence or debates. What is possible and desirable for the future of our species and for that of many others is what is currently at issue. The core question is, how fundamental does change have to be? Decarbonisation (if it proves technologically possible) seems fundamental in so far as it transforms what an industrial-consumption-focused growth system uses. But it is not necessarily fundamental in terms of what a society organises to do and how it does it – and this may be one reason why decarbonisation fails. The possibility of failure of a growth system is why Sayer suggested in 2015 that a rethinking of the very nature of economic activity was what was required: more social redesign, doing less with less, redirecting resources to low impact activity, introducing prohibitions that actually reduce and restrict activity (rather than incentivise market psychology), that is, things that we know *can* be achieved because they depend more on (re)organisation, changes that (upon reflection) we might also actually appreciate and want.

Conclusion

Support, for the kinds of changes Sayer was suggesting needed to be made in 2015, has only increased in the last five years and a great deal of work has been published under the banners of degrowth, postgrowth and social-ecological economics (e.g. Kallis et al. 2020; Spash 2020). Common to all of these is the need for strategies of 'contraction and convergence' of material and energy use but also a power-balancing grassroots democratisation of societies, and this provides yet another reason why we cannot afford the very rich.[19] Social justice as a predicate of change is not just preferable to the alternatives (up to and including a worst-case dystopic future of resource wars, climate disasters, mass-migrations and authoritarian oppression), it is one of the most plausible ways to achieve effectively managed transitions because attention to the harms that might be produced by otherwise progressive climate policy (unemployment in some sectors) is the most reasonable way of achieving necessary approval and participation from the majority. This is one reason why neoliberal states have started to co-opt the language of 'just transition', though the term does have primary meaning in terms of distributional fairness, equity and the maintenance of livelihoods (see Newell & Mulvaney 2012; Newell & Sims 2021). In any case, numerous practical initiatives have been suggested by activist groups: organising around 'sufficiency', increasing localism, redirection of activity towards core social welfare needs and services rather than expansionary conspicuous consumption and designed obsolescence, job shares, universal basic income, new financing, taxation and spending approaches, debt forgiveness that sheds the dependencies of 'developing' countries and the treadmill dependencies of the working poor in wealthy ones.

From our current geo-historical position, embedded in a growth system and socialised to think progress means a blanket commitment to more and more stuff in bigger and bigger economies (by exchange value), any radically different alternative seems alien and perhaps fantastical. But there is nothing natural about a capital accumulation system that puts profit before people and assumes human welfare can be an unintended consequence of a dynamic process of economic growth. This is just one form of social organisation, one that may appear uncoordinated but depends crucially on institutions that produce its possibility. Our current dilemma is whether we are willing to bet on this system that produced our current crises also being able to solve those crises. The evidence seems against this and so the rational (if we are to reclaim that word from its weird meaning in the mathematics of mainstream economics) thing to do is to change and what seems radical may be our best future reality. Sayer's work is a reminder that we need to stop acting like we have choices we do not have and we need to start thinking about making different ones – those still open to us to do the things that really matter to us. As Richard Wilkinson notes in the Foreword to Sayer's book,

> Any idea that we should consume less will be opposed as if it were an assault on our social standing and quality of life. But by reducing inequality, we not only reduce the importance of social status but, at the same time, we also improve social relations and the real quality of life.
> (Wilkinson 2015: p. x)

The point is not just to survive but to flourish, and over the years Andrew Sayer has done more than many to make the case for a different way of looking at the world and living in it.

Notes

1 For the climate and ecological consequences of mainstream economics, see Gills and Morgan (2021a).

2 For further work, see Ray and Sayer (1999).

3 Primarily, the World Inequality Database (WID). The 'World Inequality Lab' (hosted from Paris School of Economics) now publishes an annual 'World Inequality Report'. WID absorbed the prior World Top Incomes Database in 2015. WTID launched publicly in 2011 and was built as part of projects leading to *Top Incomes over the XXth Century* in 2007 and *Top Incomes: A global perspective* in 2010. See Morgan (2020a).

4 I have qualified 'pay' because it is not definite that anyone needed to pay for the costs, at least in the sense usually understood. Modern Monetary Theory, for example, looks at this quite differently.

5 To be clear, 'steady-state' does not mean 'unchanging' in either technology or the nature of economic activity. And not all ecological economists are wedded to this term, but all are committed to the need to measure material and energy use and remain below recognisable thresholds (a slightly different issue than whether all aspects of Earth systems should be valued in exchange terms as 'assets').

6 Goal 1 Target 1 aimed to reducing extreme poverty by 50% and was achieved five years ahead of schedule in 2010. The main metric for extreme poverty has used the World Bank figure of living on or under an average $1 or $1.25 per day.

7 And for some the transition is from locally sustainable small farming (mainly subsistence) to precarious petty commodity production in an informal economy or adverse incorporation into supply chains (so a shift from something less quantifiable in exchange terms to more quantifiable that in metrics may look like progress but is not necessarily so).

8 For example, according to the UNEP 10th Emissions Gap Report, 78% of all emissions derive from the G-20 nations (UNEP 2019, November). World Bank data clearly indicates that emissions closely track GDP ranking and that the top ten countries by GDP produce the majority of emissions. China accounts for about 30%, USA 15% and the EU collectively 10%. Note, figures can vary using per capita measures and consumption measures rather than production measures, but the *general* relation between GDP and emissions remains similar and the fact a *few* countries are responsible for the majority of emission remains the same. See Gills and Morgan (2020, 2021b).

9 A simple focus on population may distract attention from issues arising from a capital accumulation system and shift responsibility from the relatively few producing much of the problem to 'overpopulation' (Fletcher et al. 2014).

10 For background, see Fullbrook and Morgan (2019); Morgan (2016).

11 So this is interventions that affect the atmosphere, hydrosphere, biosphere and geosphere and involve climate and ecological changes.

12 As Goodman and Anderson (2021) note, 65% of global emissions from 1751 to 2010 were produced by 90 entities (of which two-thirds were corporations) and 71% of emissions from 1988 to 2015 were produced by 100 corporate and state entities. See Heede (2014); Griffin (2017); Gills and Morgan (2021b).

13 Though clearly there is also a zone of ambiguity which must be resolved regarding what steady-state level is desirable rather than merely achievable, since it is possible

to avoid further climate change effects or ecological damage in ways that have more or less care for 'stewardship', aesthetics, the rights of other species, etc. So, there is still more involved here than just numbers, if and when we hit upon minimum standards for avoiding crisis.

14 This has global context. World Bank analysis in recent years has suggested that the rate of reduction of extreme poverty had reduced and that the target reduction to 3% of global population by 2030 seemed unlikely. However the pandemic seems set to reverse even prior gains to poverty reduction etc.:

> In 2020, between 88 million and 115 million people could fall back into extreme poverty as a result of the pandemic, with an additional increase of between 23 million and 35 million in 2021, potentially bringing the total number of new people living in extreme poverty to between 110 million and 150 million. Early evidence also suggests that the crisis is poised to increase inequality in much of the world. The crisis risks large human capital losses among people who are already disadvantaged, making it harder for countries to return to inclusive growth even after acute shocks recede.
>
> (World Bank 2020)

15 1% of the world's population is far more than the number of billionaires and this serves to underscore just how much of this is concentrated amongst billionaires, see next note.

16 The largest group of 788 (28%) is in the US and the second is in China (12%). Total billionaire wealth in the US stood at 36% of global billionaire wealth ($3.4 trillion). See Ruccio's blog: https://rwer.wordpress.com/2020/08/25/billionaires-pandemic-edition/?utm_medium=email&utm_campaign=email_subscription.

17 Statista allows common use with attribution: www.statista.com/markets/
For Bloomberg parallel data and discussion visit: www.bloombergquint.com/onweb/bezos-zuckerberg-and-musk-have-made-115-billion-this-year.

18 See: www.carbonbrief.org/analysis-when-might-the-world-exceed-1–5c-and-2c-of-global-warming.

19 See the Global Commons Institute: www.gci.org.uk/links.html.

References

Christensen, J., & Olhoff, A. (2019). *Lessons from a Decade of Emissions Gap Assessments*. Nairobi: UNEP.

Dale, G. (2012). The Growth Paradigm: A Critique. *International Socialism* 134: 55–88.

Daly, H. (2015). *Essays Against Growthism*. London: WEA/College Books.

Fletcher, R., Breitling, J. & Puleo, V. (2014). Barbarian Hordes: The Overpopulation Scapegoat in International Development Discourse. *Third World Quarterly* 35(7): 1195–1215.

Fullbrook, E., & Morgan, J. (eds.) (2019). *Economics and the Ecosystem*. Bristol: World Economic Association Books.

Gills, B. K., & Morgan, J. (2020). Global Climate Emergency: After COP24, Climate Science, Urgency, and the Threat to Humanity. *Globalizations* 17(6): 885–902.

Gills, B. K., & Morgan, J. (2021a). Teaching Climate Complacency: Mainstream Economics Textbooks and the Need for Transformation in Economics Education. *Globalizations* 18(7): 1189–1205.

Gills, B. K., & Morgan, J. (2021b). Economics and Climate Emergency. *Globalizations*, 18(7): 1071–1086.

Goodman, J., & Anderson, J. (2021). From Climate Change to Economic Change? Reflections on 'Feedback'. *Globalizations* 18(7): 1259–1270.

Gore, T. (2020). Confronting carbon inequality: Putting climate justice at the heart of the COVID-19 recovery. Oxfam.

Götz, N. (2015). Moral Economy: Its Conceptual History and Analytical Concepts. *Journal of Global Ethics* 11(2): 147–162.

Griffin, M. (2017). *Carbon Majors Report*. CDP and Climate Accountability Institute: London.

Hansen, J., Sato, M., Kharecha, P., von Schuckmann, K., Beerling, D. J., Cao, J. & Ruedy, R. (2017). Young People's Burden: Requirement of Negative CO_2 Emissions. *Earth System Dynamics* 8: 577–616.

Heede, R. (2014). Tracing Anthropogenic Carbon Dioxide and Methane Emissions to Fossil Fuel and Cement Producers. 1854–2010. *Climatic Change* 122(1–2): 229–241.

Hickel, J. (2017). Is Global Inequality Getting Better or Worse? A Critique of the World Bank's Convergence Narrative. *Third World Quarterly* 38(10): 2208–2222.

Hickel, J., & Kallis, G. (2019). Is Green Growth Possible? *New Political Economy* 25(4): 469–486.

IPCC (2018, October). *Global Warming of 1.5°C: Summary for Policymakers*. Geneva: IPCC.

Kallis, G., Paulson, S., D'Alisa G. & Demaria, F. (2020). *The Case for Degrowth*. Cambridge: Polity Press.

Lamb, W., Mattioli, G., Levi, S., Roberts, J., Capstick, S., Creutzig, F., Minx, J., Muller-Hansen, F., Culhane, T. & Steinberger, J. (2020). Discourses of Climate Delay. *Global Sustainability* 3, e17, 1–5.

Lenton, T., Rockstrom, J., Gaffney, O., Rahmstorf, S., Richardson, K., Steffen, W. & Schellnuber, H. (2019). Climate Tipping Points Too Risky to Bet Against. *Nature* 575, 592–595.

Moore, J. (2015). *Capitalism in the Web of Life*. Verso: London.

Morgan, J. (2016). Paris COP21: Power that Speaks the Truth? *Globalizations* 13(6): 943–951.

Morgan, J. (2020a). Inequality: What We Think, What We Don't Think and Why We Acquiesce. *Real-World Economics Review* 92: 116–133.

Morgan, J. (2020b). Electric Vehicles: The Future We Made and the Problem of Unmaking It. *Cambridge Journal of Economics* 44(4): 953–977.

Newell, P., & Mulvaney, D. (2012). The Political Economy of the Just Transition. *The Geographical Journal* 179(2): 132–140.

Newell, P., & Simms, A. (2021). How Did We Do That? Histories and Political Economies of Rapid and Just Transitions. *New Political Economy* 26(6): 907–922.

O'Neill, J. (2007). *Markets, Deliberation and Environment*. London: Routledge.

Oxfam (2019). *Public Good or Private Wealth*. Oxford: Oxfam.

Oxfam (2020). *Time to Care*. Oxford: Oxfam.

Parrique T. Barth J. Briens F. Kerschner, C. Kraus-Polk A. Kuokkanen A. & Spangenberg J. H. (2019). *Decoupling debunked*. European Environmental Bureau. eeb.org/library/decoupling-debunked.

Ray, L., & Sayer, A. (eds) (1999). *Culture and Economy After the Cultural Turn*. London: Sage.

Ripple, W., Wolf, C., Newsome, T., Barnbard, P., Moomaw, W. & 11,258 signatories (2020). World Scientists' Warning of a Climate Emergency. *BioScience* 70(1): 8–12.

Sayer, A. (1992). *Method in Social Science*, Second edition. London: Routledge.

Sayer, A. (1995). *Radical Political Economy*. Cambridge: Blackwell.

Sayer, A. (2000). *Realism and Social Science*. London: Sage.

Sayer, A. (2004). Restoring the Moral Dimension in Social Scientific Sccounts: A Qualified Ethical Naturalist Approach. In M. S. Archer & W. Outhwaite (eds) *Defending Objectivity*. London: Routledge.

Sayer, A. (2005). *The Moral Significance of Class*. Cambridge: Cambridge University Press.

Sayer, A. (2007a). Understanding Why Anything Matters: Needy Beings, Flourishing, and Suffering. In J. Frauley & F. Pearce (eds), pp. 240–257, *Critical Realism and the Social Sciences*. Toronto: University of Toronto Press.

Sayer, A. (2007b). Moral Economy as Critique. *New Political Economy* 12(2): 261–270.

Sayer, A. (2011). *Why Things Matter to People*. Cambridge: Cambridge University Press.

Sayer, A. (2015). *Why We Can't Afford the Rich*. Bristol: Policy Press.

Sayer, A. (2019). Normativity and Naturalism as if Nature Mattered. *Journal of Critical Realism* 19(3): 258–273.

Smith, R. (2020). *China's Engine of Environmental Collapse*. London: Pluto Press.

Spash, C. (ed.) (2017). *Routledge Handbook of Ecological Economics: Nature and Society*. New York: Routledge.

Spash, C. (2020). A Tale of Three Paradigms: Realising the Revolutionary Potential of Ecological Economics. *Ecological Economics* 169: article 106518.

Spash, C. (2021a). The Economy as if People Mattered: Revisiting Critiques of Economic Growth in a Time of Crisis. *Globalizations* 18(7): 1087–1104.

Spash, C. (2021b). Apologists for Growth: Passive Revolutionaries in a Passive Revolution. *Globalizations* 18(7): 1123–1148.

Steffen, W., Richardson, K., Rockstrom, J., Cornell, S.E., Fetzer, I., Bennett, E., Biggs, R., Carpenter, S., de Vries, W., de Wit, C., Folke, C., Gerten, D., Heinke, J., Mace, G. M., Persson, L. M., Ramanathan, V., Reyers, B. & Sorlin, S. (2015). Planetary Boundaries: Guiding Human Development on a Changing Planet. *Science*, 347(6223): 736–46.

Steffen, W., Rockström, J., Richardson, K., Lenton, T. M., Folke, C., Liverman, D. & Schellnhuber, H. J. (2018). Trajectories of the Earth System in the Anthropocene. *Proceedings of the National Academy of Sciences of the USA* 115: 8252–8259.

UNEP (2018). *Emissions Gap Report 2018* (9th edition). New York: UNEP.

UNEP (2019). *Emissions Gap Report 2019* (10th edition). New York: UNEP.

Wilkinson, R. (2015). Foreword. In A. Sayer, pp. ix–xi, *Why We Can't Afford the Rich*. Bristol: Policy Press.

World Bank (2020). *Poverty and Shared Prosperity 2020: Reversals of Fortune*. Washington DC: Author.

Wunderling, N., Donges, J., Kurths, J. & Winkelmann, R. (2021). Interacting Tipping Elements Increase Risk of Climate Domino Effects Under Global Warming. *Earth System Dynamics* 12: 601–619.

Chapter 10

Hard Work
Restructuring, Realism and Regions

Jamie Peck

Introduction: Starting Out

Someone once said that it can be hard to think about something that, habitually, you think *with*. This may explain why writing this chapter has involved as much introspection as it has retrospection. The introspective part stems from my social and intellectual formation as an economic geographer in 1980s Britain, when as a somewhat unmoored and slightly wayward graduate student I initially found my bearings with the project that became known as the 'restructuring' approach, with its insistent focus on the intricacies of economic restructuring and its incumbent (if emergent) method of critical realism (see Sayer 1982a, 1985a; Lovering 1989). The retrospective part has involved revisiting Andrew Sayer's influential and sometimes controversial work from that decade, when he became a significant voice in the decidedly non-canonical field of human geography, prior to changing his disciplinary address in the early 1990s. A post disciplinary scholar before the term had any real currency, Sayer may have been a product of geography – as a weakly bounded and eclectic discipline, marked by an unruly combination of conservatism and openness – but he was disinclined to set up shop there, or indeed to call it home. Pretty much from the start, his project envisaged a different kind of intellectual terrain, and he would go on to make his own path.

This chapter takes the form of a commentary on where Andrew Sayer came from, needless to say in a situated and selective manner. It is situated in the sense that the account cannot be anything but tangled up both with my own biography and with the roiling context of Thatcher's Britain, a period in which socioeconomic dislocation was as much a visceral sensibility as it was an academic question. As a graduate student, this felt like something that I had no alternative but to engage with, long before I had any real sense of *how* to do it. At the time, graduate study in the United Kingdom was a largely unstructured, sink-or-swim experience, with nothing really resembling what would now be called 'training'. The newly formed Economic and Social Research Council was however making some of its first forays in this direction, and as a first-year student, I got the opportunity to attend a workshop on research

DOI: 10.4324/9781003247326-14

methodologies at the University of Sussex. And there was Andrew Sayer, patiently explaining the rudiments of critical realism in a way that sounded to many of us like a 'technical and obscure language (for geographers)' but which was also 'its very attraction' (Pratt 1991: 248). Speaking as one of those that were intrigued and intimidated in equal measure, it would take me a few more years before I came anywhere close to cracking the code, or at least being able to 'pass'. This was a (new) way of doing economic geography, it seemed, that reserved an important place for 'local', grounded research while at the same time offering a means to wrestle with what really did feel like big, even 'structural', changes, such as those associated with deindustrialisation, mass unemployment, and the Thatcherite offensive.

Indexed to these particular circumstances, the chapter is also selective in its concern with just one moment – albeit an extended and formative one – in Andrew Sayer's long and extraordinarily wide-ranging career, his time as an institutionally affiliated geographer (if always an ambivalent and undisciplined one) during the long 1980s. It begins with the more proximate questions of his entrance into and impact on the field of human (and economic) geography, with its turf-specific pretentions to 'regional science' and 'location theory', and its endless fretting about 'space', where Sayer's interventions proved to be quite uniquely disruptive. Next, the chapter turns to his germinal contributions to the enterprise that was organised, albeit never formally, under the rubric of restructuring a project that was destined to remain frustratingly incomplete but which would nevertheless leave an indelible trace.

Contingent Geographer

Andrew Sayer arrived on the scene asking some fundamental but awkward questions – and perhaps not surprisingly ruffling more than a few feathers, including those of geography's establishment. His doctoral dissertation, subsequently published in an extended format, took aim in a fearless fashion at the conventional wisdom in regional science and urban modelling, with its reliance on neoclassical economics, its often-unexamined functionalism, and its largely taken-for-granted positivism (Sayer 1976). In the company of David Harvey, Doreen Massey and a handful of other pioneers, Sayer embraced 'the new political economy school' in geography, taking inspiration from the likes of Joan Robinson and Maurice Dobb. Somewhat contrary, however, to the prevailing disciplinary culture of just getting on with it, he would make it his business to engage in a searching critique of the normal science of the regional science paradigm, with its positivist common sense. It was entirely understandable, Sayer acknowledged, that Harvey, Massey, and the new generation of radical geographers had been 'preoccupied with pursuing their new interests rather than spending or wasting their time on detailed, retrospective and critiques of the old paradigm', but it was nevertheless necessary to take the fight to the old guard because:

without this kind of critique, the adoption of the new paradigm may appear to be dependent on some mystical conversion experience. Worse still, the new political economy school may be dismissed as an eccentric alternative to conventional regional science which we may either take or leave. More cynically, in view of the ignorance and suspicion of its Marxian content, one suspects that many regional scientists would indeed be happy to dismiss it as outlet for 'radicals' which cannot challenge 'objective', 'neutral', regional science.

(Sayer 1976: 192)

In a field somewhat averse to 'metaphysical' contemplation, and reluctant to rake over unsettling debates about its scientific purpose and status, Sayer's critical realist critiques of the status quo exposed some deep seams of complacency and confusion, provoking a series of defensive responses from authority figures and gatekeepers (see Keeble 1980; Sack 1982; Sayer 1979a, 1979b, 1980, 1982a, 1982c, 1983; Simmonds 1980; Wilson 1978). Sayer was variously accused of occupying extreme, 'academic' and 'unrealistic' positions, detached from the practical problems of policy and planning, of hiding behind jargon, technical language, and 'Aunt Sally arguments', and of making the mistake of believing that 'everything is a matter of philosophy'. The exchanges may have been revealing, but they were hardly enlightening.

Barely concealed currents of anti-Marxism (along with an abiding suspicion of 'radicals') were certainly in play here (see Duncan & Sayer 1980), although it should also be said that Sayer was trampling all over the sacred ground of 'space', leaving few punches unpulled, while aggravating disciplinary insecurities about the position of geography in the academic division of labour. But his debunking of the conceits of spatial science was never for its own sake. It came in the service of a bracingly original understanding of the place of space (among other things) in social theory, one that was being articulated on the cusp of a wider 'spatial turn' in the critical social sciences and humanities. Yet Sayer was not about to become a cheerleader for the spatial cause, or to encourage the promiscuous embrace of 'local' sources of causality. His carefully qualified position on 'the difference that space makes' affirmed that Marx, Weber, Durkheim and other pioneers of social theory had been quite right to give generally short shrift to questions of spatial form and to spatial relations. There was important work for geographers to do, but there was not really room for them on the top tables of social theory. According to Sayer, 'the spatial' is largely a domain of contingent relations (i.e., those that are neither necessary nor impossible); it is where the synthesis of multiple determinations *takes place*. But this means that it is unlikely to serve as the locus for strong or systematic theory claims, even as geographical interactions, conjunctions, and contradictions will matter (sometimes a lot) for how causal processes, liabilities and tendencies are realised in the social world.

Abstract social theory need only consider space insofar as *necessary* properties of objects are involved, and this does not amount to much … [A]ctual concrete forms cannot be anticipated purely by reference to the implicit spatial dimension of abstract theory but must be discovered through empirical investigation.

(Sayer 1985b: 54, 59–60)

As a receipt for theoretically informed and informing empirical enquiries, Sayer acknowledged that this (philosophical) position was more a matter of specifying problems than solving them. He was not one, certainly, to underestimate the 'genuine difficulties of conducting concrete (hence spatial) research' (Sayer 1985b: 60), but there were simply no shortcuts or easy workarounds to be had, while inflated claims would just have to be put in their place. This was just as much of a problem for the Marxian research programme, he insisted, no matter what sympathies one might have with the approach. In a sign of tensions to come, Sayer took issue with David Harvey's (1982) *Limits to Capital* for its habit of 'reading off' specific and singular spatial outcomes from the abstract logic of capital, given the demonstrated 'polyvalency' of the former, the demonstrably wide range of revealed (and possible) outcomes, and the open and politically mediated nature of social systems (Sayer 1985a, 1985b). In the realm of radical (economic) geography, Doreen Massey and Richard Meegan (1982, 1985a; Massey 1984) had been setting the standard for theoretically embedded, methodologically reflexive, and empirically exploratory research practice in this proto-realist vein, although for her own reasons Massey would subscribe to a more robust interpretation than Sayer's of the difference that space makes (see Massey 1985, 1995; Peck et al. 2018; Sayer 2015, 2018).

There is no doubt that these intramural discussions were important to Sayer, even as the audience addressed in his breakthrough book, *Method in Social Science* (Sayer 1984, 1992), was evidently a much wider one. On the part of (some) geographers, there was a sense that one of the discipline's most dextrous methodologists was at risk of selling the field a bit short, and not doing all that he might to defend (and extend) its explanatory turf. Ron Johnston (1993: 475, 479), for example, read Sayer to be professing, almost sacrilegiously, that 'geography is contingent only', going on to remark in a paper in *Political Geography* prompted by the book's second edition that 'Interestingly, Andrew Sayer has recently joined the staff of the Department of Sociology at the University of Lancaster'. For his part, Sayer had little interest in (or indeed patience for) what he continued to insist was a basic misreading of his argument. The condition of polyvalency or 'spatial flexibility', he maintained, has significant implications for *how* abstract theories are applied, operationalised, and revised, since the integration, combination, and synthesis of abstract tendencies and processual mechanisms in concrete geographical contexts (and in space-time) affect if and how those tendencies and processes are realised.

Like it or not, the lot of the geographer-as-social theorist is one of navigating the resulting ontological limits and their associated explanatory challenges, rather than issuing grand proclamations.

> [I]t might seem nice for geography's status if everything were entirely dependent on spatial context, for then there would never be any circumstances in which we could abstract from geography ... [Yet this] does not mean that space is unimportant. 'Contingent' does not mean 'unimportant' or 'having no effects!' ... The limited role that space has had, and always will have, in social theory (for ontological reasons), should not be taken as a personal affront by geographers. The difference that space makes in concrete situations can never be ignored, and therefore, in that sense, 'geography matters'. It still remains tremendously important to me.
>
> (Sayer 1994: 108–109)

These were not, it should be added, remarks issued by someone who had decided to make for the disciplinary exit, since Sayer had been making them, consistently, for more than a decade. Indeed, he had earlier admitted to finding partisan commitments to capital-G Geography 'somewhat strange', insisting instead that '[d]isciplinary boundaries and jealousies merely get in the way of enquiry' (Sayer 1989: 206–207). In lieu of any doubt, Sayer would later declare: 'Down with all forms of disciplinary imperialism/parochialism, be they geographical, sociological, or whatever! Long live postdisciplinary studies!'

Restructuring Work

The substantive research programme that Andrew Sayer pursued during the 1980s, which evolved in a mutually informing way with his work on methodology and the practice of social theory, would become known as the restructuring approach. Some of the early impetus for this largely uncoordinated but nevertheless collective project grew out of critiques of the fading paradigm of industrial-location studies, which as a spatialised and 'applied' branch of orthodox economics tended, in its British form at least, to be rather eclectic and empirical, positivist in an ordinary rather than deeply principled way, and rife with what Sayer would call 'chaotic conceptions' constructed out of observed regularities and spatial patterns (see Sayer 1982a, 1982b; Massey 1985). Aspiring to 'replace' the location-theory orthodoxy, the restructuring approach was never reducible to a single hypothesis or headline theory claim, but instead set out empirically to explore the 'timing, form, and place taken by restructuring [which] cannot be known in advance precisely because it is affected by contingently-related conditions such as labour organisation, political intervention, and the development of technology' (Sayer 1982b: 68;

1982a: 122), concrete expressions of restructuring being diverse in ways routinely underestimated both in conventional analyses and in more orthodox styles of Marxism. There was no expectation, in other words, of a singular pull towards least-cost locations as an aggregate outcome of rational decision making, but neither were tendencies like workforce deskilling or the falling rate of profit ever going to be associated with mechanically predictable outcomes. The restructuring approach, in this respect, represented a mid-level analytical framework more than it did some difference-splitting third way. It was a gearbox-like analytical framework designed to problematise and intermediate the one-to-many relations between, on the one hand, abstract tendencies, transformative processes, and big-picture patterns of (macro)economic restructuring, and the revealed and socially contested diversity of empirical outcomes on the other. For example, the framework could be mobilised to specify and adjudicate between the diversity of outcomes associated with (international) product-market competition, with its 'generalised' pressures and disciplines, which might take the form of intensified innovation and skill-enhancing investments in new technology in some locations, but workforce rationalisation and cost cutting in others, the analytical and political goal being to map out implications on the ground for workplaces and local communities. The restructuring approach entailed commitments to case-study methods and dirty-hands modes of enquiry, which were often qualitative in character (although rarely ethnographic), coupled with a theoretically assisted search for underlying causes, driving processes and potential intervention points.

The restructuring approach was never associated with a 'school' as such, but rather with a loosely aligned network of leftist researchers displaying a broad spectrum of (generally quite close) connections to the labour movement, to socialist parties and projects, and to various stripes of (neo) Marxism and radical economics. Its centre of gravity was the United Kingdom, with Doreen Massey as the leading figure, but there were significant alliances too in continental Europe and North America (see Bluestone & Harrison 1982; Storper & Walker 1983; Lipietz 1987). Critical realism was, in effect, the house method, although the degree of rigorous adherence varied quite markedly. In part this reflected its freshness, its ready availability, and its apparent flexibility, but the attraction also stemmed from a shared estrangement from neoclassical location theory and positivist approaches to taxonomic classification and quantification. Most would defer to Sayer on matters of method, including at various points Massey herself, even as she was to remain a critical realist more in spirit and practice than according to the letter (see Massey & Meegan 1985b; Massey 1995; Peck et al. 2018; Sayer 2018). There was, in addition, an almost reflexive dismissal of the spatial science paradigm, along with its old guard, coupled with an interest in engaging, if typically at arm's length, with the more orthodox Marxism of David Harvey and his followers. The line was that received concepts like uneven geographical development were suggestive but 'incomplete', that it was a mistake to read off spatial outcomes from the abstract functioning of capitalism, sans mediation, and that it was necessary to transcend the normative foreclosures in radical research programmes that too often had bracketed out significant dimensions of the restructuring process along with a panoply of co-constitutive relations, such as those associated with the service sector and feminised jobs, with product-market competition and different modes of management, with cultural politics and the roles of the state, and so forth (see Sayer 1985a; Lovering 1989).

If this might seem relatively uncontroversial, it was not. David Harvey, most notably, let loose a no-holds-barred critique, aimed holus-bolus at the restructuring research programme, and the contributions of Massey and Sayer in particular. His diagnosis was that this amounted to a 'marked strategic withdrawal from Marxian theory', by way of an unnecessary detour into methodological theatrics, apparently compounded by 'an ideological resistance to theorising' (Harvey 1987: 367, 376). The second of what Harvey pointedly called 'three myths in search of a reality', the contention that Marxian abstractions are not up to the task of explaining 'the specificities of history and the particularities of geography' was laid squarely at Sayer's door, since along with Massey he had sunk into a shared state of 'deep and serious [concern] for the particularities of places, events, and processes', both having been

> deeply critical of the power of existing theory in relation to the materials they currently investigate. Sayer seems particularly exercised by the way Marxists have supposedly tried to 'read off' particular events and processes from general theory ... [He] proposes a realist philosophy that combines wide-ranging contingency with an understanding of general processes ... The problem with this superficially attractive method is that there is nothing within it, apart from the judgement of individual researchers, as to what constitutes a special instance to which special processes inhere or as to what contingencies (out of a potentially infinite number) ought to be taken seriously. There is nothing, in short, to guard against the collapse of scientific understandings into a mass of contingencies exhibiting relations and processes special to each unique event.
>
> (Harvey 1987: 370, 373)

Irritated to the point of overstating his case, Harvey maintained that 'it is in principle possible to apply theoretical laws to understand individual instances, unique events', equating his own programme with the 'investigation of universal laws' through the rigorous application of dialectical analysis, meanwhile casting aspersions on realism's ostensibly 'loose' logic as not just a cover for an incipient anti-Marxism but a recipe for 'straight old fashioned and casual empiricism' (Harvey 1987: 371, 368). In light of Sayer's own past record of goading remarks, those inclined to summon the 'mystical' power of dialectics, for which Harvey had become the poster child (Sayer 1982b, 1989), this exchange of low blows probably amounted to a low-scoring draw.

Sayer's reply to Harvey, just as pointedly titled 'Hard work and its alternatives', was offered as a 'reluctant' one, since he evidently saw this broadside attack as not only heavy-handed but masculinist and mischievous. In restating his commitments to the 'serious work' of first-hand empirical labour, linked to an anything-but-casual search for contextualised, multicausal explanations, Sayer (1987: 399) repudiated both the restricted vision of monological reasoning and the role of such gladiatorial modes of combat. Only in the experimental world of closed systems, or in the recesses of the reductionist mind, he insisted, did universal laws hold sway. On the other hand, the rigors of concrete research in open and messy systems meant sifting through, documenting, and dealing with the contingently shaped 'content' of the otherwise-empty categories of abstract theory (like capital-labour relations, uneven development, and class struggle), rather than wafting them aside, while it also called for serious engagements with parallel (non-Marxian) strands of social theory, and the ever-present challenges of intersection, scrambling, and synthesis in the (real) world of multiple determinations.

These were not the musings of an armchair prognosticator, since along with his collaborator Kevin Morgan, Sayer had been hard at work on a four-year research project on the restructuring of the electronics industry, which was about to culminate in a much-anticipated monograph (Morgan & Sayer 1988). *Microcircuits of Capital* arrived with high expectations, breaking new ground in a number of ways: rather than being foretold in a breadcrumb trail of preceding journal articles, the book arrived all at once, seeking to realise the full potential of a comparative and cross-scalar research design, one still surprisingly rare in a field – economic geography – that really ought to have been making such things its own. It set out to explore the phenomenon of uneven development, not as an ambient condition or law-like system, but in a granular and content-heavy manner, from vantage points positioned on the moving landscape made by a so-called sunrise industry; and perhaps above all, the book would be read as not just an example but a model of what could be achieved with critical realism's methodological toolkit (see Rigby 1989; Kafkalas 1990; Barnes et al. 2007).

Microcircuits of Capital was well received by reviewers in geography and sociology, where it won praise for its meticulous execution and its hard-hitting critiques of neoliberal bromides. Yet those who had hoped that the book might serve as a how-to manual for apprentice critical realists, if not a sequel to Massey's *Spatial Divisions of Labour*, were to be somewhat disappointed. Explicitly methodological issues were dispatched in a surprisingly perfunctory manner in the book itself (although see Sayer & Morgan 1985); for all their formative role, they were largely demoted to implicit or background status, surfacing in a few pages and a handful of footnotes, while reflexive discussions of actual methodological practice were absent. Substantively, offered no apology for its close-focus telling of 'a highly complex story', one that combined 'sober analysis' with 'more detail than is customary in academic writing' (Morgan & Sayer 1988: 2–3). Of two recurring targets in the book – the hype attached to high-tech as a development mantra and the pervasive resort, in scholarly treatments, to stereotypes and stylised facts – the latter effectively became a foil. The explanatory manoeuvres that had so irked David Harvey, the apparent determination to excise any hint of 'structuralist leanings', were given full rein in the book, which went to some lengths to complicate and correct even the conceptual framings with which it was more sympathetically aligned, notably 'looser' applications of the spatial divisions of labour approach. While the authors declared a willingness to 'stick their necks out' (Morgan & Sayer 1988: 9), this took the form of a commitment to explanatory specificity, rather than the development of bold theory claims.

Microcircuits was faithful to Sayer's understanding of the 'difference that space makes', in its principled refusal to countenance laws of constant conjunction between abstract tendencies, mediating conditions, and 'single species' outcomes, venturing deep in the weeds of sectoral and regional specificity, where 'so much depends on contingent factors' (Morgan & Sayer 1988: 36, 120). A refusal to 'read down' from abstract theory, through go-to heuristics and received stereotypes to revealed, 'messy' outcomes on the ground, ceded narrative dominance to the latter. And the effectively black-boxed role of critical realist methodology yielded a prophylactic effect, such that the work of reading *back* to theory remained more incomplete than was arguably necessary. In navigating their path between a principled 'refusal of reductionism' and the cul-de-sac of 'radical uniqueness', Morgan and Sayer (1988: 266) engineered substantive forays into the mediating effects of capital–capital relations and market strategies (demoting the play of capital-labour dynamics, favoured in extant restructuring studies, to secondary status), yet their frequent appeals to 'scaled' processes and uneven development ultimately amounted to little in the way of systematic analytical traction. For all the praise that *Microcircuits* won for its perceptive account of the intricacies of sector-specific restructuring (see Cooke 1990; Sassen 1990; Sklair 1990), some sympathetic reviewers remained confounded by its less-than-fully digested complexity. For Kafkalas,

> The arguments cut so deeply that they do not always build as convincingly. The instances of the concrete are overwhelming, but the movements to the abstract and vice versa are not as clear and unproblematic as the authors seem to wish. There is so much caution and distance from unsafe theoretical grounds that very little remains to be protected by argument as an alternative theoretical and methodological core.
>
> (1990: 1123)

Bagguley (1989: 457) drew a telling contrast with Allen Scott's (1988) *New Industrial Spaces*, the expositional elegancy of which differed so markedly with the contingency-bound style of *Microcircuits*, with its 'thick description that does the reader no favours'. So many of its theoretical touchpoints were, in effect, counter-stereotypical, particularly in relation to Marxian and neo-Marxian arguments, which may have done as much to frustrate potential followers and interlocutors as to enrol them. And the preference for decidedly unstylised facts surely impeded the book's travel into wider (post disciplinary) circuits, strict adherence to this mature-stage variety of the restructuring approach becoming its own kind of microcircuit.[1]

In retrospect, *Microcircuits* feels like an opportunity missed, not only to extend the restructuring approach, as a fecund generator of mid-range theory claims, but also to model practices of methodological transparency. If the presentation of this finely processed product had been complemented with insights into the practical art of this kind of sausage-making, the book could have served as a much-needed, long-form 'application' of the critical realist methodology, beyond the lessons learned from those staple (if apt) illustrations like landlord–tenant relations or the properties of gunpowder. And then there is the problem of calibrating the sausage machine itself, given the challenges of grinding through the gristle associated with local specificity and the compounding effects of uneven spatial development. One reviewer with an eye for these questions noted his surprise that 'in a book concerned with uneven development no more than one page should be devoted to its meaning' (Rigby 1989: 172). Quite out of character, uneven development becomes something like an incantation, frequently signalled but presenting more as a truistic condition or placeholder, rather than as an explicitly defined, mediating framework – let alone a potentially portable one. None of this is news to Sayer himself, of course, who has since written eloquently about the intractable challenges of narrative construction, especially where this involves contending with the defining problematic of the restructuring approach, the unruly interplay of 'variety and interdependence'. When it comes to the demanding theory-building project of 'geohistorical synthesis', must it be the fate of such granular, complexity-bearing treatments to be read as little more than 'another country heard from', in Clifford Geertz's telling phrase (Sayer 2000: 139), more additive than cumulative, with 'each successive monograph [becoming] just another book on the shelf, dealing with phenomena which are so context-dependent that scarcely any of their conclusions are applicable outside them?'

Conclusion: Getting Out

One of the last things that Andrew Sayer published as a card-carrying geographer was a rather elliptical (but nonetheless forceful) commentary on the 'localities debate' that had roiled the field in the late 1980s (Sayer 1991). If the restructuring approach had enjoyed its 'brief heyday' (Lovering 1989) around the middle of that decade, as an unorchestrated but shared project of conceptual and methodological innovation, integrated through targeted empirical enquiries, it was called to a reckoning of sorts in an unedifying (if vivid) debate around the localities research programme.[2] Even though neither were directly involved on the front lines of the research programme itself, Doreen Massey and Andrew Sayer had both been influential (and in many ways instrumental) in shaping its rationale and remit, and the localities debate was duly conducted on the terrain made by the restructuring approach, the spatial divisions of labour framework, and critical realism. Even before it was reported, the localities programme was being assailed, often in caricatured terms, as an 'empirical turn' and as a 'retreat from theory', especially Marxian theory (see Harvey 1987; Smith 1987; Harvey & Scott 1989). Allen Scott (2000: 491–492), who would later assign the localities programme-cum-debate the status of a 'brief interlude', portrayed the effort as 'an amalgam of inductive studies' unmoored from any meaningful 'theoretical anchor', hastening to add that this was a state of affairs for which Sayer himself bore no 'complicity'.

Having preferred to stay out of the fray, even as he was frequently implicated by proxy, Sayer later accepted an invitation to write about goings-on 'behind' the locality debate, which he saw as providing a 'convenient focus for a number of overlapping controversies in urban and regional studies, concerning Marxism and post-Marxism, theory and empirical research, the implications of realist philosophy, and the nature and significance of space', albeit in an amplified fashion 'quite out of proportion with its limited role in terms of research effort' (Sayer 1991: 283). Noting in passing that any complete deconstruction of the episode would call for a 'sociological' treatment, not least concerning the (low) politics of knowledge production and academic rivalry, his reflections were deliberately pitched at the level of the metaphysical – and effectively above rather than merely out of the fray. With no desire to reopen a debate from which much had been lost but little gained, Sayer nevertheless insisted on acknowledging the 'great strides' that had been made by a loosely aligned group of radical geographers during the preceding decade, especially around the issue of (industrial) restructuring and the vexing question of relationality, or the problem of difference and interdependence (Sayer 1991: 305). There may have been just a hint of wistfulness about the unrealised promise of this shared project, the fate of which had apparently been sealed by a round of disciplinary parlour games. For these, he had little to no patience, seeing them for what they were. Seen in this light, Sayer's subsequent relocation from geography to sociology, or from Geography to sociology, represented less a move from one discipline to another, more a departure from the confines of the discipline itself.

Notes

1   The wider and deeper impact of Scott's *New Industrial Spaces*, for example, is reflected in a citation footprint more than ten times the size.
2   The Changing Urban and Regional System (CURS) research programme, funded by the Economic and Social Research Council, was commissioned in 1984 as a spinoff from a research fellowship held by Doreen Massey. The CURS programme involved seven research teams, each working intensively on a separate locality for over two years, ending in 1987.

References

Bagguley, P. (1989). Review of *Microcircuits of Capital*. *Sociology* 23(3): 457–458.

Barnes, T. J., Peck, J., Sheppard, E. & Tickell, A. (2007). Methods Matter: Transformations in Economic Geography. In A. Tickell, E. Sheppard, J. Peck & T. J. Barnes (eds), pp. 1–24, *Politics and Practice in Economic Geography*. London: Sage.

Bluestone, B., & Harrison, B. (1982). *The Deindustrialization of America*. New York: Basic Books.

Cooke, P. (1990). Review of *Microcircuits of Capital*. *Progress in Human Geography* 14(1): 144–149.

Duncan, S. S., & Sayer, R. A. (1980). Debate on Geography and the Vampire Trick. *Area* 12(3): 195–197.

Harvey, D. (1982). *The Limits to Capital*. Oxford: Blackwell.

Harvey D (1987). Three Myths in Search of a Reality in Urban Studies. *Society and Space* 5(4): 367–376.

Harvey, D. & Scott, A. J. (1989). The Practice of Human Geography: Theory and Empirical Specificity in the Transition from Fordism to Flexible Accumulation. In B. Macmillan (ed), pp. 217–229, *Remodelling Geography*. Oxford: Blackwell.

Johnston, R. (1993). 'Real' Political Geography. *Political Geography* 12(5): 43–480.

Kafkalas, G. (1990). Review of *Microcircuits of Capital*. *Environment and Planning A* 22(8): 1121–1123.

Keeble, D. E. (1980). Industrial Decline, Regional Policy and the Urban-Rural Manufacturing Shift in the United Kingdom. *Environment and Planning A* 12(8): 945–962.

Lipietz, A. (1987). *Mirages and Miracles*. London: Verso.

Lovering J. (1989). The Restructuring Debate. In R. Peet & N. J. Thrift (eds), pp. 198–223, *New Models in Geography*, Volume 1. London: Unwin Hyman.

Massey, D. (1984). *Spatial Divisions of Labour*. London: Macmillan.

Massey, D. (1985). New Directions in Space. In D. Gregory & J. Urry (eds), pp. 9–19, *Social Relations and Spatial Structures*. London: Macmillan.

Massey, D. (1995). Reflections on Debates over a Decade. In D. Massey, pp. 296–354, *Spatial Divisions of Labour*, Second edition. London: Macmillan.

Massey, D., & Meegan, R. (1982). *The Anatomy of Job Loss*. London: Routledge.

Massey, D., & Meegan, R. (eds) (1985a). *Politics and Method: Contrasting Studies in Industrial Geography*. London: Methuen.

Massey, D., & Meegan, R. (1985b). Profits and Job Loss. In D. Massey & R. Meegan (eds), pp. 119–143, *Politics and Method: Contrasting Studies in Industrial Geography*. London: Methuen.

Morgan, K., & Sayer, A. (1988). *Microcircuits of Capital*. Cambridge: Polity.

Peck, J., Werner, M., Lave, R. & Christophers, B. (2018). Out of Place: Doreen Massey, Radical Geographer. In M. Werner, J. Peck, R. Lave & B. Christophers (eds), pp. 1–38, *Doreen Massey: Critical Dialogues*. Newcastle upon Tyne: Agenda.

Pratt, A. C. (1991). Reflections on Critical Realism in Geography. *Antipode* 23(2): 248–255.

Rigby, D. (1989). Review of *Microcircuits of Capital*. *Economic Geography* 65(2): 171–174.

Sack, R. D. (1982). Realism and Realistic Geography. *Transactions of the Institute of British Geographers* 7(4): 504–509.

Sassen, S. (1990). Review of *Microcircuits of Capital*. *Contemporary Sociology* 19(6): 835–836.

Sayer, R. A. (1976). A Critique of Urban Modelling: From Regional Science to Urban and Regional Political Economy. *Progress in Planning* 9(3): 187–254.

Sayer, R. A. (1979a). Philosophical Bases of the Critique of Urban Modelling: A Reply to Wilson. *Environment and Planning A* 11(9): 1055–1067.

Sayer, R. A. (1979b). Understanding Urban Models versus Understanding Cities. *Environment and Planning A* 11(8): 853–862.

Sayer, R. A. (1980). Urgent Unreal and Real Nonurgent Research. *Environment and Planning A* 12(8): 967–990.

Sayer, A. (1982a). Explaining Manufacturing Shift: A Reply to Keeble. *Environment and Planning A* 14(1): 119–125.

Sayer, A. (1982b). Explanation in Economic Geography: Abstraction versus Generalization. *Progress in Human Geography* 6(1): 68–88.

Sayer, R. A. (1982c). Misconceptions of Space in Social Thought. *Transactions of the Institute of British Geographers* 7(4): 494–503.

Sayer, R. A. (1983). Reply to Robert Sack. *Transactions of the Institute of British Geographers* 8(4): 508–511.

Sayer, A. (1984). *Method in Social Science*. London: Hutchinson.

Sayer, R. A. (1985a). Industry and Space: A Sympathetic Critique of Radical Research. *Environment and Planning D: Society and Space* 3(1): 3–29.

Sayer, A. (1985b). The Difference That Space Makes. In D. Gregory & J. Urry (eds), pp. 49–66, *Social Relations and Spatial Structures*. London: Macmillan.

Sayer, A. (1987). Hard Work and the Alternatives. *Environment and Planning D: Society and Space* 5(4): 395–399.

Sayer, A. (1989). On the Dialogue between Humanism and Historical Materialism in Geography. In A. Kobayashi & S. Mackenzie (eds), pp. 206–226, *Remaking Human Geography*. London: Unwin Hyman.

Sayer, A. (1991). Behind the Locality Debate: Deconstructing Geography's Dualisms. *Environment and Planning A* 23(2): 283–308.

Sayer, A. (1992). *Method in Social Science*, Second edition. London: Routledge.

Sayer, A. (1994). Realism and Space: A Reply to Ron Johnston. *Political Geography* 13(2): 107–109.

Sayer, A. (2000). *Realism and Social Science*. London: Sage.

Sayer, A. (2015). Critical Realism in Geography. In J. D. Wright (ed.). *International Encyclopedia of the Social and Behavioral Sciences*, Second edition. Amsterdam: Elsevier.

Sayer, A. (2018). Ontology and the Politics of Place. In M. Werner, J. Peck, R. Lave & B. Christophers (eds), pp. 103–112, *Doreen Massey: Critical Dialogues*. Newcastle: Agenda.

Sayer, A., & Morgan, K. (1985). A Modern Industry in a Declining Region: Links between Method, Theory and Policy. In D. Massey & R. Meegan (eds), 147–168, *Politics and Method: Contrasting Studies in Industrial Geography*. London: Methuen.

Scott, A. J. (1988). *New Industrial Spaces*. London: Pion.

Scott, A. J. (2000). Economic Geography: The Great Half-Century. *Cambridge Journal of Economics* 24(4): 483–504.

Simmonds, D. C. (1980). A Comment on the Papers from the BSRSA Workshop on Regional Science Methods in Structure Planning. *Environment and Planning A* 12(4): 463–467.

Sklair, L. (1990). Review of *Microcircuits of Capital* and *The Globalisation of High Technology Production*. *British Journal of Sociology* 42(1): 149–150.

Smith, N. (1987). Dangers of the Empirical Turn: Some Comments on the CURS Initiative. *Antipode* 19(1): 59–68.

Storper, M., & Walker, R. (1983). The Theory of Labour and the Theory of Location. *International Journal of Urban and Regional Research* 7(1): 1–43.

Wilson, A. G. (1978). Review of *A Critique of Urban Modelling*. *Environment and Planning A* 10(9): 1085–1086.

Chapter 11

Varieties of Unfreedom

John O'Neill

Prologue

The chapter has a long history. It was written as part of an ESRC seminar series on Unfree Labour between 2009 and 2011. A version was published in 2011 as a working paper in the Manchester Papers in Political Economy. Since then, it has gone through many updates and revisions. I offer it here as an example of the influence of conversations with Andrew Sayer on my own thinking. The ideas in this chapter owe much to a number of particularly fruitful conversations with Andrew when he was writing his classic book *Why Things Matter to People*. Three themes in particular are central. The first is the centrality of vulnerability and dependence on human life: 'Concepts of human agency emphasise the capacities to do things, but our vulnerability is as important as our capacities ...' (Sayer 2011: 5). Andrew in his work notes how the failure to recognise human neediness and vulnerability permeates the social sciences: 'the literature on social ontology rarely gets beyond discussion of structure and agency and fails to recognise humans as needy and vulnerable social beings' (Sayer 2011: 140). However, as Andrew notes this is true not just of the social sciences but also of philosophy. My conversations with Andrew echoed conversations I also had with Soran Reader in which she was developing her criticism of the 'agential conception of person' in philosophy according to which the persons and human beings are characterised purely by their agency and in particular their capacities for rational choice and action (Reader 2007). 'The other side of agency', the particular human forms of vulnerability and dependency, human 'patiency', is also constitutive of our personhood and matter just as much.

A second theme that was central to my conversations with Andrew was the significance of everyday human relationships to human lives:

> The *relational* character of human being – our dependence on others for our individuality and sense of self – is fundamental, though this is inadequately acknowledged in the liberal conception of human being dominant in modern western society ... There is not first an individual who

DOI: 10.4324/9781003247326-15

then contingently enters into social relations; relations are constitutive of the individual and their sense of self.

(Sayer 2011: 119; italics in original)

The way in which everyday human relationships are central to the constitution of the self became particularly significant to me later in a project I did with Annie Austin on living well with dementia. As a person loses memory, the ways in which social relationships hold a person into their identity become particularly evident (Lindemann 2009, 2014). As such affiliation with others becomes a 'fertile functioning' to a person with dementia (Austin 2018). It is a human functioning that is not only central to human well-being in itself but sustains and maintains other human functionings such that its loss is 'corrosive disadvantage' (Wolff & de Shalit 2007: 121–125). It is through social relationships that a person's identity, her standing and her well-being are sustained as dementia develops. The conversations during the project on unfree labour pointed at the same time to another dimension of social relationships, the ways in which they are a source of vulnerability exploited by others. A feature of many migrant workers, one that Andrew Sayer also noted, was the way in which their migration was the result of the need to discharge their obligations to family members. Relationality becomes a source of their vulnerability. The claim is central to what follows.

A third related theme that arose in conversations I had with Andrew was the significance of labour itself to human life. Good work is a central constituent of human well-being but it is unequally distributed (Sayer 2005: 111–121; 2009). This chapter explores another dimension of labour, unfree labour and its persistence in modern capitalist society.

This chapter owes much then to my conversations with Andrew and I would like to take this occasion to mark my thanks to him and to look forward to future conversations. I would also like to dedicate the chapter to the memory of both Annie Austin and Soran Reader.

The Varieties of Unfreedom

Modern capitalist societies are marked by an apparent persistence and growth in unfree labour. They are marked by the continuation of existing forms of unfree labour such as debt-bondage and an increasing number of new forms associated with trafficked and migrant labour. The 2017 ILO report *Global Estimates of Modern Slavery* put the figure of at least 24.9 million people in forced labour (ILO 2017). Sixteen million people were in forced labour in the private economy in 2016 – 51% in debt-bondage. By sector, this included domestic work (24%), construction (18%), manufacturing (15%) and agriculture and fishing (11%). The estimate for forced sexual exploitation was 3.8 million adults and 1.0 million children. There is a clear gender dimension to unfree labour where women and girls form 99% of victims of forced labour in the commercial sex industry and 57.6% in other sectors. This persistence and growth of unfree labour are reflected in policy documents addressing the issues of forced labour and trafficking (ILO 1930, 2001, 2005, 2009, 2016; Experts Group on Trafficking in Human Beings 2004; UNGA 2000a, 2000b; UNODC 2009). It is also reflected in academic debates, particularly within the Marxist tradition, about the nature and explanation of these forms of unfree labour.[1]

The continued existence of unfree labour raises problems for both classical liberal and classical Marxist accounts of the development of modern capitalism. For both, a feature of commercial society or capitalism is free labourers who are in possession of their skills or labour-power and who are able to sell them to whom they choose. The free labourer is contrasted with the unfree labourer of pre-capitalist society, with the slave, the serf or the bonded labourer who is tied to a particular master. The continued existence of unfree labour raises explanatory questions as to why forms of unfreedom appear to persist. How far should the continued existence of unfree labour be understood as survivals of old forms of unfreedom? Are there specific and distinctive forms of unfreedom in modern capitalist conditions? What are the conditions for reproduction of unfreedom? These questions raise prior conceptual questions about how we should characterise the unfreedom of workers in modern conditions. It is these conceptual issues that I address in this chapter. The central argument of this chapter is that only if we attend to the varieties of unfreedom will we be in a position to understand the reproduction and distinctive nature of unfree labour in modern capitalist societies.

Before going on to a more substantive discussion, I start with a methodological observation about how the characterisation of unfree labour should be addressed, which informs the arguments of the chapter. One obvious starting point to a characterisation of unfree labour would be to begin with a characterisation of freedom and then to consider forms in which unfree labour departs from the conditions of freedom. In this chapter, I approach the problem from the opposite direction – from a characterisation of the varieties of unfreedom. Austin makes the point thus:

> While it has been the tradition to present ['freedom'] as the 'positive' term requiring elucidation, there is little doubt that to say we acted 'freely' … is to say only that we acted *not* un-freely, in one or another of the many heterogeneous ways of so acting (under duress, or what not) … In examining all the ways in which each action may not be 'free' … we may hope to dispose of the problem of Freedom. Aristotle has often been chidden for talking about excuses or pleas and overlooking 'the real problem': in my own case, it was when I began to see the injustice of this charge that I first became interested in excuses.
>
> (Austin 1956: 6)

Not the 'positive' but the 'negative' term does the work.

There are a variety of different ways in which labour can be unfree. Consider the different sites of unfreedom in labour. Unfreedom can occur at the point of entry. Entry into the labouring process is forced or involuntary. Unfreedom can occur within the labouring process itself; violence and force can be features of the workplace; the worker may have no control over the length of the working day; and the relationship might be marked by personal dependence and domination. It is in principle possible to enter a relationship that is unfree in some of these dimensions through voluntary acts. Finally, unfreedom can occur at the point of exit. There are a variety of limits to the possibilities of exit from the relationship: legal ownership of the person, debt-bondage, the absence of citizenship rights, labour rights and other protective legal and social liberties, and the loss of freedoms of movement through passport confiscation. At different sites of unfreedom, different liberty-restricting concepts are invoked: involuntariness, domination, dependence, force and so on. Both characterising and responding to new forms of unfreedom require attention to the heterogeneity in the varieties of unfreedom, rather than the assumption of some particular conception of freedom.[2]

The chapter will be concerned with some of the varieties of unfreedom. For most of the chapter, I focus on unfreedom at the point of entry. However, I should stress at the outset that the point of entry may not be the most significant in understanding the nature of unfree labour. Features of the relationship at work itself and the constraints on exit which keep a worker within conditions of unfreedom might matter more. I return to these in the final section of the chapter. However, unfreedom at the point of entry is important to understanding the reproduction of unfree labour. A feature of most of the unfree labour, although certainly not all, in modern conditions is the absence of force at the point of entry. Consider, for example, Breman's discussion forms of debt-bondage in India:

> The manner of recruitment is the same as that of the earlier hali, who was not forced to become a farm servant but offered his services 'voluntarily' to a master who was prepared to pay him an advance, usually to enable him to marry. The bondage relationship usually started with a debt, which is also true of the laborer nowadays, who surrenders his freedom of movement at the moment he accepts an advance from the jobber. Just like the hali – the bonded farm servant who had to work for his master until the debt was paid off – the seasonal worker cannot leave the brick kiln until he has worked off the advance payment.
> (Breman 2010: 49–50)

The defining feature of unfree labour here is unfreedom at the point of exit. At the point of entry, the worker 'voluntarily' offers his services. A related feature of unfree labour is that workers who have been rescued and freed 'voluntarily' return to unfreedom. What are the conditions for this reproduction of unfreedom? Breman uses scare quotes around the 'voluntarily' in his characterisation of this point of entry. He is right to do so. What is it for entry into unfreedom to be 'voluntary' or 'involuntary'?

Consider as a starting point two influential characterisations of varieties of unfree labour from the ILO convention on forced labour and from the UN protocol on trafficking:

> *forced or compulsory labour* shall mean all work or service which is exacted from any person under the menace of any penalty and for which the said person has not offered himself voluntarily.
>
> (ILO Forced Labour Convention 1930: No. 29; italics in original)

> Trafficking in persons shall mean [1] the recruitment, transport, transfer, harbouring or receipt of a person, [2] by use of threat, force, coercion, abduction, fraud or deception, abuse of power or a position of vulnerability or giving or receiving payments or benefits to achieve the consent of a person having control over another person, for the purpose of the exploitation. [3] Exploitation shall include, at a minimum, exploitation of prostitution of others or other forms of sexual exploitation, forced labour or services, slavery, practices similar to slavery, servitude or the removal of organs.
>
> (UNGA 2000a: Article 3)

Both ILO and UN Protocol are concerned in part with entry. The implicit characterisation of the absence of freedom at the point of entry under [2] in UN protocol calls upon a heterogeneous range of conditions. Putting it in terms of the ILO definition, there is a variety of ways in which persons can fail to 'voluntarily' offer themselves into work or a service. The UN definition goes beyond the minimum conditions of 'threat, force, coercion, abduction, fraud or deception', which are included in most standard liberal accounts of unfreedom. It includes also the abuse of a person's position of vulnerability. In an interpretative note the protocol offers the following characterisation of vulnerability: 'the reference to the abuse of a position of vulnerability is understood to refer to any situation in which the person involved has no real and acceptable alternative but to submit to the abuse involved' (UNGA 2000b: para. 63). How should the phrase 'no real and acceptable alternative' be understood? What relationship does it stand to involuntary action? The sections 'Voluntary and Involuntary Action', 'Compulsion by Necessity' and 'Necessities of Obligation' of this chapter will be concerned with these questions.

Agents, Victims and Vulnerability

In answering these questions about the senses in which the worker is vulnerable and workers entry into unfreedom might be involuntary, I will also address the second set of worries that runs through the literature on modern forms of unfree labour about the acknowledgement of both the unfreedom and the agency of workers. There is a much discussed tension between vulnerability-assigning and agency-assigning descriptions of workers, between the treatment of unfree workers as vulnerable victims and at the same time as agents who are able to make choices about their own lives. The worries are captured in the following passage for the 2004 EU Experts Group on trafficking:

> Although the Experts Group explicitly wants to stress the reality of trafficked persons as victims of a severe crime and human rights abuse, it also shares the concern that the use of the word 'victim', because of its emphasis on vulnerability, passivity and powerlessness fails to recognise the dignity, courage, aims and choices of the individuals concerned. Therefore, the term 'victim' is exclusively used in direct relation to the status of trafficked persons as a victim of crime and human rights abuses.
> (EU Experts Group on Trafficking in Human Beings 2004: 59–60)

The worry expressed in this passage is that reference to the abuse of vulnerability and the relative powerlessness of those compelled into unfree labour might appear to undermine the 'dignity, courage, aims and choices of the individuals concerned'. How is the apparent conflict between vulnerability-assigning and agency-assigning descriptions to be resolved? Indeed, how far is there a conflict between such descriptions at all?

Here I make three observations about this putative conflict. The first is simply to note that one possible insidious effect of unfreedom can be a loss of agency. Consider, for example, the following passage from an interview with a labourer in debt-bondage who inherited money that allowed him to buy himself out of bondage:

> After my wife received the money, we paid off our debt and were free to do whatever we wanted. But I was worried all the time – what if one of our children was sick? What if our crop failed? What if the government wanted some money? Since we no longer belonged to the landlord, we didn't get food everyday as before. Finally, I went to the landlord and asked him to take me back. I didn't have to borrow any money, but he agreed to let me be his halvaha [bonded ploughman] again. Now I don't worry so much; I know what to do.
> (Bales 2002: 83)

Debra Satz comments on this passage that the ploughman 'places little value on his ability to make decisions' (Satz 2010: 184). He exhibits a condition of 'servility' (Satz 2010: 184). The interpretation is contestable. The problem might be the objective insecurity of the situation and options that the ploughman faces rather than a failure to properly value his ability to make decisions. One would need to know more about the details of the case. However, it may be that the ploughman has, through the experience of bondage, lost his sense of agency. Habituated to others making choices on his behalf, he has lost his capacities of choice. Adaptation to a situation of powerlessness through a shift in a person's own views of their efficacy might be one way of coping with that situation. Correspondingly, one cause of the reproduction of unfree labour can be failures of agency itself. To break the cycle of reproduction of unfreedom requires programmes that address and develop anew the capacities of agency (Bale 2002). However, cycles of reproduction of unfreedom need not be of this kind. Workers with no loss of personal agency may through objective insecurity and the absence of other options place themselves in conditions of unfree labour. It is these sources of reproduction that will be the central concern of the following sections of this chapter.

The second observation is that there are serious problems in the way the conflict between agency-assigning and vulnerability-assigning descriptions is framed by the EU Experts Group, a framing that is widespread in the literature. Why should ascriptions of 'vulnerability, passivity and powerlessness' be taken to involve a failure to recognise the 'dignity' of the workers involved? This passage and others like it in the literature on unfree labour assume what Soran Reader has usefully characterised as an 'agential conception of person' (Reader 2007). The person or human being is defined purely by agency – by capacities for rational choice and action. To describe a person as a victim, as passive and vulnerable, is taken to deny her full status as a human person. Hence, it implies a failure to recognise dignity and worth. It is to treat the person as an object and as less than fully human. However, this is to distort what it is to be a human person.

Human persons are not simply agents. As Marx puts it 'A human being as an objective sensuous being is therefore a suffering being ...' (Marx 1844: 390). The agential conception of the person fails to acknowledge the other side of the agency, that is, vulnerability. Human persons are beings that can be dominated, subjugated, humiliated, oppressed and exploited. In this condition, they are an object of personal or structural powers. The persons are in that sense passive. However, it does not follow that they become mere things (Reader 2007: 593). Persons do not necessarily lose their personhood and humanity in being passive. Rather the obverse is the case. Being the object of certain kinds of humiliation, exploitation, oppression and domination is only possible if one is a human person. Mere things cannot be the objects of these relations. Some non-human animals may be the objects of versions of such relationships. However, there are specific forms of humiliation, exploitation, oppression and domination that only human persons can suffer. Being an object of these relationships is not a form of agency, although agency can and is exercised in response to them. They are specific ways in which human beings are acted upon. Workers suffer as objects of humiliation, exploitation, oppression and domination *as* human being (cf. Sayer 2011: 5ff. and 112ff.).

It is a mistake to see the agency as what is peculiarly distinctive of personhood and humanity. Personhood and humanity are also revealed in the specifically human forms in which we are patients. As such to describe a person as powerless or passive is not in itself to deny the personal dignity. Being an object of domination or humiliation will normally involve a failure to recognise the dignity of the person by those who dominate or humiliate. However, the *description* of a worker as being in that condition does not involve any such failure. It is rather to properly describe that condition. One term that might be quite properly used in this context is that the person is a victim. Being a victim involves a particular kind of human passivity and dependence. It involves being the object of human violence and coercion that harms and injures the person. If an agential conception of the human person is assumed then this is taken to reveal a failure to realise human powers: 'The agential conception conceptualises victimhood as a failure, a falling-short of full humanity' (Reader 2007: 596). To describe a person as a victim is thereby taken to fail to recognise those features that make her human, to fail to recognise her 'dignity, courage, aims and choices'. However, this is, for the reasons just outlined, an error. While part of the injury of being a victim of violence and coercion might involve the perpetrator's failure to recognise the dignity of the worker, the description of the person as being a victim need involve no such failure.

Humans are constituted by their passive powers not just their active powers: 'Full persons – all of us – are passive, needy, constrained and dependent as well as active, capable, free and independent' (Reader 2007: 603–604). Such passivity is not just involved in relations of oppression and domination. It is a ubiquitous feature of human life. Humanity and personhood are revealed in the ways we are cared for, looked after in illness and health, supported, taught, loved and in various other forms the objects of relations with other human beings in which we are dependents and acted upon, not just agents who act. It is a mistake to see autonomy and independence as an escape from dependence. The very exercise of active powers of choice and agency is only possible against the background of constraints and dependencies. It relies on networks of social support through which needs are met and through which social powers can be realised (O'Neill 2006, 2011). Those dependencies are particularly evident in the earlier and later years of life. However, they exist throughout life. They place particular kinds of obligations on those on whom dependents depend. These facts of human dependency and the obligations they create also render workers vulnerable to particular kinds of unfreedom, which I discuss in more detail in the section Necessities of Obligation.

The third observation is that vulnerability-assigning descriptions need not deny the agency of the worker. Some vulnerability-assigning descriptions, for example, those rooted in the absence of options for workers, are quite consistent with agency-assigning descriptions. Indeed, workers exercise their agency in responding to such vulnerabilities. One way of approaching this relationship between agency- and vulnerability-assigning descriptions is through the questions I raised at the end of the last section about the relationships between the voluntariness of actions and the presence or absence of options. The interpretative note on vulnerability in the UN protocol on trafficking reads: 'the reference to the abuse of a position of vulnerability is understood to refer to any situation in which the person involved has no real and acceptable alternative but to submit to the abuse involved'. The questions I raised earlier were these: How should the phrase 'no real and acceptable alternative' be understood? What relationship does it stand to involuntary action? It is to these questions and their implications for the relation between vulnerability and agency that I turn in the next section.

Voluntary and Involuntary Action

Like Austin, I start my discussion of voluntariness with Aristotle – specifically, with Aristotle's distinction between voluntary and involuntary acts in Book III of *Nicomachean Ethics*, and in particular the category of acts which Aristotle described as mixed acts, acts that look in one sense to be voluntary and in another involuntary. Discussion of this class of acts allows insight into the ambiguities around the 'voluntariness' of the entry into unfree labour and resolves some of the apparent tension between vulnerability-assigning and agency-assigning descriptions of workers. Aristotle's account of the category had particular influence on later medieval discussions of 'compulsion by necessity'. It survives in the work of Marx who, in this regard at least, is as Tawney put it the 'last of schoolmen' (Tawney 1938: 48). It stands in contrast with at least one important strand of liberal theory on the distinction between free and unfree labour.[3]

Aristotle's account of voluntary and involuntary action starts from the observation that voluntary actions are the objects of praise or blame; involuntary actions are the objects of pardon and pity: 'Virtue, then, is about feelings and actions. These received praise and blame if they are voluntary, but pardon, sometimes even pity, if they are involuntary' (Aristotle 1999: III.1). The clear cases of involuntary actions outlined by Aristotle are those that are the result of external force or ignorance. Further qualifications need to be made to Aristotle's claims here, for example, about culpable ignorance (Austin 1956). However, here I leave these aside and turn to the category of actions that appear to be a 'mixture' of the voluntary and involuntary. The category is that of 'actions done because of fear of greater evils or because of something fine' (Aristotle 1999: III.1).

Aristotle's account of mixed actions starts from two much discussed examples: the person forced by a tyrant into shameful acts through threats to family members and the captain who throws his cargo overboard to save a ship:

> Suppose e.g. a tyrant tells you to do something shameful, when he has control of your parents and children, and if you do it, they will live, but if not, they will die. These cases raise disputes about whether they are voluntary or involuntary. However, the same sort of thing also happens with throwing a cargo overboard in storms; for no one willingly throws the cargo overboard without qualification, but anyone with any sense throws it overboard [under some conditions] to save himself and the others.
>
> (Aristotle 1999: III.1)

In one sense, these acts look voluntary: The actor 'does it willingly ... it is up to him to do them or not to do them' (Aristotle 1999: III.1). In another sense, they look to be involuntary: 'the actions without qualification are involuntary, since no one would choose any such action its own right' (Aristotle 1999: III.1).

One way of capturing the puzzle here for Aristotle is that in such mixed cases, the responsibility-attributing attitudes of praise and blame that voluntary actions invoke can come apart. One might praise the captain for the action of throwing the cargo overboard, for his decisiveness in acting the way he did to save the ship and the lives of those aboard. At the same time, one might deny that he is blameworthy for the loss of the goods. One might say that he had no choice. So here is the puzzle:

(a)   the act is the result of a choice for which praise is due.
(b)   the captain is not liable to blame since he had no real choice.

The attitudes appear to both presuppose and deny the existence of a choice.

The puzzle is not a deep one. The term 'choice' is being used in two different senses. The object of praise of the captain's decisiveness is the *act* of choice. Choice is being used to refer to the act. In contrast in denying blameworthiness, in saying the captain had no choice, the term 'choice' is being used to refer to the options or alternatives over which choice is exercised. To say that the captain 'had no real choice' is to say he had no acceptable option or alternative but to throw the cargo overboard.

The distinction dissolves some of the apparent opposition between agency-assigning and vulnerability-assigning descriptions of workers. The claim that 'emphasis on vulnerability, passivity and powerlessness fails to recognise the dignity, courage, aims and choices of the individuals concerned' is a worry that the person is being denied the capacity to make his/her own choices. To assign agency is to say the person has the ability to engage in deliberation and to author his/her own actions. Their choices are their own, and one might praise 'the dignity' and 'courage' of those who make those choices. However, making that agency-assigning description of the worker is quite consistent with a vulnerability-assigning description in the sense that it is used in the UN interpretive comment on trafficking – that the person has 'no real and acceptable alternative' but to choose a particular act. This is a claim about the alternatives that are available to an agent. It is not a claim about the attributes of the agent and his/her capacities to engage in acts of choice in these contexts. It involves no ascription of an incapacity to exercise agency.

Compulsion by Necessity

One way in which an act can be involuntary is that there is 'no real and accept-able alternative' but to choose that act (cf. Cohen 1983; Olsaretti 1998). By what criteria is an alternative acceptable or not? One possible answer is to appeal to subjective criteria to define what is unacceptable – to appeal to the desires and preferences of the agent. However, any such account looks implausible. It falls foul of the problem of expensive tastes. A person who finds warm champagne simply unacceptable is not thereby drinking the port involuntarily. Neither can a person complain that they had no alternative but to work long hours in the city since it was a condition of their maintaining their yacht in the Caribbean. A second possible response is to appeal to objective criteria, for example, to the demands of survival, welfare or eth-ical obligations. It is this second line of response that I develop further in the following sections. In particular, I will explore one line of argument that is central to treatments of voluntary action from Aristotle through the scho-lastic tradition to Marxism which appeals to an objective account: the indi-vidual is compelled by necessity.

What is it to be compelled by necessity? One starting point for an answer to that question is Aristotle's account of necessity in *Metaphysics*:

> We call NECESSARY (a) that without which, as a joint cause, it is not possible to live, as for instance breathing and nourishment are necessary for an animal, because it is incapable of existing without them; and (b) anything without which it is not possible for good to exist or come to be, or for bad to be discarded or got rid of, as for instance drinking medicine is necessary so that not to be ill, and sailing to Aegina so as to get money.
> (Aristotle 1971: V.5)

This Aristotelian account was typically appealed to in scholastic accounts of compulsion by necessity.[4] The problem with this response is that as an account of compulsion by necessity it is either too restrictive or too liberal. The problem is one that has been noted by Wiggins (1998: 25–26). On the one hand, clause (a) is too restrictive: only the avoidance of death makes an alternative below conditions of necessity. On the other hand, clause (b) is too liberal: it includes any goods that are instrumental to the achievement of some end, where that end itself is optional. If in characterising compulsion by necessity one includes only that which falls under clause (a), then only where the alternative is death can an act be said not to be free. However, if one follows clause (b), the problem of expensive tastes returns. One is not compelled by necessity when one must act in some way to fund a Caribbean yacht tip.

Wiggins' distinction between purely instrumental and absolute or categorical uses of the concept of need goes some way to resolving this problem by offering an account of compulsion by need (Wiggins 1998). Some needs-claims specify needs that are purely instrumental to the realisation of an end that is itself optional. If I am to have a Caribbean yacht trip, then I need to borrow £6,000. One is not compelled by the need since the end itself is optional. A person might respond by asking 'Do you really need the yacht trip?'. Other claims of need are not like this. They are absolute or categorical in that the ends themselves are not optional but 'unforsakeable'. A person can be said to be harmed if they are not met. The concept is characterised thus by Wiggins:

> I need [absolutely] to have x
>   if and only if
>   I need [instrumentally] to have x if I am to avoid being harmed
>   if and only if
>   It is necessary, things being what they actually are, that if I avoid being harmed then I have x.
>
> (Wiggins 1998: 10)

Absolute needs should not be confused with needs grounded in a person's biological nature. Not all biological needs are absolute, for example, the dietary needs of the fashion model. Not all absolute needs are biological. A child deprived of education and an adult deprived of the chance to make choices about his/her own life are harmed even if all biological needs are met. Some absolute needs are relative to specific cultural settings and social arrangements. They include, as Smith puts it, goods which while not 'indispensably necessary for the support of life' are such that 'the custom of the country renders it indecent for creditable people, even of the lowest order, to be without' (Smith 1776: V.11.k, p.869).

Given this account, one is able to characterise at least one dimension in which a person might be said to be compelled by necessity. The person lacks acceptable alternatives, where the concept of an acceptable alternative will appeal to something like conditions for a person to live a minimally flourishing life or realise some basic capacities for human functioning. The person has no choice but to perform some act X in the sense that his/her life would fall below some minimal conditions of human flourishing if he/she fails to do so and hence that he/she will be harmed. Necessity of this kind I will call 'prudential necessity'. Prudential necessity is what is typically appealed in observing that workers are forced into bondage through poverty. A life of extreme poverty is a 'life without options' (Bales et al. 2009: 56) in just this sense. However, prudential necessity, while it is involved in the point of entry of much unfree labour, is not the only kind of compulsion by necessity. It needs to be distinguished from a distinct class of necessities, necessities of obligation.

Necessities of Obligation

Prudential necessities do not exhaust what it means to be compelled by need. Moral and ethical considerations also determine the scope of acceptable alternatives. Consider again Aristotle's examples of mixed actions. A man does something shameful because a tyrant threatens his children. The captain throws the cargo overboard since saving the ship and its passengers is what is required of him/her as a captain. In both cases, they have no choice in the sense that this is what is ethically required of them as inhabitants of that particular role, where in this context the role is itself both ethically permissible and unforsakeable. The qualifications are important. There might be requirements of a role that is itself ethically objectionable, say of the conscientious bureaucrat in Nazi Germany or of the loyal hit man. In neither of such cases would there exist the excuse 'I had no choice …' The roles themselves should be rejected. Being a parent or a captain of a ship is not ethically objectionable in this sense. Neither is being a parent or a captain of a ship forsakeable at the point of action. While the captain may make a decision to give up the job when he/she steps ashore, at the point of action that option is not available. Some roles are voluntarily entered into carrying obligations that are not foresakeable at all. Obligations of parenthood are of this kind. Finally, some roles that are not optional at the point of entry carry obligations that are not foresakeable. Ties of kinship such as being a daughter or son, a sister or brother are of this kind. Necessities of obligation refer to what is required of a person ethically or from within an ethically permissible and unforsakeable role. A person is compelled by necessity in the sense that there is no acceptable alternative to a particular action since that action is ethically required or alternatives are ethically impermissible.

Necessities of obligation are of particular importance for understanding the grounding of many modern forms of unfree labour. They are particularly evident in accounts of unfreedom of women in which care roles involving dependents falls within the gendered division of labour. Consider, for example, the following observation about sex workers in Tijuana:

> All the sex workers I talked to had a clear understanding of the societal conditions they grew up in and knew that they had had very limited

options. Almost all of them mentioned 'necessity' as the reason for entering the sex industry. This necessity stems often from them being the single heads of households with care duties for children and other dependents.

(Hofmann 2009)

The necessities the workers here are necessities of obligation grounded in the position of head of household responsible for dependents. Prudential necessities if they enter here enter indirectly. The needs of those dependents ground the particular obligations. Consider another example of entry into indentured sex work in Cambodia:

Somnang's entry into sex work and indenture was primarily in response to her mother's illness and, as her daughter, she felt obligated to look after and support her: 'My mum is very sick and when I found out about this, I came here [to work] so I could look after her. She isn't well and she needs a lot of money to look after herself with, and so I did this for her'.
(Interview, Somnang, 22 November 2003) (Sandy 2011: 14)

There is a prudential necessity here – the illness of the mother. However, it is the necessity of obligation to care for a dependent person that compels Somnang to enter indentured labour as a sex worker.

References to necessities of obligation are prominent forms of unfree labour women entering to meet gendered obligations to care for dependents. They can lead to paradoxes of unfree labour where separation is a condition of caring for dependents:

It is terrible for us, because we are far from our children, but we are giving them food education, we are giving them everything, although staying here you are dying because everything depends on you.
(Peruvian domestic worker quoted in Anderson 2000: 118)

While necessities of obligation are particularly evident in descriptions of women's entry into unfree labour, they are not gender-specific. They are evident also in reasons that male unfree workers give for entering conditions of unfreedom. For example, the need to meet obligations to provide for dowries for sisters and daughters is common in descriptions of debt-bondage in India and among migrant workers without rights in the Middle East. Sugarcane workers report entering into unfree labour in order to meet the needs of their family (McGrath 2010: 102). An Algerian migrant male worker in France echoes the dilemma noted by the Peruvian domestic worker quoted above: 'What kind of life is it when, in order to feed your children, you are forced to leave them; when in order to "fill" your house, you start by deserting it' (Sayad 2004: 39 cited in Sayer 2011: 9).

One form of involuntary entry into unfree labour stems from the fact that the worker as a relational being is enmeshed in obligations. Women enter domestic service tied to a particular employer or forms of debt-bondage in order to provide their children or parent with prudential necessities. Male workers enter unfree labour in order to discharge obligations to family members. The worker suffers from necessities of obligation in the sense that the action is required of him or her from within an ethically permissible and unforsakeable role.

There are objections that might be raised to the claim that the worker in these cases suffers from necessities of obligation. One objection might be to simply deny that any roles are unforsakeable. All are optional. Thus one form of radical liberalism might limit obligations to others to those that agents voluntarily incur. If that is the case, it might be argued that all ethical bonds to others associated with social roles are ultimately optional. There are at least two problems with this argument. First, many roles and the obligations associated with them are not voluntarily incurred. Relations to kin – for example to parents and siblings – are relations into which people are embedded without choice and which make ethical demands on the person. Somnang's relationship with her mother is not a chosen relationship. It is one that makes serious demands upon her. Second, even where roles and attachments are engaged in voluntarily and are in that sense optional at the point of entry, once they are entered the role is not forsakeable and makes demands on the person. The choice to be a sea captain is optional. Some choices on how to act within that role are not. The captain has no choice but to throw the cargo overboard. The choice to be a parent may be optional. Once entered there are demands required by the role that are not foresakeable.

A second and more important objection is that while the particular role may not be unforsakeable, the background structure in the distribution of roles may be itself both socially optional and ethical and politically objectionable. The gendered division of labour that places women in particular roles of care for dependents, patterns of dowry obligation and other patterns in the social distribution of care and dependency are not themselves ethically defensible or necessary. For that reason, they should be the object of political contestation and change. These points are right. However, that the patterns of distribution in responsibilities are not necessary does not entail that those who inhabit particular places within those distributions of responsibility and obligation are not subject to necessities of obligation. Moreover, the roles themselves – for example, being a parent, daughter, sister, brother or son – are not objectionable. What are objectionable are the particular patterns of obligation that people are placed within and the ways in which they are exploitable. One way people are oppressed is through the exploitation of relations of care – and in the nature and extent of those obligations of necessity. The worker is trapped within cycles of social reproduction from which escape is difficult or impossible. What does follow from this observation is that tackling the reproduction of unfree labour is not simply a matter of addressing the condition of individual workers, but addressing the background social conditions that mean the worker is subject to patterns of necessities of obligations that render them open to exploitation as unfree labourers. The social support and provision for dependents, social welfare and health provision for the young, old and ill can be key to freeing the agents of exploitable necessities of obligation.

Domination, Dependence and Unfreedom

I noted at the start of the chapter the different sites of unfreedom. Unfreedom can occur at the point of entry, within the labour process itself and at the point of exit. At different sites, different liberty-restricting concepts apply such as involuntariness, domination and dependence. In the last three sections, my main aim has been to understand the ways in which the point of entry into unfree labour, while the result of an act of choice by the worker, cannot be understood to be a simple voluntary act. The worker enters into the condition through a lack of reasonable alternatives. They are in this sense compelled by necessity. These necessities include not just prudential necessities, but necessities of obligation. Recognising such necessities is important to understanding the reproduction of unfree labour. However, it is important to note the lack of reasonable alternatives at the point of entry does not define the nature of unfree labour. The lack of reasonable alternative can be why workers enter into forms of labour contract in which subsequent relations of dependence are absent and from which exit is possible. For example, the lack of reasonable alternatives can be why workers engage in dangerous forms of labour which need not be forms of unfree labour (Cohen 1983). Conversely, it is possible to enter a relationship that is itself unfree through voluntary acts. The involuntariness or otherwise of the point of entry into an exploitative relationship of unfree labour is independent of the nature of the relationship itself. The voluntariness of the point of entry matters for an understanding of the social reproduction of unfreedom – of why workers enter into and indeed often return to conditions of unfreedom. It does not answer the question of how unfree labour, and in particular modern forms of unfree labour should be characterised and understood.

This final section will consider unfreedom at the point of exit and in the relationship itself. The background questions addressed are those raised at the start of the chapter: What is the relation between capitalism and the persistence and spread of unfree labour? Are there distinctive features of the nature of unfree labour in modern capitalist society? In what sense, if any, is modern unfree labour distinctively different from older forms of unfree labour? Classically, the contrast that is used to characterise unfree labour is with the free wage-labourer who owns their own labour-power and is free to sell it (Marx 1976: ch. 26). The wage-labourer must sell their labour-power to some capitalist, and in that sense there may be a collective unfreedom (Cohen

1983). However, the worker is not compelled to sell it to any particular capitalist (Marx 1976: 1032).

On this account unfreedom at the point of exit becomes central to
characterising unfree labour. Unfree workers cannot change their master
as they wish. The slave cannot exit since they are owned by the master.
The bonded worker is similarly unfree at the point of exit: the unfree
element lies not in the bondage being imposed from the start but in the
worker's 'inability to break the bond once it has been contracted' (Breman
1993: 12). Both these forms of unfree labour persist, in particular debt-
bondage. Repayment of the debt is tied to bondage to a particular master.
Debt-bondage is also central to the unfreedom of many migrant workers.
However, the constraint of exit often lies not just in debt but in the absence
of protective labour and citizenship rights. This is most clearly evident in
confiscation of passports by employers. It exists in legal and social systems
in which the migrant worker is tied to a particular employer. Consider, for
example, *Kafala* labour in the Middle East in which the worker is sponsored
by a particular employer:

> Workers are prohibited from changing employers or quitting without
> their sponsor's permission. The *kafeel* (sponsor), who is in most cases the
> employer, has the power to send the worker back to his or her country
> at any time. Within this rigid legal framework, foreigners are effectively
> bonded to their employers for the terms of their service, which typically
> last two years.
>
> (Frantz 2009)

While the worker may enter the contract freely, they have no possibility of
exit. However, even where the legal powers of the kind in the *Kafala* system
are absent, the worker may be unfree simply through the absence of positive
protections. In particular, the illegal status of many migrant workers robs
workers of social protections that allow them to exit.

Here the forms of unfreedom stressed in the tradition of republican political theory which was developed through the contrast with classical slavery
are particularly relevant. The concepts of domination and dependence are
the central liberty-restricting concepts employed. Acting as an independent
agent is in part a matter of being protected as a citizen from domination. An
individual is dominated if they are subject to the arbitrary power of another.
As such freedom requires positive protections of citizens from the powers of
others: '[f]reedom as non-domination is a social good that comes about ... by
virtue of checks on the capacity of other people to exercise domination' (Pettit
1999: 122). Central to many modern forms of unfree labour is the absence of
such checks on domination through the absence of those protections that the
status of citizenship provides. While the worker is often formally free, she is
unprotected from the arbitrary powers and violence of others in virtue of the

absence of those forms of protection that are included in the rights of a legal citizen. The worker loses the capacity to act as an independent agent. She is effectively tied to a particular employer.

The concept of dependence is also of significance in understanding distinctive features of unfreedom in the relationship itself. Both Smith and Marx employ the concept of dependence to characterise the differences between capitalist or commercial societies and their precursors. Consider, for example, Marx's distinction between pre-capitalist and capitalist modes of production in the *Grundrisse* in terms of a shift from 'relations of personal dependence' to '[p]ersonal independence founded on *objective [sachlicher]* dependence' (Marx 1973: 158). Pre-capitalist societies in which market exchange relations are not fully developed are characterised by individuals defined by social roles which make some personally dependent on others (Marx 1973: 165). The full development of market relations within capitalist society breaks ties of personal dependence. Through contract, individuals enter into relations with each other as personally independent and free agents who are not tied to a particular social definition: 'In ... the developed system of exchange ... the ties of personal dependence, of distinctions of blood, education, etc, are in fact exploded, ripped up' (Marx 1973: 165). Personal dependence is replaced by the 'objective' dependence of agents on the impersonal workings of the market.

The claim that commercial society fosters independence is central to Smith's defence of commercial society. Commerce secures 'the liberty and security of individuals, among the inhabitants of the country, who had before lived almost in a continual state of ... servile dependency upon their superiors' (Smith 1776: III.IV.4). In pre-commercial society, the worker is dependent on the wealthy through the power of patronage and gift (Smith 1776: III.IV.5–6). Commercial society breaks these ties of personal dependence. Through exchange and the division of labour, the interdependence of individuals is disassociated from personal dependence since the income of each worker is no longer tied to that of any particular individual (Smith 1776: III.IV.11).

What is distinctive about unfree labour in modern capitalist society is that older forms of personal dependence are largely absent. While forms of personal dependence do survive in modern forms of unfree labour, including forms of personal dependence founded on birth into a particular role, these are less evident. The kinds of reciprocal dependence of older forms of unfree labour have been eroded. Unfree labour takes a contractual form. Thus for example, what Breman characterises as neo-bondage involves more contract-like forms of debt-bondage. Relations of personal dependence which involve reciprocity of duties and patronage are absent. The bondage is for limited periods of time. Intergenerational inheritance of dependence disappears. Consider Breman's observation on the condition of bonded cane cutters and kiln workers in India:

The non-economic aspects of patronage that were so characteristic of halipratha, the halis' function as an indicator of their masters' power and prestige, play no part ... They are not feudal patrons who surround themselves with clients but capitalist entrepreneurs who satisfy their time-bound demand for labor.

(Breman 2010: 50)

Similar points apply elsewhere. Consider the *Kafala* system in the Middle East. The *Kafala* system appears as a continuation of older relationships of patron and client, with the ties of dependence and reciprocity these involve. However, in its modern form, Kafala is a husk of the system. The relation is one with an employer who contracts with a labourer for a set period of time. In both cases, ties of personal dependence are no longer present in the forms they were in pre-capitalist society.

There are good reasons then to claim that many modern forms of unfree labour are not persisting pre-capitalist forms but rather new forms without relationships of personal dependence with individuals tied to particular roles. These new forms of unfree labour take place in a global marketplace for labour that is highly mobile. The blocks on the exit of the worker are increasingly bound up with the very mobility of labour which removes it from legal and social protections against domination. The confiscation of the passport as a way of tying labour to a particular employer in many ways exemplifies the combination of high mobility of labour with new forms of blocks on exit. The unfreedom of the worker is often time-bound and contractual in nature. Intergenerational inheritance of unfreedom is absent. The personal dependence of patron and client, lord and serf, of caste and estate are replaced by impersonal relations without traditional forms of reciprocity and patronage.

While pre-capitalist modes of unfree labour do survive, it would be a mistake to see the continued existence and growth of unfree labour simply as survivals of pre-capitalist forms (Rao 1999). Rather they are specifically modern ways in which unfree labour is realised. Central questions about unfree labour should be about the new forms of unfreedom and not simply the persistence of older forms. What I have tried to show in this chapter is that the key to understanding modern forms of unfree labour and its reproduction is an appreciation of the varieties of unfreedom involved. Understanding that variety is required if political and social responses are to be successful.

Notes

1 Lerche (2007) provides a useful overview of the debate. For different views, see Brass and van der Linden 1997; Brass 1999; Rao 1999.
2 The methodological point is not one that is confined to the concept of freedom. Similar points may apply to other concepts, for example, to the concept of justice. It might be argued that the negative term, 'injustice', does the work and that,

correspondingly, the most appropriate starting point is a consideration of the variety of different forms of injustice. Compare Sen 2009.
3   Hobbes' negative concept of liberty in particular involved an explicit rejection of the Aristotelian framework (Hobbes 1651 [1968]: II.21 p. 262).
4   The concept of compulsion by necessity was central to scholastic debates on the just price and usury (Langholm 1998). Exchange in conditions when one agent makes use of the need of another to enforce a particular price is unjust. The arguments typically appealed back to Aristotle's discussion of voluntary action and necessity. Typical is Aquinas' criticism of usury in *De Malo* (2003: XIII, Article 4). Usury is unjust in exploiting a person's neediness (2003: XIII, Article 4 reply to seventh argument). Aquinas' defence of the claim inherits problems from Aristotle's account of necessity noted in the text. Aquinas acknowledges a potential objection with his claim: 'people sometimes borrow with interest without any great need' (2003: XIII, Article 4 eighth argument). Aquinas' response appeals to Aristotle's account of necessity in *Metaphysics*. An alternative is unacceptable if it either falls below the conditions for life at all or more liberally if one cannot live 'so well or suitably' without it (2003: XIII, Article 4 reply to eighth argument). The problem with Aquinas' argument is one inherited from Aristotle and noted in the text: the account of compulsion by necessity is either too restrictive or too liberal.

References

Anderson, B. (2000). *Doing the Dirty Work? The Global Politics of Domestic Labour.* London: Zed Books.
Aquinas, T. (2003). *De Malo.* New York: Oxford University Press.
Aristotle (1971). *Metaphysics*, trans. C. Kirwin. Oxford: Oxford University Press.
Aristotle (1999). *Nicomachean Ethics.* T. Irwin trans. Second edition. Indianapolis: Hackett.
Austin, A. (2018). Living Well with Dementia Together: Affiliation as a Fertile Functioning. *Public Health* 11: 139–150.
Austin J. L. (1956). A Plea for Excuses. *Proceedings of the Aristotelian Society* 57: 1–30.
Bales, K. (2002). The Social Psychology of Slavery. *Scientific American* 286(4): 80–88.
Bales, K., Trodd, Z. & Williamson, A. K. (2009). *Modern Slavery: The Secret World of 27 Million People.* Oxford: One World Publications.
Brass, T. (1999). *Towards a Comparative Political Economy of Unfree Labour; Case Studies and Debates.* London: Frank Cass.
Brass, T, & van der Linden, M. (eds) (1997). *Free and Unfree Labour: The Debate Continues.* Berne: Peter Lang AG.
Breman, J. (1993). *Beyond Patronage and Exploitation: Changing Agrarian Relations in South Gujarat.* Delhi: Oxford University Press.
Breman, J. (2010). Neo-Bondage: A Fieldwork-Based Account. *International Labor and Working-Class History* 78: 48–62.
Cohen, G. A. (1983). The Structure of Proletarian Unfreedom. *Philosophy and Public Affairs* 12(1): 3–33.
EU Experts Group on Trafficking in Human Beings (2004). *Report of the Experts Group on Trafficking in Human Beings.* European Commission – Directorate-General Justice, Freedom and Security, Brussels.

Frantz, E. (2009). The *Kafala* System and the Bonding of Migrant Labour: the Case of Sri Lankan Domestic Workers in Jordan. Paper at the ESRC Seminar Series on Unfree Labour, University of Manchester.

Hobbes, T. (1651 [1968]). *Leviathan.* Harmondsworth: Penguin.

Hofmann, S. (2009). Tackling Degrees of Freedom in Tijuana's Zone of Tolerance: Women's. Experiences of Selling Sex at the US-Mexican Border. Paper in the ESRC Seminar Series on Unfree Labour, University of Manchester.

ILO (1930). *Forced Labour Convention* (No. 29). www.ilo.org/dyn/normlex/en/f?p= 1000:12100:0::NO::P12100_ILO_CODE:C029

ILO (2001). *Stopping Forced Labour. Global Report Under the Follow-up to the ILO Declaration on Fundamental Principles and Rights at Work.* Geneva: ILO.

ILO (2005). *A Global Alliance against Forced Labour.* Geneva: ILO.

ILO (2009). *The Cost of Coercion.* Geneva: ILO.

ILO (2016). *ILO Standards on Forced Labour – The new Protocol and Recommendation at a Glance.* Geneva: ILO.

ILO (2017). *Global Estimates of Modern Slavery.* Geneva: ILO.

Langholm, O. (1998). *The Legacy of Scholasticism in Economic Thought.* Cambridge: Cambridge University Press.

Lerche, J. (2007). A Global Alliance against Forced Labour? Unfree Labour, Neo-Liberal Globalization and the International Labour Organization. *Journal of Agrarian Change* 7(4): 424–425.

Lindemann, H. (2009). Holding One Another (Well, Wrongly, Clumsily) in a Time of Dementia. *Metaphilosophy* 40: 416–424.

Lindemann, H. (2014). *Holding and Letting Go: The Social Practice of Personal Identities.* New York: Oxford University Press.

Marx K. (1844[1974]). Economic and Philosophical Manuscripts. In L. Colletti (ed.) *Early Writings* Harmondsworth: Penguin.

Marx, K. (1973). *Grundrisse.* Harmondsworth: Penguin.

Marx, K. (1976). *Capital I.* Harmondsworth: Penguin.

McGrath, S. (2010). *The Political Economy of Forced Labour in Brazil.* PhD Thesis, University of Manchester.

Olsaretti, S. (1998). Freedom, Force and Choice: Against the Rights-Based Definition of Voluntariness. *Journal of Political Philosophy* 6(1): 53–78.

O'Neill, J. (2006). Need, Humiliation and Independence. In S. Reader (ed.), p. 57, *The Philosophy of Need: Royal Institute of Philosophy Supplement.* Cambridge: Cambridge University Press.

O'Neill, J. (2011). The Political Economy of Recognition. *The Adam Smith Review* 6: 164–186.

Pettit, P. (1999). *Republicanism: A Theory of Freedom and Government.* Oxford: Oxford University Press.

Rao, M. (1999). Freedom, Equality, Property and Bentham: The Debate over Unfree Labour. *Journal of Peasant Studies* 27(1): 97–127.

Reader, C. S. (2007). The other side of agency. *Philosophy* 82(4): 579–604.

Sandy, L. (2011). *Srei khnyom*: Women, debt bondage and sex work in Sihanoukville Cambodia. Paper in the ESRC Seminar Series on Unfree Labour, University of Manchester.

Satz, D. (2010). *Why Some Things Should Not Be For Sale.* Oxford: Oxford University Press.

Sayad, A. (2004). *The Suffering of the Immigrant.* Cambridge: Polity.

Sayer, A. (2005). *The Moral Significance of Class.* Cambridge: Cambridge University Press.

Sayer, A. (2009). Contributive Justice and Meaningful Work. *Res Publica* 15: 1–16.

Sayer, A. (2011). *Why Things Matter to People: Social Science, Values and Ethical Life.* Cambridge: Cambridge University Press.

Sen, A. (2009). *The Idea of Justice.* London: Allen Lane.

Smith, A. (1776). *An Inquiry into the Nature and Causes of the Wealth of Nations.* Indianapolis: Liberty Press.

Tawney, R. (1938). *Religion and the Rise of Capitalism.* New York: Penguin Books.

UNGA (2000a). *UN Protocol to Prevent, Suppress and Punish Trafficking in Persons, Especially Women and Children, Supplementing the United Nations Convention against Transnational Organized Crime* www.ohchr.org/en/professionalinterest/pages/protocoltraffickinginpersons.aspx

UNGA (2000b). *Interpretative notes for the official records (travaux préparatoires) of the negotiation of the United Nations Convention against Transnational Organized Crime and the Protocols thereto* www.unodc.org/pdf/crime/final_instruments/383a1e.pdf

UNODC (2009). *Global Report on Trafficking in Persons* www.unodc.org/unodc/en/human-trafficking/global-report-on-trafficking-in-persons.html

Wiggins, D. (1998). The Claims of Need. In *Needs, Values, Truth*, Third edition. Oxford: Blackwell.

Wolff, J., & de Shalit, A. (2007). *Disadvantage.* Oxford: Oxford University Press.

Chapter 12

The Persistent Radicalism of Andrew Sayer

Richard Walker

I first met Andrew Sayer at a workshop, for promising young geographers, somewhere in North Carolina in 1980. I have little recollection of that meeting; other than that Andrew and I hit it off talking about music one evening while at a bar and have remained good friends ever since. This is despite the yawning distance between our locales and the fact that we are rather different characters: he is quiet and self-effacing; I am loud and self-confident. But we connected through shared similar qualities of mind, such as wide-ranging curiosity and a love of logical argumentation, a mutual love of nature and the outdoors and quirky delights like singing in odd local choral groups.

That friendship has survived the long distance and infrequent get-togethers in the days before the Internet. Neither of us has been a real academic jet-setter, but our paths crossed occasionally over the years. In the distant past, I made trips to Sussex and Copenhagen to see Andrew and family, while he came to California for an AAG or two and road trips to Yosemite and down the Pacific coast. I well remember the time Andrew came here to spread the word about the coal miner's strike and fight against Thatcherism in 1984, an important moment of education for me.

In recent years, I have made the trek up to Lancaster several times and he to France, where I have a summer house, and we Skype from time to time. Spartan fare, I'm sure, compared to what many others among Andrew Sayer's friends and colleagues have enjoyed but enough to reaffirm an amicable relationship of mutual admiration, hoisting a pint or two and occasional serious discussion. I even recollect tossing out the idea for the book title, 'Why Things Matter ... ', though that may be braggadocio. Mostly, I have watched his career soar from afar and happily wrestled with his many brilliant books, having long ago acknowledged that the quiet lad from the uninspiring reaches of Heathrow is much the greater thinker and more accomplished scholar. I am still happy to bask in the glow of his success.

Looking back at our early friendship, it is well to recall that the late 1970s and 1980s were heady times of the mind, as the 1968 generation came of age,

DOI: 10.4324/9781003247326-16

moved into the universities and sought to overthrow old modes of thinking. We shared key intellectual movements of the time in the social sciences around the political economy, philosophy and radical possibilities on the Left. Sayer and I were hardly alone in forging ties across the Atlantic, because a great many British academics had fled to the United States at the time – helping, I should add, to raise the overall level of geographic thought in what was then a pretty backward discipline in the United States.

At the time, Andrew and I were both nominally economic geographers, fascinated by the revolutions afoot in industrial systems and the deindustrial-isation of Britain and the United States. He would write a solid research study with Kevin Morgan, *Microcircuits of Capital* (1988), and I would produce a series of essays and finally a book, *The Capitalist Imperative* (1989), with Michael Storper. I had the good luck in the 1980s to be surrounded by an amazing group of graduate students and colleagues at Berkeley who were driving a revolution in industrial geography, and that momentum carried me along through the 1980s and niche notoriety as an economic geographer.

A salutary influence on both Sayer and me at the time was a series of excellent gatherings of leftist geographers and fellow travellers in the Greek islands, organised by Costis Hadjimichalis. Andrew was a regular, but I could only make one in 1987 thanks to a modest salary and family obligations (Greece seemed very far away from California in the 1980s). Yet, out of that gathering came the idea of writing a book together, which is *The New Social Economy* (1991). The overarching theme was that scholars should be looking more seriously at the division of labour (both social and detail). Sadly, the idea of reviving an older tradition of highlighting the division of labour, in the manner of Smith, Marx, Durkheim and Weber, fell on deaf ears in economic geography and sociology.

While most commentators of the time were excited by the industrial cluster model of the Third Italy, we were convinced that developments in Japanese production methods were driving a global upheaval in industrial geography; that proved right, yet most studies of East Asia emphasised state-led development and production chains, not the shifting global division of labour. We were also right to criticise the bogus economic category of 'services', made up of trade, management, finance and indirect labour plus education and health; yet that perennial 'chaotic concept' never seems to die. Finally, we took seriously the vital place of household labour in social reproduction as part of the overall social division of labour, but feminist geographers left that aside to undertake a wholesale questioning of capitalist economics. In the end, we were not encouraged to keep focusing on the division of labour.

In any case, Andrew had been carving out another intellectual pathway as a philosopher of (social) science, which came to define him to most of his admirers. That road was clearly taken by the time of *Method in Social Science* (1984), which brought him widespread acclaim. He was not alone in this search for foundations, of course, and it seemed that everyone in the social sciences at the time was wrestling with the philosophical scaffoldings and political implications of our work. There was a flood of methodological books from Marxists like (D) Sayer and Mezaros, sociologists such as Keats and Urry, Giddens and Bourdieu, and postmodernists such as Rorty and Lyotard. Yet, Andrew took the whole debate to another level with his path-breaking *Method*, plus the many articles, conferences and books that followed (e.g. *Realism and Social Science* 2000).

Method became my philosophical bible, as it has served many others across the social sciences. Oddly, my great mentor from graduate school days at Johns Hopkins, David Harvey, took umbrage at critical realism and at Sayer, as if they were somehow opposed to Marxist historical materialism. While I have followed David's lead on many things, on this one I thought (and still think) he was dead wrong.

Despite his growing reputation, Sayer was badly underestimated by the powers that be at Sussex and he left in disgust circa 1992 to take a position in Sociology at Lancaster (home of John Urry and other luminaries), where he has been happily ensconced ever since. That move opened the door to a supportive environment and the intellectual stimulation to allow Sayer to expand on the philosophy of social science and other matters. But it was a move that closed the door on his economic geography.

This shows the importance of our own situated lives and thought, if I may score a geographic point. I would argue that Sayer had a crucial encounter in his early days with Roy Bhaskar at Sussex (though Bhaskar was not very approachable and Andrew says he was equally influenced by the Keat and Urry's *Social Theory as Science*). On the contrary, by leaving Geography at Sussex to join Urry at Lancaster, he lost most of his collegial connection to geographers. That dimmed his interest in geographic thought.

By contrast, I was deeply influenced by my time in Baltimore with David Harvey, who was every bit as much a geographer as a Marxist, and subsequently surrounded by a brilliant group of young geographers and colleagues Allan Pred and Michael Watts at Berkeley. I also counted Ed Soja and Allen Scott at UCLA as good friends. I was, therefore, driven to come to terms with the spatial dimension of social life. We wrestled with the same questions about the *Method in Social Science* out in California, but we came to conclusions that included the spatial dimension in social theory. Andrew did not agree.

Indeed, Sayer and I quarrelled about the philosophical importance of space in social scientific theorising, as he was dismissive of any significant, independent role for the geographic dimension. This is one of the few points on which I disagree heartily with him, and it provides a key to our very different intellectual trajectories for many years. While he continued to build the edifice of critical realism in the 1990s, I followed two influential geographers, Doreen Massey and Mike Davis, down the road of taking seriously the importance of locale and place. As a result, California would occupy most of my time over the next 20 years (e.g. Walker 1995, 2001, 2004).

While he was continuing to write about philosophical issues, however, Sayer never abandoned his love of political economy. That has been another persistent thread in his work. In fact, in the mid-1990s he produced what I consider a masterpiece of clarity and rigor, *Radical Political Economy* (1995). In that volume, Sayer provides a razor-sharp comparison of the pros and cons of conventional and radical economic theory. It is richly informed by his philosophical enquiries and especially his mastery of logic, but its principal achievement is to adjudicate fairly the wisdom and error of two competing world views. It is a paragon of brevity and acuity and a perfect instrument for teaching thoughtful, advanced students how to think about economy and society.

Nevertheless, it seems that *Radical Political Economy* was not one of Andrew's most popular books, which is a terrible shame (Google lists it after even *The New Social Economy*!). This is surely due, in part, to the reluctance of both liberals and leftists to admit the truth embedded in claims of the other side. But its eclipse probably also flowed from changing intellectual fashions and new breakthroughs in the world of philosophy, social sciences and humanities that pushed the political economy to the background in favour of poststructuralism, feminism and queer theory.

In the 2000s, Sayer's political economy veered away from the economic side and towards the political dimension of class and moral economy, as in *The Moral Significance of Class* (2005) and then towards the hermeneutics of social thought and embeddedness of social scientists, as in *Why Things Matter to People* (2011). I call this his sociological turn, which led him to highlight the importance of class relations and the way ideas and practice are woven together in social life – and in every attempt to theorise about society.

For better or worse, in the 2000s my own work on California cities, agribusiness and environmental politics had taken me far from any serious grappling with methodological foundations or class (though I had done some serious thinking about race in the meantime), so Sayer's books of that decade did not make the same impact on me as his earlier work. What brought us back together was a converging interest in the financial crisis of 2008 and the subsequent Great Recession.

Out of that economic earthquake came Sayer's *Why We Can't Afford the Rich* (2015). I immediately loved the title and the book and, most of all, the keen logic and moral fervour that infuse it. So, to round out this essay of appreciation, I want to take a closer look at this book, which I think defines man better than any other. *Why We Can't Afford the Rich* serves as a handy synthesis of Andrew Sayer's talents and career, and it highlights several qualities that distinguish him from the ordinary labourer in the vineyards of academe – as well as a couple of drawbacks of being so damned smart.

The first defining characteristic is the careful work that went into the book. All science is hard work, as Sayer has long insisted, and he is nothing if not a hard worker in the scholarly fields. Even though Andrew claimed to me that he just 'knocked it out', his most slapdash effort is still a cut above most writing by academics. He is a perfectionist, as I learned as his co-author, and would not abide any editing or revisions to his text (which is why *The New Social Economy* is two half-books joined at the hip).

One has to admit, however, that the precision and density of Andrew's mode of argumentation – leaving no stone unturned, no claptrap untapped and no bull unshat – makes the book tougher going for the average reader than it might otherwise be. I say this because the same problem haunts my own books, which I aim at the intelligent layperson but which regularly miss the mark by trying to pack in too much content (e.g. Walker 2018).

The second defining characteristic of *Why We Can't Afford the Rich* is the rigorous logic involved, particularly in dismantling every bogus argument in favour of unearned enrichment in the first half of the book. This volume is, in one sense, the economic companion to *The Moral Significance of Class*, carefully dissecting the origins of wealth and the (il)logic of the ideology of the deserving rich. I am sure that Sayer had in mind Adam Smith's unity of political economy and moral economy, which is rent asunder by mainstream economics' adoration of *The Wealth of Nations* and neglect of *The Theory of Moral Sentiments*.

The first half of *Why We Can't Afford the Rich* (Parts 1 and 2) is a model of ideology critique. Sayer takes on each of the major modes of surplus extraction – rent, interest, profit and speculation (especially in asset inflation) – and shows how they operate and why they all boil down to the exploitation of productive work and workers. He skewers all popular defences of these unearned incomes, whether rent from land, celebrity or innovation, interest as reward for risk, abstinence or money-creation, or profit as payment for non-productive investment, entrepreneurship or shareholding. Speculation in the stock market casino and the rich as job-creators are equally non-starters.

In Part 2, he queries the slippery relation of work and reward among those who are part of the productive labour force, showing that contribution and income are never related in the direct way liberal (and libertarian) theory proposes. All reward rests on 'the commons', whether temporal, spatial or natural, which determines the productivity of social labour and which no one person creates. Within that collective division of labour, individual pay diverges according to scarcity and monopoly positions in the labour market, worsened by all the well-known discriminations of race, gender and origin. Finally, high-wage (and salary) workers are almost all favoured by the advantages provided by class and family origins.

The third key reveal of *Why We Can't Afford the Rich* is the moral axis of Sayer's life and work, in a double sense. On the one hand, he is a student of what can be called 'moral economy' and the way the mechanical workings of economics must be interlaced with the human significance of how economies (as in *Why Things Matter to People*) and the way economies are socially organised and controlled by the powerful (*The Moral Significance of Class*).

That is why, for example, he is a great admirer of research into the link between inequality and social pathologies, as in the work of Richard Wilkinson (who wrote the Foreword to the book, *Why We Can't Afford the Rich*). Inequality literally makes us sick.

On the other hand, gross inequality poses a moral dilemma for the social order and is, for Andrew, personally intolerable. This moral stance is a thread that runs through Sayer's entire corpus of writings. It appears not just as a judgment against the rich and class society, but as an internal compass that guides his passion for hard work, teaching and the truth. Recall that Sayer taught us long ago that the pretence of neutrality is no defence for bad science and commitment to belief is no barrier to good research and uncovering the truth. *Why We Can't Afford the Rich* is a testament to the latter.

A fourth defining element of *Why We Can't Afford the Rich* is the return of Sayer's commitment to political economy that appears in the second half of the book (Parts 3 and 4). Part 3, on how the rich contributed to the crisis of 2008, is clearly a response to the scandal of the financial bubble and Great Recession, with its devastation of the working class across Europe and North America. Because he never stopped being a political economist or a wide-ranging scholar tracking developments in capitalism, Sayer could readily conjure up a succinct overview of what had happened and why it was linked to the financialisation and bloated wealth that preceded it – the return of the rentier, as he puts it.

That analysis grows logically from what was said in the first half of the book about the mounting enrichment of the upper classes and the way financialisation has undermined the beneficial side of capitalism's drive to raise productivity and deliver the goods. Sayer was hardly alone in rising to the opportunity to teach his readers the moral economic lessons of the great meltdown of the 2000s. Many economists felt the same need to speak out and write at that time, generating a flurry of good books and a clear shift to the left and revival of classical political economic themes like value, crisis, rent and the state (e.g. Bardhan & Walker 2011).

Yet, one ends up feeling that Sayer tried to do too much. *Why We Can't Afford the Rich* is two books in one: a dissection of the rich and their ideological defences versus a political economy of how the rich distort and control the capitalist system. It's not that Sayer's analysis of the origins of the crisis in enrichment in Part 3 is not good, but it came too late to add much to other Left critiques issuing from that crisis. Much the same can be said of Part 4 on the politics of class power and the gnawing corruption inherent in the massive parasitism of our times. Its main themes have been worked over many times by Left commentators opposed to the neoliberal and proto-fascist regimes of our times.

Sayer would have done better to split the book in two and develop the second half more fully in a separate text. Indeed, the arguments of the second half seem a bit sketchy compared to the more thorough dismantling of upper-class defences in the first half. The take-down of philanthropy would do better back in Part 1, in any case.

Now, I say this not to prove my superior wisdom but to commiserate with Andrew. My last book suffered from the same mistake of trying to cram everything I know about the San Francisco Bay Area into one 500-page brick. As a result, sales sank rather quickly under its own weight. The lesson is that those of us who wish to address the broader public in an accessible way and yet do so with careful arguments and extensive evidence simply have to keep our volumes slimmer.

Not to end on that dissonant note, I want to return to the consistent themes that provide the harmonious counterpoints weaving through all of Sayer's marvellous work. The fifth and most telling theme is the persistent radicalism of Sayer's positions on every subject. This may seem an exaggeration driven by my own desire to promote a fellow leftist, but there is more to it.

Yes, the foundational argument of *Why We Can't Afford the Rich* is that national (or global) output is the result of the collective work of the millions who toil to produce the goods and services that we all live on and the rich, whether capitalist or otherwise, live off the workers by siphoning a share of that total income into their bank accounts as rent, interest, profit and speculative gains. This is a straightforward theory of class and exploitation that could be presented as Marxist without anyone batting an eye.

Yet, Sayer is careful not to make such a claim, even as he cites Marx several times. Nor does he use the term surplus (which doesn't even appear in the index) or, even more, put the matter in the contentious form of value and surplus value. That is quite intentional, as I know from conversations we had in another century about whether it was important or useful to flag our radical positions with terms like 'Marxism' or not. I thought it was and have banged away on value theory, surplus value, capitalism and the great Marx ever since. Andrew was clear that it was not, and it is clear that he expects the truth of the matter to carry the day under any label.

My point about Sayer's consistently radical stance, however, goes beyond the idea of economic exploitation and the mechanics of capitalism. It is there in his philosophy of science, which is not simply 'realist' but 'critical' and based on a profound commitment to truth-seeking and, along with it, a belief in progress in scientific knowledge of the world and social improvement through social science. His radicalism is equally at work in his take on the hermeneutics of social life in which all social thought and practice are inextricably tied to ethics, and therefore every social theorist or political actor is a moral being and either working to better the human condition or not. And, of course, Sayer's radicalism has always been there in his unfailing support of progressive politics.

Finally, Andrew's persistent radicalism as a human being has always shone through in his personal life, as one of the kindest, most decent people one might hope to find. He truly believes in the Aristotlean goal of 'flourishing', which applies both to the individual and to the collective. That is radically uncommon and a blessing to those of us fortunate enough to be counted among his students, colleagues and friends.

References

Bardhan, A., & Walker, R. (2011). California Shrugged: The Fountainhead of the Great Recession. *Cambridge Journal of Regions, Economy and Society* 4(3): 303–22.

Walker, R. (1995). California Rages against the Dying of the Light. *New Left Review* 209: 42–74.

Walker, R. (2001). California's Golden Road to Riches: Natural Resources and Regional Capitalism, 1848–1940. *Annals of the Association of American Geographers* 91(1): 167–99.

Walker, R. (2004). *The Conquest of Bread: 150 Years of California Agribusiness.* New York: The New Press.

Walker, R. (2018). *Pictures of a Gone City: Tech and the Dark Side of Prosperity in the San Francisco Bay Area.* Oakland: PM Press.

Part IV

Social Theory, Normativity and Class

Chapter 13

A Social Scientist for Our Times

Unravelling the Moral Morass of Class, Wealth, Profit and Oppression

Diane Reay

Introduction

When Andrew Sayer wrote *The Moral Significance of Class* in 2005 and *Why We Can't Afford the Rich* ten years later in 2015, he could not have predicted how prescient both texts would turn out to be in our new coronavirus times. The role of the rich in wealth extraction, the main preoccupation of *Why We Can't Afford the Rich* has become even more troubling and unsupportable over the period of the pandemic. Equally, the ways UK society does, or rather does not, deal with the growth in class inequalities, a central concern of *The Moral Significance of Class*, has resulted in a fractured and increasingly divided society where people have either become inured to class inequalities or feel powerless in the face of them. This chapter will take both texts as guiding analytic lenses in order to develop two case studies. In the first section of the chapter, I will draw on insights from *Why We Can't Afford the Rich* to examine the current conservative government's wealth extraction from the welfare state as an example of political corruption, cronyism and profiteering, mapping the duplicity and venality of Boris Johnson's government, and its obsession with augmenting the wealth of the already wealthy. Focussing on processes of wealth extraction (Sayer 2015: 31) among politicians and their social circle, it compiles a dossier of the myriad forms of profiteering and privatisation our current government is engaged in. In the second section of the chapter, I develop a case study of educational inequality which foregrounds the moral dimensions of class Sayer so perceptively developed in *The Moral Significance of Class* to examine both class contempt and class shame as structural effects of our increasingly unequal society. In the spirit of Andrew Sayer's work on inequalities, this chapter not only engages with emotions as a subject area but is underpinned by emotions, in particular, the 'righteous indignation' that accompanies a sense of injustice (Sayer 2005: 150).

DOI: 10.4324/9781003247326-18

Wealth Extraction and the Destruction of the Welfare State

Andrew Sayer writes at the beginning of *Why We Can't Afford the Rich* that his intention is to provoke a critical examination of the rich (page 9). When Sayer wrote *Why We Can't Afford the Rich* in 2015, there were 104 billionaires in Britain. In 2019, that number had risen to 151 (Times Rich List 2019). While members of our current government are not billionaires, cabinet ministers are extremely rich. Estimates put the prime minister's net wealth at over 3 million, but compared with his cabinet peers his wealth is relatively modest. Grant Shapps boasted his riches were so large it afforded him the luxury of having a private plane, a six-bedroom mansion and a car decked out with 'every refinement you could imagine'. He is reputed to have boasted: I'm so rich my car even has a fridge in it. Jacob Rees-Mogg's net worth *is estimated* to be over £150 million, while Rushi Sunak, the chancellor, is thought to be the richest sitting MP with a net worth estimated to be around £200m. And over their time in government, they are set to become even richer as the wealthy profit from a current economic crisis exacerbated by the pandemic. According to Forbes (2020), the value of the fortunes of the 53 UK billionaires, they surveyed, leapt by 14.3% (£26.3 billion) to approximately £211 billion over the first six months of 2020. For example, Richard Branson, despite calling for a bailout of his airline and others, saw his net worth grow by £3.3 billion due to the rising value of shares in Virgin Galactic. Brexiteer boss of the Ineos chemicals group Jim Ratcliffe saw his fortune increase by half to £13.6 billion after converting part of his business to produce hand sanitiser, while Mike Ashley, the boss of Sports Direct, saw his fortune increase by 22.3% to £2.5 billion. In 2021, we can afford the rich even less than we could in 2015.

One of the many lessons we learn from *Why We Can't Afford the Rich* is to question taken-for-granted terminology. Sayer demonstrates how misleading regularly accepted terms such as wealth creation and philanthropy are. Rather, the book convincingly illustrates how the wealthy increasingly extract rather than earn or create their wealth. The slipperiness of terms like the investment is revealed with Sayer arguing that investment is more often a form of gambling with other people's money. Sayer's analysis distinguishes between contributing to the creation of something useful and just getting a return no matter what. The lack of moral assessments of financial practices has resulted in questionable activities of 'asset stripping and speculation' being viewed simply as an investment (Sayer 2015: 36). But as Sayer reflexively asserts, it is not enough to just find out how rich the rich are or to describe how they get their money and spend it. Rather, we need to question the legitimacy of their wealth and interrogate their claims of wealth creation.

One of the many claims of the Johnson conservative government is that a primary objective is wealth creation. Boris Johnson (2015) actually argued in March 2015, when he was Mayor of London, that wealth creation has a moral purpose, arguing that it resulted in the reduction of poverty and inequality. More recently, he promised a process of levelling up across UK society:

> We will double down on levelling up, and when I say level up, I don't mean attacking our great companies or impeding the success of London – far from it – or launching some punitive raid on the wealth creators.
>
> (Johnson 2020)

When Boris Johnson says 'level up' he doesn't mean challenging privilege, wealth and power in society. Unlike other European countries, the government's COVID-19 strategy was to support employers, not workers. The government directly sustained businesses with 50 billion in state-backed coronavirus loans but without any conditions in regard to saving jobs. Rather, the plutocracy Sayer wrote so cogently about in *Why We Can't Afford the Rich* became even more entrenched as a result of the government's response to COVID-19. As Saad-Filho (2020: 478) argues, faced with the calamity of COVID-19 'that could not be resolved with bribes or by blockading, sanctioning or bombing a distant land, the governments of the wealthiest countries in the world did not know what to do. Unsurprisingly, the UK and US governments fared especially badly'. In the UK, as well as the US, policies were directed at protecting the profits of the rich and powerful at the expense of the health and well-being of the majority. We increasingly saw 'the infiltration and capture of the state by the rich' (Sayer 2015: 239). The government's response to the COVID-19 crisis was to set up a supply chain comprising multiple layers of private-sector profit making, siphoning money that would normally be spent through public sector institutions to private companies including Movianto, Serco, Randox, Deloitte, G4S, Sodexo and Sitel. Throughout the first year of the coronavirus pandemic, we witnessed a rapacious private sector that combined incompetence with greed. Deloitte's contract for COVID-19 testing, Serco's commission to operate 'test and trace' and Chartwell's contract to deliver food to children in low-income households are the most notable examples but there are many more.

The result has been millions of taxpayers' money handed out in contracts for friends, family members and private donors without due process, proper tendering, transparency and accountability. To take one example, that of Deloitte the global accountancy firm, Sayer (2015: 249) describes the insidious influence of Deloitte on the Tory government in 2009, and the 'free' advice they were providing to MPs, ministers and government departments. Fast forward 12 years and Deloitte is still supplying services to a Tory government but this time at enormous profit. In what has been called 'potentially the biggest NHS privatisation in history' (Clive Lewis MP in Ramsay & Thevoz 2020), Deloitte has been handed most of the work (and money) involved in running Operation Moonshot, the 100 billion pound scheme for all 68 million people in the UK to be tested weekly (Iacobucci & Coombes 2020).

Deloitte is just one cog in the government's privatisation bandwagon. A total lack of moral compass and an ideological fanaticism pervades the entire policy of dealing with procurement in the coronavirus pandemic. During the first six months of the pandemic, the government paid out 10.5 billion in contracts, completely bypassing any legitimate tendering process and with a special priority channel for bids that were sponsored by MPs or ministers (NAO 2020a). Equally concerning, a substantial proportion of that money has been paid out to private companies with no experience or expertise in the health field. A total of 450 million was paid to the subsidiary of an interior design firm for the supply of personal protective equipment (PPE). Another firm commissioned to supply PPE outfits is a small digital marketing agency in Hammersmith (Bright 2020: 3). Cronyism is endemic, as companies with connections to Tory MPs and ministers have acquired a significant number of contracts. Contracts awarded to conservative insiders include those given to a co-author of the 2019 conservative manifesto and the company that ran the conservatives' social media operation during the 2019 general election. In the government's response to COVID-19, we have seen flagrant looting of the state and public sector, diverting money to friends and funders of the conservative party. Jolyon Maugham, the human rights lawyer, has stated that he is aware of six, but that there are almost certainly many more contracts awarded without tender to long-time associates of Dominic Cummings, Boris Johnson's ex-chief political advisor. As I write this, a further contract is being negotiated with a pharmaceutical firm that employs Boris Johnson's stepbrother. As *The BMJ* concluded, 'sensationalist schemes that are based on rough and ready science, contracted out to opportunistic companies, and funded by vast amounts of taxpayers' money risk diverting us from the direct challenges of keeping a persistent and damaging pandemic under control' (Abbasi 2020). For the neoliberal right, the pandemic has become yet another opportunity for profit, as outsourcing to corporate giants accelerates.

Writing about the financial sector, Sayer described it as 'male-dominated, macho and mean' (Sayer 2015: 274), but now we have a government that is equally male-dominated, macho and mean. The UK is already the money-laundering capital of the world (Burgis 2020); it is now competing for the title 'the most corrupt nation on earth'. When journalist Roberto Saviano (2016) first claimed the UK was the world's most corrupt nation, he singled out financial capital and not politics as the reason for his judgement. Four years later, our politics are just as tainted as our financial services industry. 2020 has been a year of U-turns, failures, dodgy deals and violations by the conservative government. However, far from being seen as the dereliction of state duty that they are, the government's abuses of power are increasingly seen 'as a jubilant establishment of a system in which there is indulgent impunity for some and merciless persecution for others' (Malik 2020: 3).

One of the key lessons of *Why We Can't Afford the Rich* is the need for a forensic excavation of the hidden abuses of power by the rich, the practices too often concealed behind mindless rhetoric and lies. In the early 2010s, 22% of money spent on management consultants in UK was paid by the public sector (FEACO 2015), since then public sector management consulting has continued to rise. In 2017–2018 *NHS* England *spent* almost 50% more on external consultancy than in 2016–2017. Brexit and COVID-19 have seen a further exponential rise. Deloitte was paid fees of 147 million from public funds for consultancy in 2019–2020 compared with 40 million two years earlier (Syal 2020). As Brooks (2020) points out, 'Contracts for managing the procurement of ventilators, PPE, and even the job of keeping tabs on all these contracts have been awarded to battalions of management consultants for hundreds of millions of pounds'. Such spending constitutes a hidden form of privatisation the general public is unaware of, but it is also yet another form for profiteering and enriching the already rich, despite bringing little in terms of improvements and efficiency gains to the public sector (Kirkpatrick et al. 2019). Consultancy websites list a range of profit margins. According to the *Consulting Fees Study 2019*, 28% of consultants enjoy an 80%+ profit margin and 17% have a 70%+ profit margin (Zipursky 2020) while The Ultimate Guide to Profit Margins for Consulting Services (Eaton 2019) works with an average of 40% across the industry. But whether we are talking of 80% or 40%, profit margins are excessive and an indication of the greed and rapacity of a sector enriching itself by selling advice to the public sector that 'is not associated with any improvements in efficiency' (Kirkpatrick et al. 2019: 90). The prescience of their words was particularly evident in the revelation in October 2020 that fees of £6,250 a day had been paid over the previous months to management consultants from the American firm, Boston Consulting Group, for failing to make the UK test and trace system more efficient (Jolly & Syal 2020). By the end of November 2,300 private-sector consultants were working on the 'Test and Trace' programme – a figure that rivals a medium-sized Whitehall department, yet a National Audit Office report (NAO 2020b) found that, by June, call handler staff working on track and trace had only been occupied for 1% of their contracted paid hours (Bright 2021).

A further key concern of *Why We Can't Afford the Rich* is global warming and carbon dioxide emissions. Sayer shows how the over consumption of the rich, along with their investment in fossil fuels, and preoccupation with growth, is destroying the planet. In the book, he combines a trenchant critique of the rich with an equally incisive green critique of capitalism demonstrating how the two are integral components of the same looming crisis. Here again, his arguments are prescient. The most recent research reveals that between 1990 and 2015, the wealthiest 1% of the world's population were responsible for the emission of more than twice as much carbon dioxide as the poorer half of the world's population. The consumption of the richest 1% caused 15% of emissions during this time – more than all the citizens of the EU and more than twice that of the 7% emitted by the poorest half of the world's population (Oxfam 2020). *Why We Can't Afford the Rich* ends with the powerful statement:

> We truly cannot afford the rich and the systems that support them. They are living beyond our means and those of the planet, and their interests are at odds with those of the 99% and the environment. We must stop supporting them.
>
> (Sayer 2015: 366)

In 2021, it is even more urgent to prevent the avarice and venality of the rich and their despoliation of our welfare state and beyond that, the planet.

The Emotional Violence of Class Inequalities in English Education

The story of class inequalities is another moral tale, less dramatic and more poignant than that of the corrupted and compromised values of the rich and powerful. It tells a very different story to that of the wealthy. In place of greed, corruption and elitism are shame, humiliation, despair and powerlessness. It speaks of exploitation and oppression and the wilful neglect of the potential of huge swathes of English society. Just as the corrupt cronyism of the right-wing affluent elite is a scandal, so too is disregard and contempt of the working classes.

In *The Moral Significance of Class* Sayer refines Nancy Fraser's conception of recognition to focus specifically on class-based understandings of recognition and misrecognition, accentuating their relationship to subjective experiences of class. He states that:

> The kind of recognition we shall be concerned with has a necessary psychological dimension that is sometimes overlooked in discussion of recognition in relation to identity … The vulnerability of individuals consists in their dependence on others not only for material support but for ongoing recognition, respect, approval and trust.
>
> (Sayer 2005: 54)

He goes on to argue that a lack of such acknowledgement from others can cause 'severe distress, shame and self-contempt' (Sayer 2005: 54). But for Sayer, it is crucial to stress that recognition and redistribution are inextricably intertwined. Recognition is materialised in the distribution of material goods.

Throughout *The Moral Significance of Class*, Sayer makes a convincing case for the need for a strong moral compass in relation to class and its myriad, largely unacknowledged discriminations. But also significant is the centrality given to emotions and the recognition that 'inequality and symbolic domination are experienced primarily emotionally' (Sayer 2005: 133). In my own work with working-class parents and children, many emotions were expressed when they talked about their own or family members' experiences of schooling, but perhaps the most prevalent emotion was that of shame (Reay 2017). As Sayer (2005: 154) asserts, 'the shaming of those who fail educationally is a structurally generated effect, even though it is felt as an individual failure'. England's obsession with meritocracy and social mobility has masked deepening economic inequalities and their power to shape educational achievement. Instead, we have become the aspiration nation (Collini 2010) in which the prevalent belief is that anyone with enough determination, hard work and talent can be whatever they want to be. As a consequence, the working classes have become the outcasts in this English aspiration dream story and, as such, are disregarded and often treated with contempt by the more privileged in society.

Nowhere is this contempt more explicit than in the regulations, rankings and assessments that permeate our educational system, sorting out the winners from the losers. Boris Johnson endorsed this sifting process in a speech where he argued 'The harder you shake the pack the easier it will be for some cornflakes to get to the top'. This is a brutal form of meritocracy which sees the majority as an undifferentiated mass who will inevitably struggle in life because they lack the intelligence of those who are successful and rise to the top. The focus on intrinsic worth – intelligence, talent and effort – ignores the biggest influence on who becomes successful, the wealth and power of parents (Brown 1990). Johnson's words are a vivid example of the elitism, competitiveness and class superiority that drives policy in our state educational system. But when reading through the insights of *The Moral Significance of Class* our attention is directed beyond policy implications to consider the emotional consequences for those most affected. Yet, the impact on the self-worth and feelings of the working-class children placed in bottom sets is an issue that is worryingly overlooked when policies of setting and streaming are evaluated. In the next section, I focus on the emotional consequences and moral bankruptcy of contemporary policies of ranking and rating in English education.

An Abnegation of Moral as well as Educational Responsibility?: Bottom Set Children

In my own research (Reay 2017), shame and abjection suffused the accounts of working-class children relegated to the bottom sets.

SATVINDER: Right now, because I'm in the bottom set for everything I don't like it, because I'm only doing the foundation paper, and I don't ... I really don't want to do that. Because from Year 6 when I left I went I'm going to put my head down, and do my work, but I never did. And then it ... like, every year I say it, but I never do it. […] I haven't even done it this year either. [...] Yeah, I could have, like, gone to a better higher place, and then I could have done everything I was hoping to.

DIANE: And now?

SATVINDER: There is no hope.

ATIK: I think I failed proper badly in the tests and that's why I'm in a proper bad set now ... I can just answer the questions really easy because there's like no really smart people and they behave quite bad as well and they influence me ... So I've just become rubbish.

JOE: The behaviour's bad. You don't learn unless you're in the first set.

SHULAH: The behaviour, it gets worse in the bottom set when like teachers don't pay attention to you. And they pay attention to like the higher ability students and like you get bored because there's nothing for you to do if you don't understand the work.

In all three quotes, low sets are clearly perceived to be places of educational failure and despair, where children are written off and have no hope of succeeding. Here we see how destructive the educational system is for those who struggle, swallowed up in a remorseless system of hierarchical ranking and a competitive counting culture. We can see the consequences for many working-class children in Jason's poignant advocacy for children like himself:

> Some kids they just can't do it, like they find the work too hard, or they can't concentrate because too much is going on for them. Then they are put like as rubbish learners and put in the bottom set, and no one cares about them even though they are the ones who need the most help. They should be getting the most help.

This is the sorry outcome of the corrupted values of those with power and wealth in English society – the discarding of those with little power and resources as educational waste – the cornflakes at the bottom of the packet.

Class Contempt and Moral Dereliction

The Moral Significance of Class discusses class contempt in detail, arguing that it results in double standards whereby the same behaviour of people from different class backgrounds is evaluated differently, judgements are made that are strongly class-biased. Throughout *The Moral Significance of Class*, Sayer draws on the work of Adam Smith, and especially his seminal text 'The Theory of Moral Sentiments' demonstrating the contemporary relevance of his insight that:

> This **disposition** to admire, and almost to worship, the rich and the powerful, and to despise, or, at least, to neglect persons of poor and mean condition, though necessary both to establish and to maintain the

distinction of ranks and the order of society, is, at the same time, the great
and most universal cause of the corruption of our moral sentiments.

(Smith 1759: 61; emphasis added)

Slights, dismissals and rejections are inevitable consequences of a pervasive
upper- and middle-class sense of social, moral and intellectual superiority.
Throughout my 25 years of research, there have been telling examples of
upper- and middle-class contempt, with both parents and their children talking
dismissively about both the stupidity and the bad behaviour of working-class
children and young people when it was clear working-class children did not
attend their elite schools or were part of their social networks. Even when
middle-class parents sent their children to the same schools as the working
classes (Reay et al. 2011), often in place of an empathetic understanding was
the feeling that the working classes were a problem to be dealt with. Joan, a
parent living in the North East, expressed condescension laced with distaste
and pity:

> I go into school frequently as a governor and I see horrendous children,
> children that you think what is going to happen to them? Where are they
> going to go? And my poor children who are really nice have to be in
> amongst them.

The key distinction here is between 'nice' middle-class children and 'horren-
dous' working-class ones. Regardless of 150 years of universal state education, the working classes continue to be positioned within the educational
system as an unknowing, unreflexive, tasteless mass from which the middle-
classes draw their distinction. Even those middle classes whose children
attended socially mixed schools had complex and difficult feelings towards
their working-class other, ranging from Joan's visceral distaste to more
ambivalent but still defended responses.

The language of class superiority articulated by parents was reinforced
by what their children said. Davina, one of the white middle-class students
commented 'It's good because if you are in set one you know you are top
of the pile', while Ollie joked 'the top sets are chav free'. Ironically, given
the many fears and anxieties of their parents, the middle-class children who
remain in non-selective state secondary schools nearly all experienced a class
segregated education in the top sets. This language of 'top of the pile' clearly
indicates a sense of superiority that processes of setting and streaming build
upon and encourage. But if the middle classes are to be, in their own words
'top of the pile' and 'top of the tree academically', someone else needs to be at
the bottom. The assumption of the vast majority of the middle-class parents
is that this is perfectly natural and to be expected. But the question we all need
to ask, drawing on the insights of *The Moral Significance of Class,* is 'is this
morally acceptable?'

Conclusion

Andrew Sayer's work shines a light on the dissembling, the awkward fumbling around the edges of class, by making a convincing case for the need for a strong moral compass in relation to class and its myriad, largely unacknowledged discriminations. This chapter examined those discriminations from both a macro and a more micro perspective, focussing initially on the moral laxity and corrupted moral values of the wealthy and powerful in English society, before providing an example of the class cruelties, rejections and slights that operate at the level of school classrooms. First, it attempted to make explicit the ways in which 'economic power is also political power' (Sayer 2015: 26), by detailing the growing influence of big business on government and providing examples of the myriad ways in which private companies are asset stripping the state. Second, as *The Moral Significance of Class* illustrated so well, it reveals class to be as much about feelings and affective responses as it is about what we do. But its main objective has been to underscore the vitally important central message of both books that inequality, and its manifestation in the form of social class, is immoral and unacceptable.

References

Abbasi, K. (2020). Covid-19: Shooting for the Moon. *BMJ* 2020;370: m3509 http://dx.doi.org/10.1136/bmj.m3509

Bright, S. (2020). Government Spends £364 Million on Coveralls but Delivers Just 432,000. *Byline Times* 1 September. At: https://bylinetimes.com/2020/09/01/government-spends-364-million-on-coveralls-delivers-just-432000/

Bright, S. (2021). Government Reveals Total Number of Private Sector Consultants Working for 'Test and Trace'. *Byline Times* 5 January. At: https://bylinetimes.com/2021/01/05/government-total-number-private-sector-test-and-trace-consultants/

Brooks, R. (2020). The Failure of Test and Trace Shows the Folly of Handing Huge Contracts to Private Giants. *The Guardian* 13 October. At: www.theguardian.com/commentisfree/2020/oct/13/failure-test-trace-folly-huge-contracts-private-giants-uk

Brown, P. (1990). The 'Third Wave': Education and the Ideology of Parentocracy. *British Journal of Sociology of Education* 11(1): 65–85.

Burgis, T. (2020). *Kleptomania: How Dirty Money is Conquering the World.* London: William Collins.

Collini, S. (2010). Blahspeak. *London Review of Books* 32(7): 7–8, April: 29–34.

Eaton, T. (2019). The Ultimate Guide to Profit Margins for Consulting Services. At: www.askcody.com/blog/profit-margins-for-consulting-services

FEACO (European Federation of Management Consultancies Associations) (2015). Annual Survey. At: www.feaco.org/site-page/feaco-annual-survey-european-mc-market

Forbes (2020). *The Richest in 2020.* At: www.forbes.com/billionaires/

Iacobucci, G. & Coombes, R. (2020). Covid-19: Government Plans to Spend £100bn on Expanding Testing to 10 Million a Day. *BMJ* 2020370:m3520 http://dx.doi.org/10.1136/bmj.m3520

Jolly, J., & Syal, R. (2020). Fees of 6,250 a Day Billed by Test-and-Trace Advisors. *The Guardian* 15 October: 2.

Johnson, B. (2015). Speech to Legatum Institute. 31 March. At: www.hitc.com/en-gb/2015/03/31/labour-will-take-britain-back-to-nasty-1970s-says-boris-johnson/

Johnson, B. (2020). New Deal for Britain. 30 June. At: www.gov.uk/government/news/build-build-build-prime-minister-announces-new-deal-for-britain

Kirkpatrick, I., Sturdy, A. J, Blanco-Oliver, A. & Veronesi, G. (2019). The Impact of Management Consultants on Public Service Efficiency. *Policy & Politics* 47(1): 77–96.

Malik, N. (2020). For the Tories, Breaking the Law is Just a Sign of Strength. *The Guardian* 14 September.

NAO (National Audit Office) (2020a). *Investigation into Government Procurement During the COVID-19 Pandemic.* London: NAO.

NAO (National Audit Office) (2020b). *The Government's Approach to Test and Trace in England – Interim Report.* London: NAO.

Oxfam (2020). Confronting Carbon Inequality: Putting Climate Justice at the Heart of the COVID-19 Recovery. Oxfam Media Briefing, 21 September.

Ramsay, A., & Thevoz, S. (2020). Deloitte Gets Another Huge COVID Contract – For 'Crazy' Plan to Test Millions Each Day. *openDemocracy* 21 August. At: www.opendemocracy.net/en/dark-money-investigations/deloitte-gets-another-huge-covid-contract-for-crazy-plan-to-test-millions-each-day/

Reay, D. (2017). *Miseducation: Inequality, Education and the Working Classes.* Bristol: Policy Press.

Reay, D., Crozier, G. & James, D. (2011). *White Middle Class Identities and Urban Schooling.* Houndmills: Palgrave.

Saad-Filho, R. (2020). From COVID-19 to the End of Neoliberalism. *Critical Sociology* 46(4–5): 477–485.

Saviano, R. (2016). *Zero, Zero, Zero.* London: Penguin Books.

Sayer, A. (2005). *The Moral Significance of Class.* Cambridge: Cambridge University Press.

Sayer, A. (2015). *Why We Can't Afford the Rich.* Bristol: Policy Press.

Smith, A. (1759). *The Theory of Moral Sentiments.* Indianapolis: Liberty Fund.

Syal, R (2020). 450 Million Fees Bonanza for Whitehall Consultants. *The Guardian* 7 October: 1.

Zipursky, M. (2020). Consulting Fees Guide: How Much To Charge For Consulting (3 Formulas & Examples). At: www.consultingsuccess.com/consulting-fees

Chapter 14

The Elephant in the Room
Sayer on Social Class

Graham Scambler

Introduction

Part of the attraction to the work of colleagues is overlapping interests and outlooks. In the case of Andrew Sayer, these attractions are complemented by the sheer pleasure of reading his texts. I confess that I am most interested in *what* colleagues working in similar fields to my own have to say, not *how* they say it: for me content trumps erudition every time. But Sayer offers us the best of both worlds. The comprehensiveness, depth, delicacy and potency of his theorising are communicated in the most eloquent prose. In this brief chapter, I focus on a number of specific themes that have emerged in his writings on social class and comment and elaborate on them with reference to my own studies. Although I refer to others of his texts, I concentrate in particular on his *The Moral Significance of Class* and his more recent *Why We Can't Afford the Rich*.

The themes I have selected can be broached with certain preliminaries in mind. The first of these celebrates Sayer's *analytic subtlety*. The critical realist frame that subtly informs his thinking and writing allows for the recognition that social phenomena are not only complex elements of an essentially open society but also products of a rich admix of different types of causes (Sayer 1992). Those of us working in the social sciences are conscious of what might be called the *Pendulum of Complexity*. On the one hand, it is part and parcel of the social scientific project to discern meaningful patterns in human practices and activities and to offer credible explanations in the form of theories for why these patterns have emerged. But on the other hand, when the pendulum swings the other way, such theories seem open to the charge that they are ill-advised simplifications of what are in fact complex, dynamic and evolving practices and activities. It is often said that sociologists sit on one side of the pendulum, historians on the other. In his discussions of social class, Sayer manages to strike an enviable balance in that his theorising on class in contemporary society reveals and offers explanations for patterns of social action *and* emphasises and does justice to the complex and shifting

DOI: 10.4324/9781003247326-19

character of human social action and interaction. He manages to retain a grip on the pendulum even as it swings first this way then that.

A second point to note at the outset is Sayer's distinction between class inequalities and those attributable to gender and race or ethnicity. While the latter is produced, he argues, primarily by sexism and racism, class differences would persist even if the upper and middle classes were entirely respectful to the working class. This is because class prejudice, or classism, is more a response to economic inequalities than a cause of them. Enduring sexism and racism on the other hand would have a major impact on gender and race relations. He continues:

> Neoliberals – New Labour for example – can appear quite progressive about gender, race, sexuality, disability and condemn those who discriminate against people on these grounds. Unsurprisingly, **the elephant in the room is economic inequalities or class difference**. Though it never admits it, neoliberalism is a political-economic movement that seeks to legitimise widening economic inequalities and defend rentier interests above all others. Rentiers can live off others regardless of their gender, race, sexuality and so on'.
>
> (Sayer 2015: 170; emphasis added)

My third preliminary remark rests on a distinction reflected in another point made by Sayer (2005: 172):

> it is not unusual for individuals, especially those with plenty of economic, cultural and social capital, to imagine that class differences can be neutralised by ignoring them and treating others as equals, as if class were purely a product of misrecognition.

At stake here is the contrast between 'identity-neutral mechanisms' and 'identity-sensitive mechanisms'. Capitalism is *not* dependent on identity, and for Sayer one of the great disappointments of recent research on inequalities has been 'a tendency to invert the former neglect of identity-sensitive, cultural influences by denying the co-presence of identity-neutral mechanisms' (Sayer 2005: 87). We must acknowledge the contingent co-presence of identity-neutral and identity-sensitive mechanisms in determining inequalities. I have made a kindred point by distinguishing between 'objective class relations', which have in my view assumed greater causal power in post-1970s financialised or rentier capitalism, and 'subjective class relations', which have diminished in salience over the same period (Scambler 2018a). In other words, class has come to exercise more influence over people's material well-being even as it has provided less fuel for the formation of their identities.

A final introductory point picks up on Sayer's (2015) assertion that we are now governed by a plutocracy in Britain, and that this is constituted by a tiny minority: that is, less than the 1% popularised by the Occupy Movement. This exactly accords with my contention, though I have used the term 'governing oligarchy' rather than plutocracy (Scambler 2018a).

A Few Theses

In discussions of the widening 'health gap' in Britain, reflected in differential morbidity and mortality rates by socio-economic group (Scambler 2012), I have presented and defended the thesis that the most powerful explanatory mechanism is the *class/command dynamic*. As Coburn (2009: 44) has rightly insisted, socio-economic groupings are a result of class forces:

> The nature of the capitalist class structure, and the outcome of class struggles, determine the extent and type of socio-economic inequalities in a given society, and the socio-economic inequalities in turn shape the pattern of health – and of health care.

My contention has been that during what Sayer calls rentier capitalism, the class/command dynamic – that is, the relations of class compared with the command relations of the state – has shifted significantly in favour of class. If as the American historian Landes (1998) has claimed, those with wealth have long been able to buy those with power; they get considerably more for their money now than they could in post-WW2 welfare state capitalism. Indeed, if Gill's (2018) research on the progressive inclusion of the corporate elite in American Presidential Cabinets is echoed in the UK, as it surely is, then the wealthy may well be personally exercising as well as buying the power to make policy in their interests.

This thesis might be captured by the formula: capital buys power to make policy conducive to its further accumulation. The more precise applicability of this formula since the 1970s has led to a substantial increase in health inequalities. These inequalities are the largely unintended consequences of decisions taken by bankers, CEOs of transnational corporations and major shareholders, constituting a hardcore of 'capital monopolists' that comprise a mere fraction of the Occupy Movement's 1%. It is these decisions, clandestine, unaccountable and motivated by material self-interest, that lie behind the decimation of trade union rights and the statutory safeguards and backstops of wage-labour, free or cheap labour via internships, zero-hours contracts under-written by tax-payer benefits, outsourcing, benefit cuts inaccurately and misleadingly portrayed as austerity measures designed to cut what is actually a growing deficit, and the closure or downgrading of final-salary pension schemes.

I have contended that the lining of the pockets of the less than 1% kills people, especially those within the bottom decile (Scambler & Scambler 2015: 342). I have postulated a series of seven *asset flows* as the means by which class relations – via the command relations of the state – impact health and longevity (i.e. constitute the media of enactment of the class/command dynamic in the domain of health). It is by restricting the flows of biological, psychological, social, cultural, spatial, symbolic and, above all, material assets, each of which is known to be salient and positive for health, that the health of people is compromised, sometimes fatally. Why 'flows'? Because people do not either 'have or not have' these assets, rather they wax and wane, varying in strength over time. Also, there can be and often there is compensation between asset flows. If someone is unexpectedly made redundant, the negative effect on that person's health via a diminished material asset flow might yet be mitigated by strong flows of biological, psychological and social assets. This is entirely consonant with the socio-epidemiological and quantitative social scientific research (although those with positivistic mindsets baulk at notions like flows because they see them as presenting measurement problems). Two further points should be noted: (i) both strong and weak flows tend to cluster, so that a weak flow of material assets tends to be accompanied by weak flows of social, cultural, spatial and symbolic assets for example; and (ii) this clustering of flows is especially significant at critical junctures in the life-course, most significantly in infancy and early childhood, with ramifications for health well into adulthood (Scambler 2018a).

It is worth adding here that the advent of COVID-19 in 2020 has predictably exacerbated class-related health inequalities (Marmot 2020). In what I have come to call the 'fractured society', extant cracks and fissures that have been increasingly visible since the 1970s have been widened by COVID-19 (Scambler 2018a, 2020a). Moreover, the enhanced susceptibility of members of BAME (black, Asian and minority ethnic) communities to COVID-19 has its genesis, it seems, in 'social determinants' and is at least in part due to class: the virus has most afflicted, and with the direst consequences, those already experiencing a clustering of weak asset flows.

A second thesis, if that is not too grandiose a term, picks up on Sayer's distinction between identity-neutral and identity-sensitive mechanisms with regard to class and his insistence on their contingent co-presence in determining inequalities. While it is true that people's (subjective) identities owe less to their (objective) class locations than hitherto, it is possible to contend that the 'postmodernisation' of identity formation over the last generation has been functional for the governing oligarchy/plutocracy. Lyotard's (1984) distinction between *grand* and *petit* narratives is useful here. The cultural shift that Lyotard alludes to arguably antedated the structural transition from welfare statist to financialised capitalism: there is no case for claiming the former to simply be the cause of the latter. However, the displacement of well-established *grand* narratives announcing alternate routes to 'progress' – capitalism versus socialism for example – so familiar since the European Enlightenment by a richer mix of *petit* narratives is of salience for class relations and class struggle.

Contemporary culture would seem to invite people to choose the self they want to be from a multiplicity of options, like a child in a sweetshop. Culture, in other words, comprises a mosaic of identities, each one part and parcel of a *petit* narrative. This amounts to a 'relativisation' of culture. There can no longer be any rationally compelling case for any particular view of self or society: the inhibiting presence of a handful of *grand* narratives has given way to a disinhibiting freedom of choice of *petit* narratives. I have likened this disinhibition to that following the consumption of much alcohol. It is wrong to regard it as emancipatory in any meaningful sense. There are several important points to be made here. The first is that there has indeed been real change that can be appropriately cast in terms of a postmodernisation or relativisation of culture. The second is this does not mean that sociology must itself tread in the footsteps of these processes. As Habermas (1987) insists, there is an evident 'performative contradiction' in affirming and celebrating cultural relativism since this very affirmation pleads to escape the processes it celebrates. Habermas (1984, 1987) argues for an Enlightenment-based but *reconstructed* 'project of modernity', and I have posited this as an epistemological starting point for the contemporary sociological project (Scambler 1996).

A third point, which is particularly germane to the present discussion, is that it is not necessary to claim that Britain's class-driven governing oligarchy purposefully introduced or promoted a cultural reorientation in order to argue that it is nevertheless 'fit for their purposes'. This is Habermas' (1989) point about what he calls 'the new conservatism'. A postmodern or relativised culture as I have described it rules out of court, or at least undermines, any attempt to venture a rationally compelling representation of, or alternative to, the status quo. Sociologists, as already intimated, must hold their nerve and resist being seduced into going with the relativistic flow. The passing of postmodernism as an intellectual fashion does not mean this threat has altogether diminished.

My fourth and final thesis returns to the issue of gender and race. While I share Sayers' differentiation between class on the one hand and gender and race on the other, there is no disputing the fact that capitalism was from its onset in Europe in the long 16th century both gendered and racialised. From the very moment of their formation, classes and class divisions and conflicts ran on pre-established gendered and racialised tracks. This is the essence of the growing insistence on intersectional thought and research. Gender and racial relations and differences do not reduce to those of class; on the contrary, they might be said to be *intrinsic to them*. Feminist and post-colonial thinkers have fought for and won this argument.

In an earlier text on the sociology of sport, I experimented with what I called the 'jigsaw model' (Scambler 2005: 168–169). There were three aspects: a 'best guess', which is an *overall picture* of the dynamic complex and highly differentiated world we inhabit; a series of models, articulated in terms of *logics, relations* and *figurations*; and a process of *dialectical reasoning* by means of which the sense of the overall picture informs the applications of models and the application of models informs the overall picture. For example, the logic of 'capital accumulation' is associated with relations of class, and the logic of 'the mode of regulation' is associated with relations of state or command. The class/command dynamic cited earlier applied these logics and relations to the context or figuration of the nation state. There are of course many other models, including, as I then described them, the logic of 'patriarchy' and its relations of gender, and the logic of 'tribalism' and its relations of race or ethnicity. I stressed that the same figuration, be it the nation state, a discrete community, neighbourhood or street, or an individual household, could and should be profitably revisited under the aegis of several different models. Thus in one figuration, relations of class might prevail, in another those of gender and in another those of race. Independent of its merits and limitations, the heuristic or device of the jigsaw model makes my point. Empirical enquiry shows that in many figurations multiple logics and relations are simultaneously at play, some dominant, others derivative or subsidiary, some active, others passive, a fact that a critical realist perspective accommodates very well.

These theses coalesce in many ways in the 'fractured society', which features the following sets of characteristics.

> *Environmental Threat*: we have, as the planet's most incendiary species, now penetrated what for the bulk of our history was regarded as a natural and impenetrable environmental 'given'. Human nature too is being prised open. Beck's 'risk society' (1992), plus its 'boomerang effect', is with us.
>
> *The Nomadic Proletariat*: the rate of migration, variously occasioned by war, persecution, poverty, unemployment and wanting to be with kin, is extremely high. A staggering one in 110 people worldwide are presently 'displaced' and many are seeking safe-havens.
>
> *The New Inequality*: high levels of wealth and income inequality or their equivalents have been omnipresent through history, the post-WW2 era of western welfare state capitalism being something of an exception. However, since the mid-1970s, inequality has grown substantially. The UK now has its 'super rich'. While they and their professional and managerial allies have fared well, the middle classes have been squeezed and the working classes have generally experienced a decline, sometimes precipitous, in living standards and well-being.
>
> *Class and Precarity*: the increasingly transnational 'capital executive', of which the capital monopolists constitute a hardcore, is a product of

reinvigorated objective relations of class, and privileges capital accumulation above all else. Standing (2011) is right to emphasise widespread 'precarity', which captures the new insecurity around jobs and wages, but it is wrong to consider the 'precariat' as a class in or for itself.

Post-national 'Othering': nation states and political power elites remain vital global players, but included in their arsenal now are options for the expedient, 'populist' othering of vulnerable segments of populations, most obviously the racial othering of migrants, but extending to the long-term sick and disabled and those in need of benefits.

Gender Dissolution: capitalism has been gendered and racialised from the outset, and emergent relations of class utilised and exploited those of gender and race. Financial capitalism has experienced a 'feminisation of poverty'; and in the UK a cultural and right-based challenge to long-standing gender (and sexual) binaries has occurred under the rubric of the fourth wave of feminism. This has divided and fragmented the women's movement.

Cultural Disorientation: like agency, culture is structured without being structurally determined. Its postmodernisation or relativisation has led to a deconstruction of the established Enlightenment agenda for 'progress towards a good society': a delegitimation of compelling narratives, an era of post-truth in which issues of truth and falsity have become matters of the power to persuade, a disorientation of electorates and a search for new certainties or 'fundamentalisms'.

Disconnected Fatalism: some people in financial capitalism have fallen beyond disorientation to feelings of abandonment, bitterness and hopeless. This disconnected fatalism is class-related but cuts across all classes. The Brexit phenomenon was in part a quasi-fundamentalist reaction to disconnected fatalism.

It has already been intimated that the class/command dynamic is a pivotal mechanisms for describing and explaining the transition from welfare statist to financialised or rentier capitalism, but it is of course one among many pertinent structural and cultural mechanisms. In *A Sociology of Shame and Blame: Insiders versus Outsiders* three other significant mechanisms are outlined (Scambler 2020b).

Stigma/Deviance Dynamic: stigma or infringements against norms of 'shame' is being *weaponised* in financial capitalism by the appending of 'deviance', or infringements against norms of 'blame': people are being held culpable for non-conformity to norms of shame. This is being exploited as a political strategy to minimise public sympathy for those exposed to welfare cuts under the UK austerity programme (Scambler 2018b).

Insider/Outsider Dynamic: the insider–outsider binary is omnipresent, but financial capitalism has witnessed its overt racialisation, which has fuelled support for alt-right and proto-fascist populist politics (Scambler 2020c). This dynamic has also skewed the command relations of the state, leading to former UK Prime Minister May's 'hostile environment' policy, the Windrush scandal and continuing, crude othering of migrants and refugees.

Party/Populist Dynamic: there is a new fluidity and unpredictability to conventional party political politics in financial capitalism. The UK's 'first past the post' two-party politics is under challenge. As Fraser (2019) notes, the 'hegemonic bloc' of progressive neoliberalism is under threat: waiting in the wings are, on the one hand, 'reactionary populism', and on the other, 'progressive populism'.

There exists a strand in sociology which insists that the days of capitalism are numbered, that the fractured society represents its end-stage (Wallerstein et al. 2013; Streeck 2016). This may be, but sociologists should exercise caution. I have considered four *possible* scenarios, given the present state of affairs.

1   *Statist Authoritarianism*: this most closely approximates a return to the status quo. It anticipates a degree of state repression to this end, with further curtailments of democratic processes and a second bout of political austerity to claw back COVID-related expenditures via a new programme of public expenditure and welfare cuts, skewed to hit the many rather than the few, together with a further tranche of privatisations.

2   *Proto-fascistic Populism*: this signals a break with conventional parliamentary politics in the wake of a COVID-precipitated crisis of capitalism and subsequent populist demand for transformative change. Twinned with Brexit, it would likely feature a platform of economic and cultural nationalism/isolationism in an England-based identity politics of white supremacism.

3   *Statist Paternalism*: this scenario sees the electoral displacement of the conservatives by a centrist labour administration or coalition committed to an ameliorated form of neoliberalism. It might be characterised as neo-Thatcherite but is further removed from the post-WW2 era of welfare statism than its predecessors. Its commitment is to piecemeal social engineering.

4   *Radical Left Populism*: this is also emergent from populist demand following a COVID-generated crisis of state legitimation and of capitalism itself. This time it heralds a regime committed to a radically transformative manifesto oriented to left-progressive change and a reformed or post-parliamentary system of democratic politics.

At the time of writing the first scenario seems most likely, indeed underway.

Revisiting Sayer

The theses outlined here are, I believe, consonant with Sayer's writings, not least in their exploration of the continuing salience of social class. They define class as a social structure or set of relations that, as a generative mechanism, has causal power. This can be supported empirically via quantitative and qualitative/ethnographic examinations of events using what critical realists term retroduction and abduction, respectively. Expressed differently, for material, social and, in their wake, health inequalities to expand as rapidly as they have following the welfare statist era, itself an exceptional or 'stalled' phase in the unfolding of capitalism, the class/command dynamic *must exist and have become more potent causally during financialised or rentier capitalism.* That this is critical for the fracturing of society is I think more than plausible, for all this is but one part of a large and complex jigsaw puzzle.

I hope that in this short piece, I have managed both to celebrate and to build upon Sayer's analysis of class without doing it too much injustice, though I am conscious that I have in the process made some bold claims. In conclusion, I want to insist that Sayer's writings provide a special resource for social theorists and empirical researchers alike. They are detailed and nuanced, but they also take us on a full journey from Archer's (2003) 'internal conversations' that donate past, present and future to our thinking as individual actors; to the everyday decision making of mundane lifeworld activities; to the cultural and subcultural recipes available to us; to the social institutions that both enable and constrain; to the deeply entrenched social structures – like class, gender and race/ethnicity – that underpin and inform social actors and action at the macro-level. In other words, a journey from *Why Things Matter to People* (Sayer 2011) to *Why We Can't Afford the Rich.*

References

Archer, M. (2003). *Structure, Agency and the Internal Conversation*. Cambridge: Cambridge University Press.

Beck, U. (1992). *Risk Society*. London: Sage.

Coburn, D. (2009). Inequality and Health. In L. Panitch & C. Leys (eds), *Morbid Symptoms: Health Under Capitalism*. Pontypool, UK: Merlin Press.

Fraser, N. (2019). *The Old is Dying and the New Cannot Be Born*. London: Verso.

Gill, T. (2018). The Persistence of the Power Elite: Presidential Cabinets and Corporate Interlocks, 1968–2018. *Social Currents* 5(6): 501–511.

Habermas, J. (1984). *Theory of Communicative Action, Volume One: Reason and the Rationalization of Society*. London: Heinemann.

Habermas, J. (1987). *Theory of Communicative Action, Volume Two: Lifeworld and System: A Critique of Functionalist Reason*. Cambridge: Polity Press.

Habermas, J. (1989). *The New Conservatism*. Cambridge: Polity Press.

Landes, D. (1998). *Wealth and Poverty of Nations*. London: Little, Brown & Co.

Lyotard, J-F. (1984). *The Postmodern Condition*. Manchester: Manchester University Press.

Marmot, M. (2020). Society and the Slow Burn on Inequality. *The Lancet* 395: 1413–1414.

Sayer, A. (1992). *Method in Social Science: A Realist Approach*, Second edition. London: Routledge.

Sayer, A. (2005). *The Moral Significance of Class*. Cambridge: Cambridge University Press.

Sayer, A. (2011). *Why Things Matter to People: Social Science, Values and Ethical Life*. Cambridge: Cambridge University Press.

Sayer, A. (2015). *Why We Can't Afford the Rich*. Bristol: Policy Press.

Scambler, G. (1996). The 'Project of Modernity' and the Parameters for a Critical Sociology: An Argument with Illustrations from Medical Sociology. *Sociology* 30(3): 567–581.

Scambler, G. (2005). *Sport and Society: History, Power and Culture*. Maidenhead: Open University Press.

Scambler, G. (2012). Health inequalities. *Sociology of Health and Illness* 34(1): 130–146.

Scambler, G. (2018a). *Sociology, Health and the Fractured Society: A Critical Realist Account*. London: Routledge.

Scambler, G. (2018b). Heaping Blame on Shame: 'Weaponising Stigma' for Neoliberal Times. *Sociological Review* 66(4): 766–782.

Scambler, G. (2020a). Covid-19 as a 'Breaching Experiment': Exposing the Fractured Society. *Health Sociology Review* 29(2): 140–148.

Scambler, G. (2020b). The Fractured Society: Structures, Mechanisms, Tendencies. *Journal of Critical Realism* 19(1): 1–13.

Scambler, G. (2020c). *A Sociology of Shame and Blame: Insiders Versus Outsiders*. London: Palgrave Macmillan.

Scambler, G., & Scambler, S. (2015). Theorizing Health Inequalities: The Untapped Potential of Dialectical Critical Realism. *Social Theory and Health* 13(3–4): 340–354.

Standing, G. (2011). *The Precariat: The New Dangerous Class*. London: Bloomsbury.

Streeck, W. (2016). *How Will Capitalism End?* London: Verso.

Wallerstein, I., Collins, R., Mann, M., Derluguian, G. & Calhoun, C. (2013). *Does Capitalism Have a Future?* Oxford: Oxford University Press.

Chapter 15

From Dispositions to Interaction and Relations

Nick Crossley

Much of Andrew's reflection upon moral matters, particularly in *The Moral Significance of Class*, is structured around a critical engagement with Bourdieu (Sayer 2005, 1999). Bourdieu's focus upon social class is clearly appealing to him, and the former's concept of 'symbolic violence' captures much of the moral injury, suffered by the working class that Andrew wants to highlight and explore. In addition, following Bourdieu, Andrew's account centres upon a 'social field' involving struggle between various groups, particularly classes – though, departing from Bourdieu, Andrew strives to bring other social divisions, particularly gender, into consideration too. This field is structured by way of an uneven distribution of goods and resources, theorised as forms of 'capital' by Bourdieu (1984), and the action of actors within it is explained by reference to dispositions which Bourdieu captures by way of his 'habitus' concept. However, Andrew is critical of Bourdieu's 'habitus', calling for a reworking of it and, in particular, an incorporation of 'ethical dispositions' within it. Moreover, he questions the exclusive focus upon exchange value in Bourdieu's conception of 'capital', arguing for a consideration of both 'use value' and, following MacIntyre (2013), 'internal goods'. Goods, in some cases, are genuinely good and not, or at least not only tokens of social power, according to Andrew's respecification, and actors sometimes pursue the good. Their motivations are not restricted to striving for dominance and power, as they often seem to be in Bourdieu's work.

Andrew's engagement with Bourdieu is interesting and insightful, but it constrains his thinking in an unhelpful and unnecessary way, particularly in relation to 'dispositions'. Whilst the concept of 'dispositions' is invaluable for sociology, the specific way in which it is used and foregrounded by Bourdieu, which rubs off in Andrew's account, is problematic because it tends to locate phenomena such as morality *within* discrete individuals when they are better conceived as existing *between* social actors; in their interactions, it is the relations and the agreements (e.g. norms) they arrive at. A disposition is a property of the individual, even if it was acquired via socialisation from a wider group, and the concept encourages us to think of the social world as

DOI: 10.4324/9781003247326-20

an aggregate of individuals and their properties rather than, and notwithstanding Bourdieu's claims to the contrary, in a more relational manner. The 'relations' Bourdieu focuses upon are social distances; to reproduce a quote cited approvingly by Andrew:

> 'Social reality' ... consists of a set of invisible relations, those precisely which constitute a space of positions external to one another and defined by their relative distance to one another ... the real is the relational.
> (Bourdieu 1987: 3 cited in and abridged by Sayer 2005: 81)

For example, some are in a 'richer than' relation to others; the 'distance' between them being a function of the differences between the resources available to them. And social reality is thus conceived as a set of individuals, positioned at varying distances from one another and disposed to act in particular ways as a consequence.

Social distance is important, but it only amounts to a relation in a special and very limited sense. I am no more related to others via social distance than by geographical distance because 'distance' *per se* does not involve interdependence, influence or contact. Living 200 miles away from somebody and earning twice as much as them, in and of themselves, do not constitute connections and might characterise entirely independent lives. The relations which impact upon and influence me, including those with my employer, family, friends and the Inland Revenue, involve interdependence, interaction and the various levers of influence these create between us. Bourdieu's neglect and occasional dismissal of such 'visible' (or 'empirical' as he sometimes calls them) relations, based upon actual contact,[1] generate an atomised representation of the social world, which fails to fully grasp its relational nature, creating various theoretical problems as a consequence.

Andrew's account corrects this to some extent – subtly and tacitly removing some of the individualistic biases in Bourdieu's thinking whilst simultaneously critiquing, more explicitly, what he identifies as its 'Hobbesian' (utilitarian) underpinnings. Moreover, he offers an extensive critique of 'the habitus', which at times, on my reading, suggests a need to go not only beyond this particular concept but beyond 'dispositions' altogether and towards concrete relations of the sort just mentioned. However, he repeatedly draws back to 'dispositions' and to the idea of 'moral sentiments', which he borrows from Adam Smith (2000) and regards as a type of disposition centring his 'ethical turn' upon them. I am not convinced that sentiments *per se* are dispositions. We can be disposed to certain sentiments, but they are more usually episodic and often transient, both qualities which are antithetic to the concept of 'dispositions'. More to the point, however, both concepts locate morality within the individual. In this respect, the criticisms that follow are an attempt to push Andrew further along a road that he has already tentatively stepped upon.

Beyond its individualising effect, I am also concerned that 'disposition' can become something of a problematic 'black box' in the work of Bourdieu and his followers. Bourdieusians, including Andrew in places, explain individual actions and differences in lifestyles by reference to 'the habitus' as if that somehow resolved the issue, neglecting to consider that habitus are merely sediments of earlier actions which require their own explanation. Explanation by habitus amounts to little more than saying 'because that is how they and people in their group typically act'. The answer to the question 'where do habitus come from?' is often answered by reference to 'socialisation'. Members of the working class are socialised in one way, members of the middle class in another and therein lies the explanation for their different habitus. Except, of course, it doesn't because it begs the further question of why socialisation patterns differ in the first place.

At this point Bourdieu and his fellow travellers become vague. Bourdieu sometimes invokes 'history' but that only tells us when habitus were formed (in the past) not how or why. Another common explanation centres upon the structure of social space: differences in habitus are 'explained' by the fact that some actors have a greater volume of capital than others or a different ratio of economic to cultural capital. In particular, Bourdieu argues that the working class habitus is shaped by closer proximity to 'necessity' (an argument that Andrew repeats in *Moral Significance*). This is important and most people would probably agree that lifestyles are shaped by the resources available to actors. However, this is still not an explanation. How we get from resources to dispositions remains unclear. The mechanism is missing.

Furthermore, it is important to avoid the determinism that would suggest that a particular volume and combination of resources necessarily results in a particular set of dispositions, not least because Bourdieu himself acknowledges that what characterises a working or middle-class disposition varies both across national societies and within the same society over time, whilst their positions and resourcing remain constant. Position does not determine disposition. This in turn begs a further question, moreover, of how and why actors in similar social positions appear to have similar dispositions. If position doesn't determine disposition, then we might expect to find different and competing dispositions at the same position (of course we do to some extent but for present purposes, I am reflecting upon similarities).

A proper explanation of class (and other group-specific) dispositions requires a focus upon interaction and status homophily (Crossley 2022). Dispositions that are not biologically hard-wired are simply ways of acting that have been selected by the actor (often without conscious awareness or volition) for habituation. They are sediments of earlier (inter)actions. If members of a social group share dispositions, it is because they tend to interact disproportionately with one another (status homophily), influencing one another's actions and the selection processes whereby some are habituated. Likewise, if members of different groups typically have different dispositions, this is due to a lack of meaningful, positive contact and influence between them; that is, because of the status homophily that allows us to consider them distinct groups in the first place (ibid.). Class habitus are the individualised, internalised form of a class culture, and as the concept of 'culture' better suggests, they are a product of interaction between members of a class. Indeed, the concept of 'culture' is in many ways preferable to that of habitus/disposition because it suggests an interworld formed and maintained between members of a group rather than individualised inclinations.

In what follows, I want to push back further against the anchoring role which Andrew, following Bourdieu, accords to dispositions. Before I do, however, I want to briefly introduce the distinction between 'the good' and 'the right' and to briefly make a case for prioritising the latter. Andrew dismisses this distinction in a footnote (2005: 8), claiming that it is 'fuzzy' and not useful for his purposes. However, it is no more fuzzy than any of the many distinctions he does make use of and, whilst the two notions are mutually implicating to some extent, can be stated fairly clearly. What is 'right' is what is considered obligatory for everybody, a matter of duty, and is embodied in norms. 'The good', by contrast, is a matter of values and that which is considered worthy, virtuous and/or life enhancing within specific communities or traditions.

Much of what Andrew discusses leans towards 'the good' and this perhaps partly explains the appeal of 'dispositions' to him. The Aristotelian theory of 'the good' – which many subsequent theories, including MacIntyre's (2013), draw upon – accords a key role to 'hexis' – a Greek concept which translates as 'habitus' in Latin and 'disposition' or 'habit' in English (Aristotle 2004). However, he does stray into the domain of 'the right' on occasion, blurring an important distinction in a confusing way. More to the point, the distinction between the right and the good is very important for anybody seeking to tackle the moral issues of pluralistic and increasingly fractious societies such as our own. The many communities and intersectional groups that make up contemporary societies have very different and often conflicting definitions of the good, and it would require Herculean optimism to imagine them ever agreeing upon such matters. However, peaceful co-existence demands agreed upon 'rules of engagement', that is, a negotiated agreement as to what is 'right'. We do not have to agree about what is 'good' and probably never will, but we do have to agree upon a shared set of rules (norms) to live by, that is, we have to agree upon what is 'right'.

Importantly, moreover, issues of distribution and recognition, which are central to Andrew's concerns about class, belong to discussions concerning 'the right'. At one point in *Moral Significance*, Andrew approvingly quotes a remark by Diane Reay to the effect that solving class inequality is not a matter of making the working-class middle-class but rather of redistributing resources which attach to the status of latter (2005: 137). This argument effectively hinges on the distinction between the right and the good. It suggests that there is no need for the classes to agree on their lifestyles and senses of the good so long as a fair ('right') system of distributing resources between them can be found. I am sure all involved recognise the many complexities this aspiration raises, but it suffices to illustrate how the good/right distinction matters in relation to the discussion Andrew initiates.

Ethical Dispositions and Beyond

I am not convinced that the concept of 'ethical dispositions' is the best way to capture the moral dimension of social life. To put my argument crudely: the moral/ethical aspects of our lives concern what happens *between* us and cannot be adequately captured by the concept of dispositions because a disposition, even if socially acquired and typical of a particular social group, is a property of the individual. This is not to say that dispositions play no role in moral life and it is certainly not to deny their sociological importance. Dispositions (both biologically and socially rooted) are an evident fact of human social action and agency. However, they are only one element in the process comprising action and agency and abstracting and foregrounding them in the way that Bourdieu does, and which Andrew's revision of the habitus concept echoes, puts sociological reflection upon an unhelpful footing, particularly if we seek to explore the moral dimension of social life. It reduces a relational property (morality) to an individual property.

As noted above, Andrew's critique of Bourdieu's 'habitus' touches upon problems which, in my view, extend to the concept of 'dispositions' more generally, and he likewise suggests revisions which, to my mind, take us beyond 'dispositions'. He gives us sufficient reason to doubt that 'dispositions' can do the work he apparently wants it to do. However, he sticks with the concept. In what follows I want to make a case for moving beyond the concept of dispositions towards a more relational framework. Drawing upon the abovementioned distinction, I will develop my argument first in relation to 'the right' before turning to 'the good'.

Insofar as norms are internalised and a sense of duty cultivated the concept of 'dispositions' may have some role in elucidating 'the right'. However, as agreements (albeit often tacit, inherited from previous generations and sometimes forced), norms originate and exist *between* social actors. They are forged in response to exigencies of co-existence (e.g. coordination problems and conflicts of interest), and they are not properties of individual actors but rather of *relations between actors*. They are socially binding and, as Durkheim (1974) stressed, the weakness of our internalised sense of duty is often such that they have to be enforced, in interaction, by way of sanctions. Indeed, many sociological accounts suggest that norms often come into conflict with deep-rooted dispositions. Dennis Wrong's (1961) classic article, 'The Oversocialised Conception of Man [sic] in Sociology', identifies this conflict in both its external and its internalised forms, and various 'homo duplex' models of the human social actor, including Durkheim's (1973) and that of Norbert Elias (1984), similarly engage with it.

Wrong tends to portray the dispositions that conflict with norms as natural tendencies, rooted in the body, and Durkheim and Elias tend to portray the conflict as one between our 'primary' (biological) and 'secondary' (socialised) nature (with Elias (e.g. 1996) often using the term 'habitus' to capture socialised nature). I am not convinced by this nature/society dualism. Whilst it is no doubt true that our nature has to be tamed in accordance with social norms, it is also true both that the desire to transgress norms is social shaped (e.g. by interests deriving from social position and/or the social desirability of certain goods) and that empathy and cooperation have played a role in our evolution and therefore find some support in our biology (Wilson 2013). Nevertheless, these writers do draw out an important tension between individual inclinations and moral demands, demonstrating the inter-individual nature and origin of the latter. The force of morality derives from the collective to which the individual belongs and with whose other members they interact.

Norms are sometimes understood by advocates and critics alike in over-simplified terms as external impositions of a society which is external to us, with no justification or at least no justification beyond their social function. They are 'what society tells us to do'. This view is misleading and unhelpful. Norms are the product of human interaction: created, modified and sometimes rejected by human actors. And they are enforced (through sanctions) in and through interaction. Their generation can be largely unintended. As Durkheim (1964) and Becker (1982) both suggest, the ways in which we happen to interact can over time become ways in which we agree that we ought to act; ways that we demand others to act and learn that they demand of us. However, as Mead (1967) and, building upon him, Habermas (1987) in particular have argued, norms can be and often are the result of deliberative negotiation. When our desires, interests and/or dispositions come into conflict we either fight over who is right or we argue, negotiating rules which strike a compromise between the preferred alternative of all parties. Moreover, such negotiation *can be* rational in Habermas' (1991) 'communicative' sense; that is to say, parties *can* seek to understand one another's different points of view and to resolve their differences through the force of argument alone.

There is an interesting and important convergence of sociology and Kantian moral philosophy in the work of Habermas and Mead. The latter thinkers accept the key cornerstones of Kant's (1999) moral theory, including the imperative that others be treated as ends and that norms be rationally justifiable and universalisable. However, they re-envisage what Kant (1999) imagines happening within the (solitary) moral thinker as a (social) debate involving competing parties who insist upon being treated as ends, serve as a check upon one another's particular interests and justifications and put universalisation to the test in their efforts to reach an agreement. Moral rules do not derive from the rational individual but from (communicatively) rational interaction between parties to a debate.

This is moral philosophy-in-action and simultaneously society-in-process. Mead and Habermas have one eye on Kant but the other on what Parsons[2] (1967), drawing in turn upon Hobbes (1978) called 'the problem of order'. Hobbes asked how it is that society doesn't descend into a 'war of all against all', given the many competing and conflicting desires and interests of its members. Mead and Habermas are not so sociologically naïve as to suggest 'talk' as a complete answer to that question. Both recognise the facts of military conquest, violent repression, domination, power imbalances and so on. However, they argue that the negotiation of norms has played an important role, historically, alongside those other interaction forms, and that, to the extent that this process and the norms it gives rise to are 'communicatively rational', the order they effect is legitimate. Of course negotiation may only ever approximate communicative rationality and is often, to invoke another of Habermas' (1970) concepts, 'systematically distorted', but this only qualifies the point. It does not negate it.

To return briefly to the abovementioned 'homo duplex' model, the conflict that an individual may sometimes experience between their desires and their internalised moral sense may also entail a sense of the rational justification for certain norms and duties. Actors may refrain from action for fear of sanctions (or employ strategies to avoid such sanctions), but they may equally comply with norms and duties because they believe them to be 'right' (if also inconvenient). Alternatively, they may feel that a norm lacks rational justification and challenges the agreement in the wider community which forms its basis:

> we must not forget this other capacity, that of replying to the community and insisting on the gesture of the community changing ... We are engaged in a conversation.
>
> (Mead 1967: 168)

This observation belongs to Mead's account of 'internal conversation' and 'self'. Andrew has a conception of the former and, as I read him, comes much closer to Mead in his understanding of it than to Archer (2003), whom he tends to refer to when using the concept. Archer, who rejects Mead's version as too 'socialised', links 'internal conversation' to what she believes to be a pre-social sense of self and suggests that internal conversations separate the individual from society (albeit if only to subsequently transform it or transform their position in it). Andrew, as I interpret him, understands 'internal conversations' as (simulated) continuations of external conversations – conversations which, I would suggest, are constitutive of society. In this respect, he comes much closer to Mead's version of the concept and thereby avoids the shortcomings of Archer's (overly individualistic) conception (on Archer's individualism see

King 1999, 2004). Whichever version of 'internal conversation' we prefer, however, it is important to note that, whilst in some respects dispositional, it introduces reflectiveness, reflexivity and interaction (of the actor with themselves and, for Mead at least, indirectly thereby with others) into our concept of agency, taking it beyond Bourdieu and any simple dispositional model of the actor. Andrew gestures in this direction. Indeed, in his discussion of Adam Smith (2000), he appears to gesture towards a conception of 'self' akin to Mead's. This forward step is ultimately undone, however, by his repeated return to and use of 'dispositions' and 'sentiments' as anchor points for his theory.

A brief discussion of Mead's concept of 'self', a *process* wherein conscious actors achieve and maintain a degree of *self-consciousness*, would be useful here. Like Smith (2000) (whom, along with Hegel (1979), he draws upon), Mead argues that consciousness can only fully become conscious of itself by achieving an external perspective upon itself, which it does by learning to see itself from the perspective of the other. The actor must learn that their perspective upon the world is indeed a perspective, distinct from the world itself, and is just one perspective amongst many. Moreover, they must learn that others have a perspective upon them and, crucially, must learn to empathise with other perspectives so as to imaginatively perceive their own activities from the point of view of others. Much of Andrew's discussion, at least when focused on Smith (2000), engages this intersubjective dimension, deeming it, as Mead does, integral to the moral nature of the actor (on Mead's moral thought see Abbott 2019, 2020). We are moral, in large part, for Andrew, because we recognise others and recognise that we exist for them. This is crucial but we cannot fully understand and appreciate it if we anchor and centre our account upon dispositions, as Andrew tends to insist. We must look beyond individuals, taking interactions, relations, intersubjectivity and the selves formed within them as our point of departure.

One final point on this issue: anticipating the scepticism of his readers, Andrew suggests that it is difficult to explain how our intersubjective sense of the perspectives of others comes about. It is, however, within the interactionist tradition which he largely ignores and, in particular, in Mead's (1967) account of the role of games plays in the cultivation of empathy and Cooley's (1902) account of the mirroring role of the other, we have a good place to start. Moreover, though the moral aspects of their respective conceptions of self have often been downplayed, it is integral (on Mead's moral aspects see Abbott 2019, 2020). Both were acutely aware that the social relations that are central to their theories are inherently moral relations.

My aim in the above discussion was to illustrate that the aspect of our moral lives captured by the concept of 'the right' is only very partially served by the concept of 'ethical dispositions' which, irrespective of their socialised content and origin, are properties of the individual and that a better focus and starting point would be interaction and social relations. Of course interaction and relations, however much they form individual actors, are only possible and only do so for beings disposed in certain ways but that does not necessitate that we take the individual and their properties as our starting point in sociological reflection or moral theory, not least because individuals, whatever their properties, always-already belong to networks of social relations and interactions. 'The individual' is an abstraction and often an unhelpful one.

We can turn now to 'the good'. As noted above, there is a philosophical affinity, in the Aristotelian tradition, between the concept of dispositions and that of the good. However, this is because actors acquire good habits (hexis), indeed they are trained, within communities that both encourage and support this, and which define the good for their members. Dispositions (or sentiments) are not the source of our sense of the good or its guarantee, as they often seem to be in Andrew's account. They are the desired goal. The focus is upon the process of cultivating good dispositions, through self-conscious effort but also by working with others, and measuring one's success against the criteria defined within a particular community. Foucault's (1988) 'technologies of the self' capture something of this and so too does MacIntyre's (2013) concept of 'practices', which Andrew borrows in his discussion of 'internal goods'. Actors strive to improve within a practice, in pursuit of a state of excellence (a disposition) defined within a community of practice. The language of 'practices' can be misleading here, tending to remove agency and encourage reification, but in MacIntyre's work at least they rest upon *agreement between* members of a community as to a good or goods and the legitimate and best means by which they can be achieved. Again there is a relational element here that the foregrounding of dispositions tends to obscure.

This, moreover, entails that individuals do not necessarily know, themselves, how 'good', 'virtuous' or indeed 'bad' they are, and insofar as they do know, they do so only by stepping outside of the immediacy of their lived experience to view their actions, thoughts and intentions from the perspectives of others, and in particular what Mead (1967) called 'the generalised other' (i.e., a perspective shared by the members of one or more of the social circles to which they belong). Feeling that I am a good chess player, to use an example which MacIntyre (2013) uses in his discussion of internal goods, and feeling that I understand the finer points of the game are not the same as actually being good and properly understanding. The criteria for both are emergent from interaction within the community of chess players, and I can only know by way of engagement with that community and the judgements of its participants. Judgements of goodness are necessarily intersubjective.

We can make a similar point in relation to the 'moral sentiments' that Andrew borrows from Adam Smith (2000). Their relationship to morality, as Andrew notes, is often far from clear. Not only are sentiments not necessarily 'good' or 'right', but their moral standing can be ambiguous and open to debate. Indeed, their very identity is often contestable. The feelings and behaviours constitutive of envy can be the same as those constitutive of righteous indignation – likewise concern and condescension. And unless we are prepared to posit a self-transparent, Cartesian subject, and I assume we are not, then the actor themselves is no arbiter in such matters. My jealousy may be more apparent to others than it is to me. I might believe that I am justifiably irritated. The identity of sentiments depends not only upon behaviours and sensations but on their broader context and effect, and for this reason it is typically contestable and open to debate (see also Crossley 1997). In this respect, whilst moral debate might be triggered by felt and expressed sentiments, the moral content of those sentiments is only fully realised in a context of intersubjective debate where their identity, justification and implications are debated. Again, morality arises *between* actors, in interaction and relations, not within them in *dispositions* and *sentiments*.

Conclusion

In this brief chapter, I have sought to challenge the weight which Andrew accords to dispositions and sentiments in his reflections on moral life. I agree that human actors have both dispositions and sentiments, and I agree that both are sociologically important. However, there is a danger in foregrounding them, in the way that Andrew does, because they are individual properties and there is a danger that focusing upon them reduces phenomena that exist *between* actors, in agreements, interactions and relations, to the individual. At points in his work Andrew recognises this, criticising Bourdieu's 'habitus' in ways which, I believe, extend to the concept of 'dispositions' more generally and suggesting revisions that effectively point in a more relational direction. In the final analysis, however, because he picks Bourdieu as his sparring partner and seeks to reform the Bourdieusian approach, 'dispositions' and 'sentiments' remain key conceptual anchors in his approach.

Bourdieu declares his sociology 'relational' but his focus is restricted to 'invisible' relations that are, in effect, social distances, and he tends to reject the attention afforded to 'visible'[3] relations (involving actual interdependence and interaction) in some sociological perspectives. We would do much better to prioritise these visible relations, in my view, albeit also exploring their interplay with the social distances that Bourdieu describes as 'invisible relations'.

Notes

1   Though this is often metaphorical and even those relations that Bourdieu deems and rejects as 'visible' and merely 'empirical' cannot be observed directly and have to be inferred.
2   Habermas engages directly with Parsons' work. Mead's work predates that of Parsons and he can only be said to have anticipated it..
3   Which, as noted above, aren't actually visible either.

References

Abbott, O. (2019). *The Self, Relational Sociology, and Morality in Practice.* London: Palgrave.

Abbott, O. (2020). The Self as the Locus of Morality: A Comparison between Charles Taylor and George Herbert Mead's Theories of the Moral Constitution of the Self. *Journal for the Theory of Social Behaviour* 50(4): 516–533.

Archer, M. (2003). *Structure, Agency and the Internal Conversation.* Cambridge: Cambridge University Press.

Aristotle (2004). *The Nicomachean Ethics.* Harmondsworth: Penguin.

Becker, H. (1982). *Art Worlds.* Berkeley: University of California Press.

Bourdieu, P. (1984). *Distinction.* London: Routledge and Kegan Paul.

Bourdieu, P. (1987). What Makes a Social Class? *Berkeley Journal of Sociology* 32: 1–17.

Cooley, C. H. (1902). *Human Nature and the Social Order.* New York: Scribner.

Crossley, N. (1997). Emotion and Communicative Action. In Bendelow, G. & Williams, S., (eds), pp. 16–38, *Emotions in Social Life.* London: Routledge.

Crossley, N. (2022) A Dependent Structure of Interdependence: Structure and Agency in Relational Perspective. *Sociology* 56(1): 166–182.

Durkheim, E. (1964). *The Division of Labour.* New York: Free Press.

Durkheim, E. (1973). The Dualism of Human Nature and its Social Conditions. In Bellah, R. (ed.), pp. 149–163, *Emile Durkheim on Morality and Society.* Chicago: Chicago University Press.

Durkheim, E. (1974). The Determination of Moral Facts. In E. Durkheim, pp. 35–80, *Sociology and Philosophy.* New York: Free Press.

Elias, N. (1984). *The Civilising Process.* Oxford: Blackwell.

Elias, N. (1996). *The Germans.* Oxford: Blackwell.

Foucault, M. (1988). Technologies of the Self. In L. Martin, H. Gutman & P. Hutton (eds), pp. 16–49, *Technologies of the Self.* Cambridge: University of Massachusetts Press.

Habermas, J. (1970). On Systematically Distorted Communication. *Inquiry* 13(3): 205–218.

Habermas, J. (1987). *The Theory of Communicative Action II.* Cambridge: Polity Press.

Habermas, J. (1991). *The Theory of Communicative Action I.* Cambridge: Polity Press.

Hegel, G. (1979). *The Phenomenology of Spirit.* Oxford: Oxford University Press.

Hobbes, T. (1978). *Leviathan.* Harmondsworth: Penguin.

Kant, I. (1999). *Critique of Practical Judgement.* Cambridge: Cambridge University Press.

King, A. (1999). Against Structure. *Sociological Review* 47(2): 199–227.

King, A. (2004). *The Structure of Social Theory.* London: Routledge.

MacIntyre, A. (2013). *After Virtue.* London: Bloomsbury.

Mead, G. H. (1967). *Mind, Self and Society.* Chicago: Chicago University Press.

Parsons, T. (1967). *The Structure of Social Action* (2 Vols). New York: Free Press.

Sayer, A. (1999). Bourdieu, Smith and Disinterested Judgement. *Sociological Review* 47(3): 403–431.

Sayer, A. (2005). *The Moral Significance of Class*. Cambridge: Cambridge University Press.

Smith, A. (2000). *The Theory of Moral Sentiments*. New York: Prometheus.

Wilson, E. O. (2013). *The Social Conquest of Earth*. New York: Liveright.

Wrong, D. (1961). The Oversocialised Conception of Man in Modern Sociology. *American Sociological Review* 26(2): 183–193.

Chapter 16

Ordinary Inequality
Sayer, Political Theory and the Human Good

Gideon Calder

Introduction

Here are two senses in which inequality has an 'ordinariness' about it. The first is that we have got used to levels of inequalities of income and wealth far, far beyond what would once have been imagined. Countries such as the UK and the USA have seen the gap between the richest and the poorest rise vastly in the period since the late 1970s. In its way, despite its sheer scale, the gap has become unremarkable. For those who find this abhorrent, its very ordinariness stands for a resounding and enduring political defeat. The other sense reflects the fact that meanwhile, inequality is lived out mundanely: witnessed, felt and navigated in the everyday flows of experience. It is there in 'that world' far from the articulations of political struggle, as Raymond Williams once put it, 'in which people live as they can as themselves, and then necessarily live in a whole complex of work and love and illness and natural beauty' (Williams 2007: 116). There too, it may be so familiar a part of the furniture as not to be noticed much for what it is. But the lowering of expectations, the adaptation of preferences, the acceptance of injustices as givens and the maintenance of dignity even in the face of them – all of these are entirely compatible with, and best understood at least partly as responses to, inequalities of deep and persistent kinds.[1]

Andrew Sayer's work has shed an extraordinary degree of light on the contours and implications of inequality in both of these senses. It is vividly written, acutely observed and performs expert gymnastics in moving between the structural and the intimate, the macro and the lived, and between the parameters of divergent disciplines. It is also read more by sociologists than by political philosophers – despite inequality being a staple item on the agendas of both. In this chapter, I make some suggestions as to why Sayer's work should matter to political theorists, and why political theory should matter to Sayer. Before that, it is worth telling a short cross-disciplinary backstory.

DOI: 10.4324/9781003247326-21

Three Divides

For people like me who found their footing in political theory in the 1990s, any journey through the discipline would encounter some forks in the road. At such points, one faced choices between conceptual vocabularies, styles of writing and ways of framing issues. In my own case, three divides were particularly prominent.

One was between liberals and communitarians. Or, to put that in a fuller way: between universalist, mostly Kantian, liberal individualists and more particularist, maybe Humean, maybe Aristotelian, communitarians. For some, this unpacked mainly as a clash between ideological agendas, or alternative political doctrines. But for me, the most compelling aspect of this split centred not so much on the content of value systems, but on their derivation and scope – and the relation of normativity to philosophical anthropology. Liberal individualists could be painted – as Michael Sandel (1982) so effectively did, in his critique of Rawls' *A Theory of Justice* (1971) – as securing universalism only on the basis of a drastically 'unencumbered' model of the subject. This in turn could be depicted as an isolated, featureless stick figure, bereft of any of the 'thick' attachments, affinities and orientations which might seem required in any plausible account of our normative being, and how we come to hold the values we do. Meanwhile, their communitarian counterparts were easily enough portrayed as reductionist relativists, so submerging the self within networks of local tradition that the very possibility either of a transcultural discourse of emancipation or of any kind of critique of in-place norms seemed to wither away. Of course, neither caricature was wholly accurate or fair – and of course, as soon as the cartoon opposition between liberalism and communitarianism became ensconced, people from either camp or neither began to chip away at its foundations. Yet, however contrived in some respects, the polarity between them seemed important. For one thing, it illuminated the need to find a way of doing justice to the fact that both caricatures seemed intrinsically problematic (Calder 1998). It made urgent, we might say, some kind of accommodation between the critical leverage – the alertness to the potential oppressiveness of convention – afforded by liberal methodology and the communitarians' richer, thicker, more *realistic* picture of what it is to be an agent making value judgements.

The second was within egalitarian thinking. This boomed in the closing decades of the 20th century, just as neoliberalism bit in societies such as the UK and USA and, as we've mentioned, the gap between rich and poor began to yawn ever wider, to unprecedented levels and with worsening effects (Wilkinson & Pickett 2009; Dorling 2014, 2018; Lansley 2021). There grew to be a complicated menu of egalitarian positions – and answers to the question posed famously in 1980 by Amartya Sen: equality of *what?*

(Sen 1980). Resources, access to advantage, welfare and capabilities: each of these was distinct metrics or 'currencies' of egalitarian justice (Cohen 1989). Over time, these debates dug their way down to a minute level of finer points, epitomised in the agonised debates among those batched together as 'luck egalitarians', for whom the point of distributive justice is the equalisation of outcomes with respect to fortune, under which rubric choice-based losses through (for example) gambling would not be compensable, but the sheer 'brute bad luck' of being struck by lightning would (Dworkin 1981a, 1981b). Other egalitarians found this industry nit-picking and point-missing – precisely because it became so fixated on questions around the parsing and weighing of individuals' responsibilities, talents, efforts and tastes. On the one hand, this ceded too much of the discussion to terrain favoured by conservatives, by focusing on questions of lifestyle and desert. On the other hand, it neglected, as Elizabeth Anderson observed, 'the much broader agendas of egalitarian movements', for which the proper aim of egalitarian justice 'is not to ensure that everyone gets what they morally deserve, but to create a community in which people stand in relations of equality to others' – in other words, to end oppression (Anderson 1999: 288–289). Because other egalitarians argued about what *that* looked like – for example, about the relative weight of redistribution and recognition (see Fraser 1995, 1997; Young 1997; and for penetrative analysis, Sayer 2005: ch. 3) – this made for two separate kinds of conversation about the conditions and shape of a more equal society, each with its own internal debates.

And the third schism was between modernists and postmodernists. Well, that's much too neat a way of putting it – but the general terrain will be familiar enough. Again this was – mostly – a methodological dispute, about the presumptions of theory and the ways it presented itself, rather than reflecting substantive divergences on this or that normative issue. I doubt that any of the figures looming up in those debates – Habermas, Foucault, Derrida, Lyotard, Rorty, Marxists and post-Marxists, liberal and poststructuralist feminists, realists and social constructionists about science – disagreed much at all with any of the others about the death penalty, abortion, the desirability of equalising pay between the genders or whether a second presidential term for George H.W. Bush would be a good thing. But the debates about the nature and scope of normative critique – the kind of enterprise that critical thinking is, and whether or not it might take its direction from the philosophical ambitions of the European Enlightenment – were deep and fractious. And again, each side could be easily enough positioned by their opponents in a problematic-looking place. So on the one hand, we had imperialistic modernists, unseverable from the assumption that the West was somehow intrinsically best, nonchalant about how every universalism masks a particularism and of the abuses to which the supposedly progressive, humanitarian, inclusive ideals of the Enlightenment had been put. While on the other were feckless, jargonistic, discourse-fixated Nietzschean relativists ready to undo the many progressive achievements of modern society with their intoxicated mash-up of paranoia about its central intellectual foundations and a complacent ease in taking those achievements for granted – as if the abolition of slavery or the formation of the United Nations were as oppressive or as hostile to difference as other 'products' of modernity like the Gulag and the atomic bomb.

Coming up against such splits, we had to orientate ourselves somehow, tune in and tool up. In doing so, what became for me most useful were the resources which allowed thinking through and across those divides, in ways that allowed the tensions at stake to be productive and illuminating, rather than just irrevocable and thwarting. Sometimes those resources could be found within political theory itself – for example, among those thinkers like Fraser, Rorty, Habermas and Geras, who could move limpidly between the vocabularies of continental and analytic philosophy. In the case of Andrew Sayer's thinking, they came in from another direction.

Sayer, Political Theory and the Human Good

Sayer's work is neither positioned as political theory nor much discussed in its mainstream. I encountered it via an affinity with the broad church of critical realism, which I had picked up while looking for conceptual resources to help articulate why I found neo-pragmatism both alluring and flawed (Calder 2007a). So it was with Sayer the (exceptional) explicator of realist theory and methods (*Realism and Social Science* 2000; *Method in Social Science* 1992) that I was first acquainted. But it was on reading *The Moral Significance of Class* (2005) that the luminosity and resonance of Sayer's work really sank in. The resonances happened both in a general way – through his insistence on the centrality of normativity to social science and the profundity of class in shaping our lives, but also through his take on specific aspects of the terrain. That book kept throwing up insights, angles and ways of putting things which gave excellent tools to work with, particularly if, like me, you wanted to work constructively in and across the three divides depicted above.

Why though did it seem so distinctively rich? This was partly down to that movement between the structural and the intimate, mentioned earlier – between the two senses of inequality's ordinariness. Earlier *Radical Political Economy* (Sayer 1995) had provided tools with which to rethink the critique of capitalism in the wake of the rippling impacts of neoliberalism and opened up the question of the relation between critical social science and normative theorising. But *The Moral Significance of Class* started out instead from lay normativity and the lived experience of the class. The account it gave was compelling in itself, in ways very well-captured elsewhere in this book – see Diane Reay's chapter, for example. But the richness lay largely in the mode in which Sayer did his work. Reviewing it, I tried to convey how his ' "post-disciplinary" approach, moving between sociology and moral philosophy ... is something itself to be valued', and that

> One of the most valuable things about Sayer's book is that it shows that a better understanding both of what class does to us, and the kinds of beings we must be for it to have these effects, is a central plank of the moral critique of those effects.

(Calder 2007b: 259, 260)

Since then, I have come to think this even more strongly, partly under the influence of Sayer's ways of working. So that point about sociology and philosophy is worth expanding upon.

In the hands of political philosophers and applied ethicists, 'applying' theory often happens like this. One adopts a theoretical position from a range on offer and then tests it out against the competition by applying it to items from a menu of given topics, and seeing how it stands up. Those topics become more or less reified, presented as self-contained, off-the-peg items for discussion. We can call this a 'top-down', or 'first choose your theory' approach, in a sense contrasted by Jonathan Wolff with those which start out instead from the 'real-world' subject-matter, get a grasp of the moral difficulties generated there and then aim to 'be able to connect those difficulties or dilemmas with patterns of philosophical reasoning or reflection' (Wolff 2020: 8). Within this alternative line of approach, the task of political theory is descriptive and explanatory, as well as normative: it is, in the words of John Dunn, 'to diagnose practical predicaments and show us best how to confront them', a task which begins with 'ascertaining how the social, political, and economic setting of our lives now is and in understanding why it is as it is' (Dunn 1990: 193). Viewed this way, critical normative theorising is ambidextrous, requiring a sensitivity to the contours both of social research and philosophical exchange. Its task is a kind of mediation between the two.

Now it is not at all automatic that political philosophers can do this – even the pop stars of the field. 'Smartness' in political philosophy debates has all too often consisted chiefly in the sharp deployment of the thought-experiment, semantic twist or counter-example. This feeds the kinds of divide we summarised earlier, where competing approaches jostle for position at (in Wolff's terms) the top. Alternatively, setting off from the diagnosing of practical predicaments, we reach for the normative insights that connect best with that ontological terrain. It is highly unlikely that these will be simply liberal *or* communitarian, attach to one kind of egalitarian conversation *or* the other, or be available exclusively under the heading of modernism *or* postmodernism. And they will have arisen via different disciplines.

Thus part of the special value of Sayer's approach in *The Moral Significance of Class* and *Why Things Matter to People* is that it feeds into exactly this kind of mediation and possesses just this kind of ambidextrousness – precisely because it labours away at the seam between the positive, the explanatory and the normative. For Sayer, of course, that seam itself is porous and an interface rather than a divide. Among other implications, this means that when we locate the significance of a social issue, it will already be freighted with lay normativity. The most important questions people tend to face in our everyday lives are *already*, before any light at all may be shed on them by this or that abstract theoretical framework, 'normative ones of what is good or bad about what is happening, including how others are treating them, and of how to act, and of what to do for the best' (Sayer 2011: 1). But it is not just that the significance of lived reality is already normative. It is also that frameworks of values will themselves always carry, and be assessable in relation to, ontological assumptions about what it's like to be a human being (Calder 2008). Some political philosophers acknowledge this and avoid talking (as some liberals and a lot of postmodernists do) as if *any* assumptions about human beings carry within them an effect of violence.

Charles Taylor, sometime protagonist in the liberal/communitarian face-offs of the 1980s, had a helpful habit of noting the insecure nature of that kind of stance. There are no coherent means by which to bracket ontology from questions of social justice. So, for example: 'different principles of distributive justice are related to conceptions of the human good, and in particular to different notions of individuals' dependence on society to realize the good' (Taylor 1985: 291). Bernard Williams expands upon a similar point: human beings are alike in ways beyond the capacity to speak a language, use tools, live in societies – but ways 'more likely to be forgotten'. Thus (with allowances for the 1970s nouns and pronouns):

> These respects are notably the capacity to feel pain, both from immediate physical causes and from various situations represented in perception and in thought and the capacity to feel affection for others, and the consequences of this, connected with the frustration of this affection, loss of its object, etc. The assertion that men are alike in the possession of these characteristics is, while indisputable and (it may be) even necessarily true, not trivial. For it is certain that there are political and social arrangements that systematically neglect these characteristics in the case of some groups of men, while being fully aware of them in the case of others; that is to say, they treat certain men as though they did not possess these characteristics, and neglect moral claims that arise from these characteristics and would be admitted to arise from them.
>
> (Williams 2005: 99)

There is a particular reason for quoting this passage in full. It dates from the early 1970s, as part of a take on the reach and scope of political philosophy that was already contentious. It is cited by Amartya Sen in his early book *On Economic Inequality* (1973). The reason for quoting it here is that it helps convey why Sayer's work should resonate with political philosophers (including Sen) even when it is targeted at sociologists. For Sayer too, 'some conception of the nature of human being must be at least implicit in any ethical theory' (Sayer 2004: 96). But if we rely on political philosophy for that conception, it will be inevitably incomplete – just as it will if we rely on economics. We will need to furnish ourselves with wider resources: from across the social sciences, and from anthropologists, psychologists and biologists. It is one thing to admit that we just *do* have to think about the nature of human beings, to think adequately about normative questions. It is another to offer a nuanced account of what that means.

And that's exactly what we get in Sayer's later theorising, in a way which (as I read it) extends right down from his earliest work in geography: there is no rupture or swerve as his thinking unfolds. And the thinking gets steadily more detailed on questions of human beings and the human good. One of my favourite sequences in his writing comes in the chapter on 'Dignity' in *Why Things Matter to People*, in which the analysis progresses from abstract uses of that term in places such as the UN Declaration of Human Rights to relationality and vulnerability, the body and animality, hierarchy and inequality, before culminating in a discussion of the phrase 'dignity at work'. We find there an account of why a consideration of dignity – often hastily dismissed as a conceptually vapid term – is necessary to any account of well-being, multi-dimensional, and understandable only in relation to the roles of 'social structures that make people's lives objectively unequal within their society' (Sayer 2011: 215). The care with which Sayer treads this terrain is typical of the ways in which he handles the relation between other concepts, attributes and concerns – for example, sentiments and dispositions, reason and emotion, redistribution and recognition – and offers sympathetic criticisms of resources to hand: Bourdieu (Sayer 2005), the capabilities approach (Sayer 2011), virtue ethics (Sayer 2020) or – in a rare direct foray onto the terrain of political philosophy itself – contributive justice (Sayer 2009). This allows him to combine so effectively critical attention to both senses of the ordinariness of inequality.

Concluding Note: Sayer and the Political

The idea mentioned earlier that 'smartness' consists in a kind of sparring at the level of thought experiments is characteristic of what Raymond Geuss calls 'ethics-first' political philosophy, for him typified by Rawls and Nozick – which makes the mistake of assuming that 'one could come to any substantive understanding of politics by discussing abstractly the good, the right, the true, or the rational in complete abstraction from the way in which these items ... impinge, even if indirectly, on human action' (Geuss 2008: 28). Geuss counterposes 'ethics-first' political theory to a version of realism – a road down which here we need not go. But stress on the status and role of the political in the navigation of the human good points to questions that lie adjacent to Sayer's work, but remain unbroached. There is no Sayerian political theory: no treatment, for example, of the field of deliberation, contestation, conflict and the negotiation of plurality which has preoccupied a good deal of political philosophy – analytic and continental – since Rawls. And while that's not a *flaw* ('post disciplinary' doesn't mean 'all-encompassing') that field does crucially matter, on his terms as well as otherwise. For while there is so much of value in the retrieval of the ordinary, in Raymond Williams' sense, there is also much to interrogate in the supposition that it sits separately from political struggle. Sayer's work helps show us why. *Why We Can't Afford the Rich* (2015) should be read, alongside all the other things it offers, as a political provocation. That goes for *Why Things Matter to People*, too. *The Moral Significance of Class* should be read by every political theorist plying their trade in an egalitarian vein. The ordinariness of inequality is part of what makes the need for all this reading so acute.

Note

1 Sometimes the unremarkableness of hardship is captured best in fiction. At one point in Douglas Stuart's compelling novel *Shuggie Bain*, with the character Leanne describing sexual violence at home, he writes: 'She yawned like it was too ordinary to explain' (Stuart 2020: 391). The second sense I'm trying to invoke here is there in exactly *that* kind of ordinariness.

References

Anderson, E. (1999). What is the Point of Equality? *Ethics* 109(2): 287–337.
Calder, G. (1998). Liberalism without Universalism? In B. Brecher & J. Halliday (eds), pp. 140–159, *Nationalism and Racism in the Liberal Order*. Aldershot: Ashgate.
Calder, G. (2007a). *Rorty's Politics of Redescription*. Cardiff: University of Wales Press.
Calder, G. (2007b). Feeling better? (Review of Sayer, *The Moral Significance of Class*). *Imprints: Egalitarian Theory and Practice* 9(3): 250–260.
Calder, G. (2008). Ethics and Social Ontology. *Analyse & Kritik* 30(2): 427–443.
Cohen. G. (1989). On the Currency of Egalitarian Justice. *Ethics* 99: 906–944.
Dorling, D. (2014). *Inequality and the 1%*. London: Verso.
Dorling, D. (2018). *Peak Inequality*. Bristol: Policy Press.
Dunn, J. (1990). Reconceiving the Content and Character of Modern Political Community. In J. Dunn, pp. 193–215, *Interpreting Political Responsibility*. Cambridge: Polity Press.
Dworkin, R. (1981a). What is Equality? Part 1: Equality of Welfare. *Philosophy & Public Affairs* 10(3): 185–246.
Dworkin, R. (1981b). What is Equality? Part 2: Equality of Resources. *Philosophy & Public Affairs* 10(4): 283–345.
Fraser, N. (1995). From Redistribution to Recognition? Dilemmas of Justice in a 'Post-Socialist' Age. *New Left Review* 212: 68–93.

Fraser, N. (1997). A Rejoinder to Iris Young. *New Left Review* 223: 126–130.

Guess, R. (2008). *Philosophy and Real Politics*. Princeton: Princeton University Press.

Lansley, S. (2021). *The Richer, The Poorer: How Britain Enriched the Few and Failed the Poor*. Bristol: Policy Press.

Rawls, J. (1971). *A Theory of Justice*. Cambridge, Mass: Harvard University Press.

Sandel, M. (1982). *Liberalism and the Limits of Justice*. Cambridge: Cambridge University Press.

Sayer, A. (1992). *Method in Social Science: A Realist Approach*, Second edition. London: Routledge.

Sayer, A. (1995). *Radical Political Economy: A Critique*. Oxford: Blackwell.

Sayer, A. (2000). *Realism and Social Science*. London: Sage.

Sayer, A. (2004). Restoring the Moral Dimension in Social Scientific Accounts. In M. S. Archer & W. Outhwaite (eds), *Defending Objectivity: Essays in Honour of Andrew Collier*. London: Routledge.

Sayer, A. (2005). *The Moral Significance of Class*. Cambridge: Cambridge University Press.

Sayer, A. (2009). Contributive Justice and Meaningful Work. *Res Publica* 15(1): 1–16.

Sayer, A. (2011). *Why Things Matter to People*. Cambridge: Cambridge University Press.

Sayer, A. (2015). *Why We Can't Afford the Rich*. Bristol: Policy Press.

Sayer, A. (2020). Critiquing – and Rescuing – 'Character'. *Sociology* 54(3): 460–481.

Sen, A. (1973). *On Economic Inequality*. Oxford: Oxford University Press.

Sen, A. (1980). Equality of What? In S. M. McMurrin (ed.), *The Tanner Lectures on Human Values I*. Salt Lake City: University of Utah Press.

Stuart, D. (2020). *Shuggie Bain*. London: Picador.

Taylor, C. (1985). The Nature and Scope of Distributive Justice. In C. Taylor, pp. 289–317, *Philosophy and the Human Sciences: Philosophical Papers 2*. Cambridge: Cambridge University Press.

Wilkinson, R., & Pickett, K. (2009). *The Spirit Level*. London: Allen Lane.

Williams, B. (2005). The Idea of Equality. In B. Williams, pp. 97–114, *In the Beginning Was the Deed: Realism and Moralism in Political Argument*. Princeton: Princeton University Press.

Williams, R. (2007). *Politics of Modernism*. London: Verso.

Wolff, J. (2020). *Ethics and Public Policy*, Second edition. London: Routledge.

Young, I. M. (1997). Unruly Categories: A Critique of Nancy Fraser's Dual Systems Theory. *New Left Review* 222: 147–160.

Part V

Responses

Chapter 17

Responses to the Contributors

Andrew Sayer

I hadn't expected to be the subject of a festschrift so it was a lovely surprise when Gideon and Balihar suggested it. I feel honoured, uplifted and
very grateful. I am touched by the care and attentiveness the contributors
have given to my work and have enjoyed reading their contributions and
the stimulus of their criticisms and differences. Often they have spotted
connections and implications – and gaps and errors – that I hadn't noticed.
I would like to thank them for making me think further, both in the past
and now. Writing academic books and articles can be a lonely pursuit, especially when you're not sure if there's anyone out there who'll be interested,
but the whole collection is a reminder of how our work is thickly intertwined
with that of others. In this context, I would like to thank others not present
here: former colleagues at Sussex University including Tony Fielding (also
my DPhil supervisor), Mick Dunford, Peter Dickens and Fred Gray; and
at Lancaster, Norman Fairclough, Anne-Marie Fortier, Betsy Olson, Larry
Ray, Celia Roberts, Beverley Skeggs, Sylvia Walby, Alan Warde, Ruth Wodak,
Linda Woodhead and the late John Urry; also John Allen and the late Doreen
Massey at the Open University, Costis Hadjimichalis and Dina Vaiou in
Greece, Frank Hansen in Denmark, and Eric Clark in Sweden.

As Dick Walker notes, our early careers owed much to the institutional
and wider political environment of universities in the 1970s and early 1980s,
before neoliberalism, the New Public Management, and online working
eroded so many key ingredients of university life – in particular, the time for
daily agenda-free conversations with colleagues, through which we picked
up invaluable ideas and information and formed a sense of belonging. I was
particularly lucky to start my career at Sussex University at the time of
its exciting experiment (now sadly abandoned) of 'redrawing the map of
learning' by making both teaching and research interdisciplinary, so that
by 1978, I realised that I did not want to identify as a member of a single
discipline (I was originally a geographer), but as a social scientist. While
I moved to a department of sociology at Lancaster University in 1993, it has
always been an adventurous and open-minded department that accepted
my 'post disciplinary' stance and has never tried to 'discipline' me in either

DOI: 10.4324/9781003247326-23

teaching or research. My distaste for identifying with any single discipline is not meant to deny that they have something to contribute; it's just that while adopting disciplinary blinkers allows one to focus, it also invites reductionism, disciplinary imperialism and misattributions of causality (Sayer 2000c).

Dick Walker, Kevin Morgan and Steve Fleetwood also mention the crucial role of friendships and life outside academia, and here I would like to thank Hazel Ellerby, John Sayer, Liz Thomas, Richard Light, Norman Fairclough, Bridget Graham, Sue Halsam, Iain Hunter, Grazyna Monvid, Jill Yeung, Pat Batteson, Ann McChesney, the Lancaster Millennium Choir and especially my daughter Lizzie Sayer.

But to come on to the contributors' chapters, given space limitations I can only respond briefly, and inevitably I have more to say about disagreements than agreements. I have grouped the responses into six themes: space, theory and economic development; critical realism; ethical life, habitus and naturalism; moral economy; inequality and the rich; and environment.

Space, Theory and Economic Development

This concerns a debate that took place in geography in the 1980s, concerning the place of space in social science, and which some have seen as a challenge to geography's raison d'être; **Dick Walker** and I have argued many times about it. I hold that we can't expect social scientific *theory* to say much about space, beyond noting that it makes important differences that must be taken into account in concrete research, because most social phenomena have a considerable degree of flexibility as regards their particular spatial forms – and necessarily so if they are to exist in many different contexts; as critical realists would say, they exist in open systems in which there are never more than temporary and approximate regularities. And since one of the characteristics of theory is that it seeks to identify the necessary and sufficient conditions for the existence of its objects, then usually it can only say that an object must be accessible to those conditions, though that, of course, says very little about how that works out spatially. Thus, labour markets can take a variety of spatial forms – particularly so with the development of the internet and home working – so there's not much that 'spatial theory' can say about them in advance of particular empirical studies of their contingent forms. And this is borne out in practice: words like 'geographies', 'space' and 'scalar' are *mentioned* frequently in the theoretical literature in geography, without saying anything specific *about* their referents, other than to give a few examples of *contingent* spatial forms. I still believe that *empirical research on concrete situations* needs to take the difference that space makes into account, so in supervising PhD theses – with topics ranging from women and the 'dual shift', neoliberal economic policy, gentrification to multiculturalism and migration – I have often urged students to do so. So my line on space and social theory doesn't mean that I think geography doesn't matter, a conclusion some jumped to when I joined a sociology department!

As **Jamie Peck** notes, I cut my teeth in the 1970s developing a critique of positivist models in geography by drawing on critiques of mainstream economics, particularly those by Maurice Dobb and Joan Robinson, and later critiques developed through critical realism. When it came to substantive theory capable of understanding capitalism's production of inequalities and uneven development, Marxism provided a much more plausible account than mainstream economics and traditional economic geography. After an initial phase of exploring Marxist and other radical theory, some of us sought to develop empirical studies of concrete cases. As Jamie and Dick note, this became a source of much contention in the 1980s, as some researchers were not willing to venture far from what was already contained in that theory and regarded those who found they had to consider things beyond it as guilty of both lapsing into empiricism and deserting radicalism. *Microcircuits of Capital* (which I co-authored with Kevin Morgan) was very definitely a concrete, empirical study, and it was informed by that radical theory (Morgan & Sayer 1988), but as Jamie indicates, some readers were not sure what the theoretical conclusions were.

Perhaps what puzzled some, I imagine, was that the book scarcely mentioned 'Fordism' – then a key concept for so much political-economic research. That was quite deliberate, because we felt that particularly with reference to labour processes, the concept was greatly overstretched in the radical literature, to the point where it became the subject of a lazy grand narrative that obscured more than it revealed. Only a small minority of workers in capitalism were ever mass-production workers, and while work intensification (speed-up) and automation are common responses to capitalist competition, for many of the electronics firms we studied the main problems were not how to reduce labour time through process innovations and controlling the workforce – the classic challenge of Fordist labour processes – but how to innovate products, form ties with customers (mostly other firms) and break into distribution networks and markets or form new ones; contrary to Marx's account in *Capital* that commodities are never merely 'thrown onto the market'. While capital–labour relations are quite understandably the focus of radical political economy, and while these are strongly related to competition between capitals, responses to competition are often not centred on the labour process.

Implicit in all this was a broader theoretical lesson, one which was developed in *The New Social Economy* and *Radical Political Economy* (Sayer & Walker 1992; Sayer 1995): the underestimation in the radical economic theory of the effects of an enormously complex, geographically extended, social division of labour. This really does divide labour and eludes centralised control, as was found both in theory (Hayek and others) and in practice (the former Soviet Union). It is also far too complex to be planned democratically. Alternatives to capitalism need not only to change the ownership of the means of production but to find ways of coordinating vast numbers of producers, users and products in socially just and sustainable ways. So, all in all, though it may not have been apparent, *Microcircuits of Capital* was not only theoretically informed but in the long-run theoretically informative – and politically suggestive.

Critical Realism

As critical realist philosophy of social science implies, the besetting sin of positivism and its strange rationalist variant in economics is its casual attitude to how it conceptualises its objects, and in particular how it goes about the tricky business of abstraction. Ordinary language is full of abstractions, and while they may be good enough for getting by in everyday life, a much more careful approach is needed in social science. **Steve Fleetwood's** forensic analysis of abstraction complements his earlier important work on the realism of assumptions, an issue that is central to explaining the dire state of mainstream economics.

I see abstraction as particularly important for non-experimental science, inasmuch as it tries to provide a substitute for experimentation, so that instead of physically separating the object of interest from other objects not of interest in the experiment, we do so in thought.[1] Here, as Steve notes, it's important to ask whether the social phenomenon A that we have abstracted from B and C in our theorising could actually exist independently of them. Sometimes there may be real situations where A does exist independently of them, but even where A is always found with B and C in all known cases, I would argue that it is still important to ask if this is an historical accident or because B and C are necessary conditions for the existence of A. It's no surprise that capitalist businesses in England use English as their language, but it doesn't follow that using English is a necessary condition of being a capitalist business. If we don't know an entity's conditions of existence, we don't know much about it. What I have termed 'associational thinking' assumes that what is found together must go together (Sayer 2000a); it fails to distinguish 'can' from 'must'. This is particularly common in radical social science interested in 'bads' like race, class and gender: to be sure they commonly intersect, often in ways that reinforce one another, but it is still important to ask if these combinations are necessary ones. There is a danger in radical research that in wanting to show what is problematic about some situation, it is tempting to claim that its component parts all *necessarily* depend on one another, as this seems grander and more radical than an account which says there are several bads, some of which can or could exist separately. This is far from an academic point of no practical import: if the former is the case, then nothing can be changed until everything is changed; or if the latter, change is easier.

Notwithstanding the importance of abstraction and the move back to the concrete, it is only part of what is needed, for developing powerful concepts also requires imagination and metaphor. Some objects of interest – the meaning of discourses, for example – are too indivisible and open to 'the play of difference' for abstraction to be appropriate. And while abstraction narrows down what we think about, when it comes to analysing concrete situations we must also draw upon all we know, which requires an opening out. We need both careful analysis (left-brain dominant) – as illustrated in Steve's chapter – and a more open kind of thinking (right-brain dominant).

Bob Jessop discusses further how we move from abstract concepts, through hybrid ones, to concrete concepts. While he has provided an excellent summary of my own work on this – and on the connections to moral economy and ethics – he doesn't mention some of his own contributions on the subject. I think critical realists – and others – should take more note of his 'strategic relational approach' and use of evolutionary concepts in explaining how structures are selective with respect to actions, how actions can be selective with respect to structures and how the interaction of different elements of a conjuncture interact depends on their spacing and timing (Jessop 2005).

Doug Porpora raises a more philosophical basic issue: my take on truth as being about practical adequacy (Sayer 1992, 2000b). I would say that the latter should not be interpreted in instrumentalist fashion as simply that which is 'useful' to believe, as if it were a matter of convenience, but as what appears to be the case, based on the fullest and most rigorously assembled evidence, the best arguments we can find, and the best practical tests we can conduct. Hence, I believe the statement that 'six million people were murdered in the Holocaust' is true because the evidence and arguments provided by historians and witnesses put it beyond reasonable doubt that this happened; their accounts are the most adequate.

Ethical Life, Habitus and Naturalism

This theme, owing much to Bourdieu, Adam Smith, neo-Aristotelian virtue ethics and the feminist ethic of care literature, was explored in my *Why Things Matter to People*, building on initial work in relation to class in *The Moral Significance of Class*. Both books were critiques of reductive accounts of behaviour in social science, especially sociology.

Nick Crossley raises some important issues about how we should understand everyday morality and regarding the limitations of Bourdieu's concept of habitus. I accept that I probably should have taken Mead's work on morality into account. However, I continue to find the distinction made by some moral and political philosophers between the right and the good unhelpful. Why would we consider something to be obligatory – for example, respecting others' autonomy – if we didn't think it was good for people? It seems to me that the right is just a lowest common denominator form of the good, one that attempts to identify a kind of minimum requirement for people, whatever their culture; I don't see it as qualitatively different from the good.

I agree with some of Nick's reservations about the concept of habitus, particularly regarding our lack of understanding of the formation of dispositions, and indeed the wider fundamental question of how socialisation works. Too often, social scientists assume a blank slate model of socialisation, which completely fails to explain what it is about human beings that allow them to be socialised. Trying to explain socialisation without answering this question is like trying to clap with one hand. Somewhere, Bourdieu said that the concept of habitus was a social-psychological one and that further investigation was needed into the processes that form what it identifies. I agree, but the black box is beginning to be opened up. The exceptional neuroplasticity of humans enables learning and socialisation, but the paradox of neuroplasticity is that it can also allow the development of durable neural circuits and hence dispositions that are difficult to change (Doidge 2007). Also in neuroscience, Antonio Damasio refers to 'somatic markers' that code experiences positively or negatively, and which then come to shape our spontaneous, rapid responses to events. This suggests our dispositions – and hence our habitus – are evaluative (Damasio 2000). Studies of attachment processes in developmental psychology – which are precisely about the key, formative social relations in our early years when neuroplasticity is at a peak – also need to be taken seriously by sociologists if they are to understand socialisation. In psychology, according to 'dual process' theories there is both fast action, based on acquired dispositions that enable us to do much with little or no conscious monitoring, and slow responses based on deliberation. This supports the position of those who have argued against Margaret Archer that we need to acknowledge the dual roles of habitus and reflexivity in determining action (Archer 2009).

Regarding Nick's doubts about the match between social position and dispositions, it's clear from the diagrams in Bourdieu's *Distinction* and subsequent empirical studies of the sociology of taste that this is usually only approximate (Bourdieu 1984). I suggest the relationship is complicated and blurred by two things: firstly, as I argued in *The Moral Significance of Class*, by the concern people may develop for the internal goods of certain practices regardless of their social coordinates in terms of relations of proximity/distance in the social field, and secondly, by the visible, substantial relation*ships* between people (e.g. within families and among friends) that Nick notes and Bourdieu often ignored, and which have a major formative influence on us. Nevertheless, while social location does not uniquely determine dispositions, it does have significant influence.

Although there is a lot on dispositions and the habitus in *The Moral Significance of Class*, I don't see any conflict between this and acknowledging the importance of social relations and interactions. The book is also about relations of recognition and associated *social* emotions such as pride, guilt, shame and sense of (in)justice, and their dependence on empathy or fellow-feeling. As I argued in *Why Things Matter to People*, we are relational beings, but our interactions are not determined just through conversation, negotiation and power but in relation to our capacities to flourish or suffer; this naturalist element cannot be ignored, as it so often is in social science and philosophy.

Virtue ethics, particularly via the work of Martha Nussbaum, was another major influence on both books. Like Bourdieu, this emphasises the importance of acquired dispositions (virtues and vices), but it acknowledges that the acquisition involves a mix of habituation through repetition and conscious learning, and it recommends that the exercise of those dispositions in actions requires some conscious monitoring to make adjustments for specific contexts. It also emphasises the importance of emotions in relation to dispositions: the exercise of virtues like kindness or justice involves or should involve appropriate emotions, like compassion and resentment at injustice.[2] This was one of the reasons why I felt that Bourdieu's concept of habitus needed to be modified to take account of the way in which our learned responses can also be emotional, and how emotions mediate their acquisition. We do not just accommodate indifferently to prevailing situations as Bourdieu implies: we feel good or bad about them in various ways, so, for example, we do not adjust to contempt and exploitation as easily as we do to respect. Unless we acknowledge this, it is hard to explain resistance in social life.

I agree that there is a tendency in Bourdieu to underplay culture in the sense of shared meanings and practices, but there's also a tendency in cultural studies and sociology to reduce morality to mere norms, conventions or power, as if it had no particular connection to human flourishing. Morality has a multi-level character, involving dispositions, emotions, fellow-feeling, meanings, norms and discourses, and in practice these are all influenced by our biological affordances and constraints, attachment processes, socialisation and power relations. The challenge of understanding everyday morality is to work out how to synthesise these elements. It needs a post disciplinary approach to avoid the biases produced by the restricted concerns of particular social science disciplines.

Justin Cruickshank's thoughtful discussion of practical knowledge and theoretical knowledge within academic life and of relations between academics and laypeople links some of the concerns of *Why Things Matter to People* to the issue of critical social science. Perhaps academics do need to reflect more on how their own thought can become habitual and resistant to change, even though they believe that it is open to revision. I very much agree that education needs to be more dialogical. As regards the relation between academic and lay thought, Justin draws upon Freire and Gadamer, to discuss the issue in critical social science (CSS) of the asymmetry of knowledge and cognitive resources between experts and laypeople in addressing problems, and the danger of CSS becoming a monologue rather than a dialogue. Habermas' discourse ethics is relevant here in that the ideal speech situation requires equality, including equality of cognitive resources, among participants so they can seek the best arguments and evidence and arrive at 'uncoerced agreement'. While I still think they also need some conception of flourishing and suffering as objective forms of being, I was wrong to say that Habermas' discourse ethics was neither necessary nor sufficient for flourishing. While it's not sufficient, being able to discuss with others as equals, so that each person both listens to others and feels listened to by them, is certainly an important ingredient of flourishing (see Fricker 2007). The problem is how to move closer to such an ideal? Justin mentions cooperative universities as a way forward for higher education; citizens' juries and assemblies are another way of reducing cognitive inequality and empowering lay people on specific issues.

The difficulties are particularly severe in highly unequal societies like the UK where the everyday political arguments one sees in both traditional and social media have more in common with a brawl than a seminar. Dog-whistle populist political discourse encourages anti-intellectualism in order to silence science-based critiques. In this regard, as George Lakoff shows, responses to political issues are often influenced less by evidence and argument than by how they are framed in relation to underlying values and emotions (Lakoff 2014). But then discourse is not always the best way of changing minds – exemplary individuals and actions may make a bigger impact.

As **Doug Porpora** notes in his generous comments on *Why Things Matter to People* and on emotions, it was primarily subjective mattering – caring or being concerned about things – that I discussed in that book. In retrospect, I think it mainly showed *how* things matter to people. Although I did say that the reason why things matter is that they affect whether we flourish or suffer, that is a somewhat truncated explanation, for it omits what makes us care about this. I now realise that *at base*, things matter to us because of our biology: as living beings, we are kept alive by bodily homeostatic systems that produce responses to the world that tend to keep us safe and well; in addition, as a highly advanced form of life, we have the capacity for oversight, reflexivity and learning to guide our responses. So normativity is at base biological, as philosophers like Philippa Foot, Hans Jonas and Mary Midgley have argued, though of course through emergence and our capacities for reasoning and for forming commitments and attachments, normativity goes far beyond this (Foot 2001; Jonas 2001; Midgley 2003). In social science and much of philosophy, a combination of the scholastic fallacy and neglect of biology ('biophobia') makes it impossible to understand this. At the time I wrote the book, I was unaware of this biological underpinning, so my account of emotions, which was heavily influenced by Nussbaum, made too little of the physiological aspect of emotions. Although this is different from their cognitive aspect, it is not generally irrational from the point of view of flourishing, for emotions involve some of our homeostatic systems, and as evolved capacities they generally help protect us by forcing problems and opportunities into our consciousness. Even those social practices and norms that appear to have nothing to do with human biology draw some of their power by recruiting emotions, though to do this they have to be compatible with our socialised mind-body's powers and susceptibilities; otherwise they do not 'push our buttons'.

I think we can worry too much about what distinguishes us from other animals, and, of course, human exceptionalism has had disastrous effects on our behaviour in relation to the global ecosystem; we should be open to both our similarities and our differences and the extraordinarily complex webs of dependence that link us to other species. Biological normativity applies to all living things, which is not to say that everything from viruses to humans has equal worth; there is a hierarchy of worth, as Andrew Collier argued (Collier 1999). I didn't intend to base normativity wholly on sentiments, though, for there are other considerations at a social level regarding how we live with others in ways that promote the flourishing of all. Here I agree that I need to say more about personhood as a distinctive element of *human* flourishing, though I think it was implicit in what I wrote on dignity. I take it to be emergent from our social being (and as such dependent on it), and again, to involve the recruitment through downward causation of our emotions. All in all, and unlike Doug, I'm inclined to shift *further* towards naturalism.

Like **Ted Benton**, I was much impressed not only by realism but also by Marx's ideas on our relationship to nature. Regarding concepts of nature, Ted recommends paying more attention to 'attempting to specify some underlying feature or condition in virtue of which the being in question is able or liable to manifest the range of behaviours or powers that we can observe or expect'. Explaining social life without considering what it is about us that makes us susceptible to socialisation and enables us to do the things humans do, including developing an extraordinary variety of cultures, leads to one-sided explanations, and sociological reductionism. So I agree that biology should certainly not 'be held at arm's length'; indeed, there needs to be a dialogue between biologists and social scientists. 'The social' covers a number of ontological levels, including the biological affordances and constraints that make us and many other mammals 'social animals', dependent on other members of our species throughout our lives. Again, our exceptional neuroplasticity allows our extraordinary variety of forms of socialisation or acculturation. This involves a process of morphogenesis in which, at each moment, how we experience the world and what we can do are constrained and enabled by our brain-bodies, which in turn have been modified by experience and actions at previous times. Here it is not only necessary to acknowledge emergence – in particular, mind or thought from the workings of the brain-body – but also downward causation through which what we think, do and experience modifies those workings (van der Kolk 2014). I also accept that social science should take more interest in paleoanthropology and evolutionary biology, so we are open to the possibility that some things we generally regard as wholly cultural phenomena, such as love of nature, are in fact emergent cultural elaborations of universal biological tendencies or affordances.

Moral Economy

As **Bob Jessop** notes, this interest grew out of a long-standing interest in political economy and coevolved with ideas about CSS's need for a normative basis, but I should add that it was also a delayed product of having to teach a course at Sussex called Foundations of Social Science, covering some key texts of Smith, Marx and Mill. Having been strongly influenced by Marx's political economy, I later went back to Smith and his work on *The Theory of Moral Sentiments* and *The Wealth of Nations*. It seemed to me that these pre-disciplinary authors' work on classical political economy or what was once called moral philosophy was a good model for contemporary post disciplinary studies of political and moral economy. An additional influence was conversations with **John O'Neill**, and reading his book *The Market: Ethics, Knowledge and Politics* (O'Neill 1998), which got me interested in Aristotle, not just in relation to economics, but social science generally.

John's contribution on unfree labour shows the value of bringing philosophy and social science together, albeit in a different way from most approaches. First, it differs in emphasising 'patiency' (vulnerability and dependency) rather than just agency. Second, because of its separation from social science, moral and political philosophy today is dominated by ideal theory, which tends to ignore social structures or adopt idealised versions of them. Such philosophy also tends to focus on the good, as if injustice and evil were just the absence of the good. By contrast, in most social science disciplines, oppression, exploitation, injustice and violence are discussed with little or no discussion of *why* they are bad, perhaps because of a misguided belief that value-freedom is necessary for objectivity. Hence, philosophy and social science have complementary strengths and weaknesses that invite resolution. Examining a concrete example of injustice, John demonstrates that to explain what unfree labour is and how it arises we need to *evaluate* it, and in a way that includes the structures and contexts in which it occurs. This also helps us realise that in addition to more obvious solutions of improving employment legislation, there are more indirect ones – for example, providing support for the dependants of unfree workers in order to reduce the economic pressure on such workers to resort to such work. He also notes that in thinking about labour and freedom, one can get much further by considering actual forms of *un*freedom – a conclusion also arrived at by Amartya Sen in his book on justice (Sen 2009). I had the same experience in trying to make sense of *dignity* in *Why Things Matter to People*; philosophical definitions of it were unenlightening, and it was only when I looked at how the word and especially its antonyms are used in everyday life that it became possible to understand its nature and significance.

Dave Elder-Vass has made important contributions to both critical realism and moral economy (Elder-Vass 2016). As he notes, I initially defined my version of moral economy as addressing the influence of morality on economic behaviour and the effects of economic forces on morality. However, in the last ten years, I have come to see it primarily in terms of interrogating the constitutive norms, rules and power relations governing economic practices – particularly property rights in capitalism – to assess how reasonable or unreasonable the justifications of them are. More specifically, Dave rightly draws attention to the importance of gifts in the contemporary digital economy, though when it comes to assessing the new gift economy, I would add that it is vital to acknowledge the extent to which this is coupled with the harvesting of platform rents – an economic process for which there is no moral justification in terms of payment for work. This source of unearned income is a key component of contemporary rentier capitalism (Christophers 2020).

Regarding his query about my reservations about universal basic income policies, these include the belief that work – that is, contributing to the good of community/society through provisioning and care – should be seen as both a duty for those able to work and a fundamental component of individual well-being; a duty because otherwise it allows unwarranted free-riding on others' labour, and a right or capability in that being able to contribute to society in ways that benefit others as well as oneself is a source of dignity and self-worth. To enable this, the state – local or national – needs to be the employer of last resort and provide appropriate welfare support for those unable to work. There also needs to be adequate support for those doing unpaid childcare and eldercare work. As regards poor quality jobs (unpleasant/hazardous/insecure/low paid), the solution is to improve their quality or, if the tasks are unavoidably unpleasant, etc., share them out among all workers so each has some pleasanter, more fulfilling tasks too. We need not only distributive justice but 'contributive justice' (Gomberg 2007; Sayer 2009).

I agree with **Kevin Morgan** that the idea of the foundational economy (FE) has much to commend from a moral economic point of view. Kevin and I explored the zero-sum competitive tendencies of the high-tech industry in our research on electronics in the 1980s (*Microcircuits of Capital*), and while many have noted these features and the predictable failure of regional development policies based on them, promoting high-tech unfortunately remains the default option for many economic policies, despite the limited numbers employed in such industry. If we are to stop runaway global heating we have to abandon this fetish and work towards combining a green new deal and FE.

A striking feature of the thinking behind the FE movement and one that differs from most radical political economy is that it is prescriptive about the kind of *use-values* that should be prioritised, instead of focusing just on exchange value and how much money different groups get out of the economic process – a focus that mirrors capitalism's pursuit of money as its ultimate goal. Green imperatives also oblige us to consider the nature of *what* is produced and consumed. Real economic wealth consists of use-values, but some of these are much more important for our well-being than others.

Accordingly, FE champions universal basic services rather than universal basic income, which could – as Right-wing advocates hope – co-exist with a radically shrunken public sector, where what used to be provided collectively has to be purchased by individuals. Of course, as Kevin notes, ways of financing FE have to be devised, and here I would suggest that green or FE Individual Savings Accounts (ISAs)[3] issued by the local and central government to fund FE and greening the economy may win popular support and give people a stake in its success. At the same time, especially for the foundational sector of housing, it is important to shift finance *away* from promoting asset inflation and indebtedness, and more generally to reverse the shift towards rentierism. In view of the current hold of rentier interests and big capital over governments, this is an enormous challenge.

Balihar Sanghera and **Elmira Satybaldieva** are right: in writing about inequalities and moral economy, I have said far too little about resistance, whether in research on the lived experience of class or moral economy and the rich. One reason is probably an overreaction against the tendency of radicals to exaggerate and romanticise the rebelliousness of the oppressed and exaggerate the precariousness of the social order (forecasting 6 of the last 3 crises … as the joke goes) and to suppose that, but for strategies of legitimation, mass resistance would surely break out. E.P. Thompson, who popularised but did not originate the concept of moral economy, was an example of this tendency, though in response to critics, he did acknowledge he had ignored the 'flag-saluting, foreigner-hating, peer respecting side of the plebian mind' (Eastwood 1995). I also felt that radical political economists tended to gloss over divisions within classes, including the division of labour and skill, and differences in cultural capital among those who were, at least in a Marxist sense, workers. The same surely goes for gender and race. Research on intersectionality highlights these divisions.

In opposition to radical wishful thinking, I was much taken with Bourdieu's explanation of the lack of resistance by reference to the naturalisation of contingent social forms and limitation of individuals' horizons and aspirations by 'the sense of reality', as Balihar and Elmira note. But Bourdieu took this too far – and not surprisingly, because as already noted, he treated the formation of the habitus as indifferent to whether its formative conditions were harmful or beneficial, as if we could accommodate to being despised and exploited as easily to being respected and empowered. He therefore ignored emotional resistance. Even then, emotional resistance does not always transform into political resistance; problems may just be registered as personal misfortunes. Resistance can also be deflected by divide and rule strategies, such as the Right's attempt to stir up 'culture wars' and deflect working-class attention from the financial upper class onto the liberal Left; a tendency facilitated by the remoteness of the upper class from the rest of the population but also sometimes reinforced by middle class 'class racism'. Further, given that emotions are often mixed, there can be complex mixes of resistance and consent, willing or reluctant. For my part though, I accept that while I have written about emotions such as shame or resentment of injustice, I have not gone into what determines how they are acted upon, if at all, or how they are contingently politicised.

Gideon Calder's chapter illuminates why anyone interested in what is problematic about inequality will not find many answers in political theory, despite its focus on justice. I have to agree that sadly, in many cases, political theory comes across primarily as a vehicle for demonstrating cleverness rather than identifying actual injustice. In its dominant focus on 'ideal theory' – models of ideal forms of social organization that support liberty and fairness – it shares a similar malaise to that of mainstream economics with its preoccupation with idealised models of markets and lack of attention to actually existing economic processes and structures. Significantly, in neither case do they pose much threat to contemporary capitalism, which, of course, could account for their dominance. As I noted in my response to John O'Neill, it's a casualty of the divorce of normative thinking from positive social science that has emerged over the last 150 years. Hence, in trying to develop an approach to moral economy and economic justice, I found that Aristotle, Smith, Marx, Tawney, Veblen, Hobson and more recent authors such as David Graeber, Ann Pettifor, Nancy Fraser, Elizabeth Anderson and Michael Hudson had more to offer than the kind of political theory that Gideon critiques. And as he notes, starting from actual injustices requires a pluralistic approach to theory: as highly complex beings with diverse capacities, forms of dependence and vulnerability, it is surely no surprise that what is required for us to live together justly and in ways that promote the well-being of all cannot be covered by the kind of one-dimensional theories that dominate contemporary political theory. I appreciate Gideon's generous comments on my work, but as for what a more pluralistic and realistic or worldly political theory should look like, I'm not currently able to say.

Inequality and the Rich

Health inequalities are not something I have studied before,[4] so it is gratifying to know that my more general work on inequality has been helpful in that field. As **Graham Scambler's** work has shown, much research on health inequalities doesn't go far enough back along the causal chain to identify what *produces* the inequalities in income, status, education and environment that correlate with health inequalities. Positivist research treats such correlations as in themselves the key to explanation. I suspect that most health researchers are reluctant to examine the underlying processes not only because they are schooled in positivist rather than critical realist methods, but because things like economic exploitation, class contempt and racism are seen as too far removed from their own topic and also 'too political'. While positivist research on health inequalities tends to suggest sticking-plaster policies involving allocating extra resources at various points so as to reduce the impact of things like low income, or lack of support, critical realist research implies more radical policies that change the *determinants* of low income or poor educational outcomes.

Graham presents some interesting ways of examining the relations and processes that generate these common empirical associations, such as by reference to the 'seven asset flows' he mentions. In the case of material asset flows, these are of course very much the focus of *Why We Can't Afford the Rich*. The complication of economic inequality and objective class relations over the last half-century referred to by Graham owes much to the shift to rentier capitalism. This has been associated not only with the return of the rich but also with the rise of small-time rentiers, whose earned income is supplemented by capital gains in housing, and by private pensions based on rentier sources of income.

Graham mentions my distinction between identity-sensitive sources of inequality – such as those of racism and sexism – and identity-indifferent sources – such as market forces.[5] As regards the former, I should perhaps add a comment here, because I am sure some critics would want to say that this ignores the 'structural' aspect of racism and sexism. If the use of the word 'structural' is to be more than just a way of upping the rhetorical *ante*, we need to identify the structures that tend to anchor or embed inequalities of race, ethnicity and gender. Examples are the unequal division of labour between better paid, good quality jobs and poorly paid, poor quality ones; the spatial segregation of urban areas by income and ethnicity; and selective schools and their catchment areas. In each of these, women and BAME people are over-represented in the more disadvantaged positions within these structures, so that *in addition to* conscious and unconscious racist and sexist discrimination, people's lives are shaped by their location in these structures in ways that reinforce racial and gender inequalities. In everyday life, differences in placement within these structures tend to be seen as a reflection of differences in what individuals deserve, and, in turn, differences in recognition tend to reinforce inequalities in distribution.

Diane Reay's outstanding research on schools, class, gender and race has been a major influence on my work on the lived experience of inequalities. Regarding her observations on education, meritocracy and the view from the bottom set, I recall reading somewhere of psychological experiments on the effects of teachers' expectations on their pupils' performance: when teachers showed confidence in their pupils' ability it actually enhanced their performance, and when they communicated doubt in their ability, pupils performed worse than with teachers who were neutral or more positive about them. In practice, as Diane's examples indicate, this positive or negative feedback comes not only from teachers but from the highly unequal structural contexts in which education takes place, where inequalities of class in terms of economic and cultural capital are misread as evidence of unequal potential and ability.

The quality of the physical environment of the school and local area can also affect how pupils feel about themselves. Thus, the differences between the lavish grounds and facilities of the private school and the limited facilities of a cash-strapped state school[6] indicate how their respective pupils are valued and send powerful confidence-building or confidence-eroding signals to them.

Relations between the working and middle classes have been widely studied in sociology, but for various reasons relations between these and the upper class have not, even though in the case of upper-class politicians we see it every day in the news media. Recently, some authors have argued that the upper-class practice of sending children to boarding school – a form of deliberate parental neglect – creates certain common pathologies that can last into adulthood. Notable among these is a refusal of pupils to acknowledge their own vulnerability in order to avoid being bullied. Presenting an impression of impregnable confidence and assurance and lack of need of others is a vital form of self-preservation in the boarding school environment. This also leads to difficulties in accepting others' vulnerability and in sustaining relationships in later life (Duffell 2014; Beard 2021; Schaverien 2015). Ironically, when combined with a sense of superiority and entitlement, these pathologies tend to benefit them in the competitive struggles of public life. Of course, they also have all the advantages of economic, social and cultural capital, but I suspect more needs to be said about the social psychology of the upper class and their relation to members of other classes with whom they interact and who often allow them to get away with assuming positions of dominance.

This brings me to the other topic discussed by Diane – the growth of corruption in politics. Since *Why We Can't Afford the Rich* came out in 2014, we have seen a strengthening of what I termed (adapting a phrase from Bob Jessop) 'plutocracy in the shadow of democracy'. As Diane shows, it has become increasingly corrupt and brazen in facilitating wealth extraction. This is particularly clear in the extraordinary expansion of cronyism (or 'coronyism') in which hugely generous contracts have been given to donors and friends of Conservative party with no competitive tendering or checks. Legal challenges to these practices have so far made little impression. To paraphrase a comment attributed to Frank Wilhoit, while for the rich, the law protects but does not bind, for the rest the law binds but does not protect. How do they get away with this? The usual explanations cite the combination of the UK's first-past-the-post electoral system, a weak and divided opposition, and a supine and sycophantic news media dominated by billionaires. But important though all these are, it is still difficult to understand why so many voters should vote against their own interests and support such an irresponsible, dishonest, corrupt and manifestly incompetent group of politicians. The rise of populism is something I didn't mention in *Why We Can't Afford the Rich*; what I still find difficult to understand is the psychology of reception of this populism. Although we must never lose sight of the structural forces of the rise of rentier capitalism in deepening inequalities, nor should we ignore the strange psychology of the popular reception of a Right-wing government packed with boarding school-damaged 'reckless opportunists', apparently able to 'con' the public through confidence and fake conviction (Davis 2018).[7]

In other words, although *Why We Can't Afford the Rich* was far too long,[8] as Dick Walker notes, there is so much else that needs to be said – ranging from the economic to the cultural and psycho-social – in explaining the return of the rich.

Environment

Jamie Morgan expands and updates another theme from *Why We Can't Afford the Rich*: the diabolical double crisis of economy and environment. As Jamie – a heterodox economist – knows better than I do, mainstream economics retains its disastrous monopoly control of the subject, and one of the reasons I wanted to write the book was to present an alternative.

As he notes, I use a financial definition of wealth in the book, because that is most relevant to understanding the rich. However, from a normative point of view, I would again want to emphasise that economic wealth consists of use-values. Prices are poor indicators of this kind of value, and the only reason why we treat them as if they were measures of value is that our dependence on money for access to goods forces us to do so. As K.W. Kapp wrote, capitalism is 'a system of unpaid costs', and however useful markets and prices are for coordinating the world's extraordinarily complex social division of labour, they fail to reflect the environmental and social costs incurred by capitalism (Kapp 1978). What mainstream economics sidelines as a matter of 'externalities' has never been more central. If I were to write a more academic book on moral economy, I would probably begin with economic evaluation as a matter of dealing with incommensurable things, such as the need for food and education, and hence which cannot be represented in a single value, such as a price. The growth of the division of labour and globalisation has concealed what is clear to subsistence producers – our total dependence on the biophysical environment. Further, the environment itself, including features that have no use to us for provisioning, is central to any conception of wealth that goes beyond the narrowly economic. We have not only to change the meaning of economic wealth but to resist the reduction of wealth to its economic aspect. As Ruskin said, 'There is no wealth but life'.

I fully accept the point raised both by Jamie and Dave Elder-Vass that particularly in view of the climate and ecological crises, we have to consider our dependence on other species and ecosystems, which also need to flourish, and physical systems such as those of climate. Hence, as regards the concept of flourishing, I agree that it must go beyond that of humans to other species and not just to individual species but especially the flourishing of ecosystems.

I certainly agree with Jamie that unless a green transition safeguards the living standards and indeed benefits the working class, there is little chance of it gaining democratic approval. The response of the 'gilets jaunes' in France is salutary; it is understandable that those struggling to pay their bills put this before saving the planet. It is hardly surprising that workers in climate-harming sectors like aviation are reluctant to see their sectors radically downsized. Greening the economy will require rapid structural change on an unprecedented scale and major changes in ways of life, so unless the state – central and local – provides those most affected with economic security and alternative work, it won't happen. I used to think Gramsci's slogan – 'pessimism of the intellect, optimism of the will' – was a bit too glib, but now, in the truly desperate situation we're in, there's no rational alternative.

Notes

1 I'm not sure that the difference between extracting the thing of interest and removing the things not of interest is a difference that makes a difference.
2 Dispositions and emotions are not quite the same thing: in critical realist terms, dispositions are causal powers or potentials, while moral sentiments or emotions may be involved in their activation/actualisation.
3 This idea was proposed by Caroline Lucas, Clive Lewis, Colin Hines and Richard Murphy in 2021: www.theguardian.com/politics/2021/may/14/a-green-recovery-bond-will-enable-the-government-to-fund-its-climate-pledges.
4 But see Sayer and McCartney (2021).
5 A recent example of identity-indifferent sources of inequality is redundancies in the retail sector, which have been the consequence not of discrimination against retail workers, but of the rise of online shopping.
6 English public (i.e. private) school fees are 90% higher than state spending per school pupil (www.theguardian.com/education/2021/oct/08/english-private-school-fees-90-higher-than-state-school-spending-per-pupil).
7 As Aeron Davis argues, there are also structural forces that tend to select and groom such individuals: in the case of those running major companies, these include the pressure to meet short-term demands of shareholders for profits, which encourages CEOs to sacrifice long-term strategy and to pocket their winnings and move on before the damage is revealed. Similar incentives exist in the public sector with the rise of New Public Management, while in Parliament, a host of constraints and incentives obstructs the pursuit of the public good (Hardmann 2019).
8 I did think of bringing out an abridged version called 'Why We *Simply* Can't Afford the Rich', but that never came to anything.

References

Archer, M.S. (2009). (ed.) *Conversations about Reflexivity*. London: Routledge.
Beard, R. (2021). *Sad Little Men: Private Schools and the Ruin of England*. London: Harvill Secker.
Bourdieu, P. (1984). *Distinction: A Critique of the Judgement of Taste*. London: Routledge.

Christophers, B. (2020). *Rentier Capitalism: Who Owns the Economy and Who Pays for it*. London: Verso.

Collier, A. (2007). *Being and Worth*, London Routledge.

Damasio, A. (2000). *The Feeling of What Happens*. London: Vintage.

Davis, A (2018). *Reckless Opportunists: Elites at the End of the British Establishment*. Manchester University Press.

Doidge, N. (2007). *The Brain that Changes Itself*. London: Penguin.

Duffell, N. (2014). *Wounded Leaders: British Elitism and the Entitlement Illusion*. Berwick upon Tweed: Lone Arrow Press.

Eastwood, D. (1995). E. P. Thompson, Britain, and the French Revolution. *History Workshop Journal* 39 (Spring): 79–88.

Elder-Vass, D. (2016). *Profit and Gift in the Digital Economy*. Cambridge: Cambridge University Press.

Foot, P. (2001). *Natural Goodness*. Oxford: Oxford University Press.

Fricker, M. (2007). *Epistemic Injustice*. Oxford: Oxford University Press.

Gomberg, P. (2007). *How to Make Opportunity Equal*. Oxford: Blackwell.

Hardman, I. (2019). *Why We Get the Wrong Politicians*. London: Atlantic Books.

Jessop, B. (2005). Critical Realism and the Strategic Relational Approach. *New Formations* 56: 40–53.

Jonas, H. (2001). *The Phenomenon of Life: Toward a Philosophical Biology*. Evanston, Illinois: Northwestern University Press.

Kapp, K.W. (1978). *The Social Costs of British Enterprise*. Nottingham: Spokesman.

Lakoff, G. (2014). *Don't Think of an Elephant*. Hartford, Vermont: Chelsea Green Publishing Company.

Midgley, M. (2003). *Heart and Mind*. London: Routledge.

Morgan, K., & Sayer, A. (1988). *Microcircuits of Capital: Sunrise Industry and Uneven Development*. Polity Press: Cambridge.

O'Neill, J. (1998). *The Market: Ethics, Knowledge and Politics*. London: Routledge.

Sayer, A. (1992). *Method in Social Science*, Second edition. London: Routledge.

Sayer, A. (1995). *Radical Political Economy*. Cambridge: Blackwell.

Sayer, A. (2000a). System, Lifeworld and Gender Associational versus Counterfactual Thinking. *Sociology* 34(4): 707–725.

Sayer, A. (2000b). *Realism and Social Science*. London: Sage.

Sayer, A. (2000c). For Postdisciplinary Studies: Sociology and the Curse of Disciplinary Parochialism/Imperialism. In J. Eldridge, J. MacInnes, S. Scott, C. Warhurst, & A. Witz, (eds), pp. 85–97, *Sociology: Legacies and Prospects*. Durham: Sociologypress.

Sayer, A. (2009). Contributive Justice and Meaningful Work. *Res Publica*. 15(1): 1–16.

Sayer, A., & Walker, R. (1992). *The New Social Economy. Reworking the Division of Labour*. Cambridge: Blackwell.

Sayer, A., & McCartney, G. (2021). Economic Relationships and Health Inequalities: Improving Public Health Recommendations. *Public Health* 199 (October): 103–106.

Schaverien, J. (2015). *Boarding School Syndrome: the Psychological Trauma of the 'Privileged' Child*. London: Routledge.

Sen, A. (2009). *The Idea of Justice*. London: Allen Lane.

Van der Kolk, B. (2014). *The Body Keeps the Score*. London: Allen Lane.

Index